The Family in Early Modern England

This is the first single volume in recent years to provide an overview and assessment of the most important research that has been published on the English family in the past three decades. Some of the most distinguished historians of family life, together with a new generation of historians working in the field, present previously unpublished archival research to shed new light on family ideals and experiences in the early modern period. Contributions to this volume interrogate the definitions and meanings of the term 'family' in the past, showing how the family was a locus for power and authority, as well as personal or subjective identity, and exploring how expectations as well as realities of family behaviour could be shaped by ideas of childhood, youth, adulthood and old age. This pioneering collection of essays will appeal to scholars of early modern British history, social history, family history and gender studies.

HELEN BERRY is Reader in Early Modern History in the School of Historical Studies, University of Newcastle upon Tyne. Her previous publications include *Gender, Society and Print Culture in Late-Stuart England* (2003) and, with Jeremy Gregory, *Creating and Consuming Culture in North-East England, 1660–1830* (2004).

ELIZABETH FOYSTER is Lecturer in History and Fellow of Clare College, Cambridge. She is the author of *Manhood in Early Modern England: Honour, Sex and Marriage* (1999) and *Marital Violence: An English Family History 1660–1857* (2005).

Anthony Fletcher

The Family in Early Modern England

Edited by

Helen Berry and Elizabeth Foyster

CAMBRIDGE
UNIVERSITY PRESS

CAMBRIDGE UNIVERSITY PRESS
Cambridge, New York, Melbourne, Madrid, Cape Town, Singapore, São Paulo, Delhi

Cambridge University Press
The Edinburgh Building, Cambridge CB2 8RU, UK

Published in the United States of America by Cambridge University Press, New York

www.cambridge.org
Information on this title: www.cambridge.org/9780521858762

© Cambridge University Press, 2007

First published 2007

Printed in the United Kingdom at the University Press, Cambridge

A catalogue record for this publication is available from the British Library

ISBN 978-0-521-85876-2 hardback

Contents

vi   Contents

Preface

The selection of a theme for a volume of essays dedicated to our teacher, mentor and friend Anthony Fletcher was a peculiarly difficult task. His contribution to the field of early modern history has, in the course of a lifetime's career, encompassed a wide range of research interests. From his early studies on county history, notably of Sussex, to his powerful and meticulous account of the outbreak of the English Civil War, from his analyses of the dynamics of office-holding among local magistrates and county gentry, to the influence of the Protestant religion upon household and government in the early Stuart period, it is extremely difficult to categorise him as a particular *type* of historian. His name is familiar to most former 'A' level history students as the author of *Tudor Rebellions* (now in its fifth edition), a book which first inspired many young people to study early modern history through its engagement with archival material and clear communication of the excitement of interpreting primary historical documents. The impact of this book nationally was brought home at one of the present author's weddings, where a guest (a former 'A' level history student, now turned city lawyer and not usually given to over-excitement) glanced at the seating plan and exclaimed 'That's not *the* Anthony Fletcher is it?'

A former schoolteacher, Anthony's long-standing interest in the history of education, which has currently evolved into a large-scale research project on the history of childhood, reflects his own dedication as an educator who has inspired generations of undergraduate students at the Universities of Sheffield, Durham and Essex, some of whom (as this volume attests) went on to benefit from his tutelage at postgraduate level. Anthony's book-lined study, in which the inquisitive student's eye was drawn to his collection of framed prints and engravings (here, a portrait of Oliver Cromwell, there, his *alma mater*, Merton College), and his eclectic collection of colourful china jugs, was the setting for tutorials and – perhaps most memorably of all – group seminars, through which Anthony skilfully steered the attendant gathering of novitiate historians with just the right combination of probing queries and gentle corrections, listening attentively to what each student had to say, and displaying a willingness always to share his evidently vast knowledge of the social and political history of the early modern period. Whether the subject was Cromwell's Major-Generals, or the lesser-known early-Stuart conduct writers, he always had the ability to make his subject engaging, and to inspire his students to want to learn more.

The thirtieth anniversary of the publication of Lawrence Stone's *The Family, Sex and Marriage in England, 1500–1800*, following Anthony's retirement and sixty-fifth birthday, seemed a fortuitous coincidence that aided the process of selecting a theme for this collection. The contributors, chosen from among Anthony's former colleagues and students and representing the different stages of his career, were invited to present their latest research and to reflect upon the current state of early modern family history three decades after *The Family, Sex and Marriage*. Each responded to the call to honour Anthony in this way with enthusiasm, and more than fulfilled their remit. We would like to thank the contributors for their dedication to meeting the demands of editorial deadlines, and Patrick Collinson, Julie Gammon and John Morrill for their additional support.

To some, it may seem peculiar to have chosen Stone's book, rather than one of Anthony's, as a starting point for this collaboration. This deliberate stratagem was pursued, however, much in the manner of organising one of the seminars which the dedicatee of this volume so relishes, provided they are *colloquia* in the true sense of the term. Anthony's long-standing interest in the family may be traced back to his studies of local gentry families in Sussex, but came much more to the forefront of his research during the 1990s, marked with the publication of *Gender, Sex and Subordination* (1995). His influential publications on gender, the household and family form a rich seam of reference in each of the chapters that follows.

It is also fitting that a collection dedicated to someone for whom good teaching has been as much a part of his achievement as a distinguished list of publications should be accessible to the newcomer to early modern family history, as well as to the expert, and it is with this in mind that an over-view of the relevant historiography relating to Stone and his subsequent critics is included in the Introduction, as well as a Select Bibliography. For a historian who is as forward-looking and research-active as Anthony, who enjoys the stimulating friendship of impertinent youth as much as the august company of his eminent peers, it is also appropriate that this volume should not only highlight the past and present state of the field, but indicate the new directions that might be taken in the future. We dedicate what follows to him, with gratitude and affection.

HMB and EAF

Notes on contributors

JOANNE BAILEY is Senior Lecturer in Early Modern History at Oxford Brookes University. Her publications include *Unquiet Lives: Marriage and Marriage Breakdown in England, 1660–1800* (2003), and a number of journal articles on marriage and the law. Her current research is on parenting and childhood in the long eighteenth century.

HELEN BERRY is Reader in Early Modern History at the University of Newcastle upon Tyne. She is the author of *Gender, Society and Print Culture in Late-Stuart England* (2003) and has published articles on the history of print culture, gender and sexuality, and consumer culture in early modern England.

BERNARD CAPP is Professor of History at the University of Warwick and a Fellow of the British Academy. His books include *Cromwell's Navy* (1989), *The World of John Taylor the Water-Poet* (1994) and *When Gossips Meet: Women, Family and Neighbourhood in Early Modern England* (2003). He is currently preparing a book on the 'culture wars' of England in the 1650s.

ELIZABETH FOYSTER is a College Lecturer in History and Fellow of Clare College, Cambridge. She has published in edited collections and journals on subjects such as childhood, parenting, marriage and widowhood. She is the author of *Manhood in Early Modern England: Honour, Sex and Marriage* (1999), and *Marital Violence: An English Family History 1660–1857* (2005).

STEVE HINDLE is Professor of History at the University of Warwick. He is the author of *The State and Social Change in Early Modern England, c.1550–1640* (2000), and *On the Parish: The Micro-Politics of Poor Relief in Rural England, c.1550–1750* (2004). His next monograph will be a study of social structure and social relations in the Warwickshire parish of Chilvers Coton, provisionally entitled 'The social topography of a rural community'.

R. I. MOORE is Emeritus Professor of Medieval History at the University of Newcastle upon Tyne and a Corresponding Fellow of the Medieval Academy of America. His many publications include *The Origins of European Dissent* (1977), *The Formation of a Persecuting Society* (1987, 2nd edn 2006), and *The First European Revolution, c. 970–1215* (2000).

TIM STRETTON is Associate Professor and Chair of the History Department at Saint Mary's University in Halifax, Nova Scotia. His publications include *Women Waging Law in Elizabethan England* (1998) and a document volume for the Camden Series, *Marital Litigation in the Court of Requests 1542–1642* (forthcoming).

INGRID TAGUE is Associate Professor of History and Chair of the History Department at the University of Denver. She is the author of *Women of Quality: Accepting and Contesting Ideals of Femininity in England, 1690–1760* (2002). She is currently working on a history of pets and pet keeping in eighteenth-century England.

GARTHINE WALKER is Senior Lecturer in History at Cardiff University. She is the author of *Crime, Gender and Social Order in Early Modern England* (2003), editor of *Writing Early Modern History* (2005), and co-editor of *Women, Crime and the Courts in Early Modern England* (1994), and has written a number of articles and essays on early modern gender and crime and on historiography. Her current projects include aspects of subjectivity and emotion, and rape and sexual violence in the early modern period.

JOHN WALTER is Professor in History at the University of Essex. He is the author of *Understanding Popular Violence in the English Revolution* (1999), awarded the Whitfield Prize by the Royal Historical Society, and of *Crowds and Popular Politics in Early Modern England* (2006), and he has published articles on famine, early modern crowds, and popular politics. He is currently working on a monograph on the Protestation Oath and popular political culture in the English Revolution.

Anthony Fletcher

R. I. Moore

A certain kind of English crime novelist might describe Anthony Fletcher, with restrained approval, as a certain kind of Englishman. That, born in 1941, he was shaped not in the golden age of that genre but in that of post-war nostalgia for it, goes some way to accounting for the striking combination of traditionalism in his concerns with the fabric and institutions of English country life, and the increasingly radical individualism, not to say rebelliousness, of his sympathies and approaches. He came from just such a background as our novelist might have invented for him. His father was a distinguished scientist in government service, and in later life an antiquarian who pioneered the use of dendrochronology in dating medieval buildings; an uncle was a Labour MP and junior minister. On his mother's side soldiers and Anglican clergymen – including Richard Chenevix Trench, archbishop of Dublin at the time of the disestablishment of the Irish church – abound; in the Merton room in which Anthony lived in his second year a plaque commemorates a Chenevix Trench killed in the Great War.

I met Anthony in early October 1959, two of Merton College's ten History freshmen eyeing one another with all the suspicion and unease of a first tutorial meeting. Alone among us he wore a tie (and out of doors, it became apparent, a scarf) in the colours of his old school – an unpleasing combination which quickly became familiar, since it denoted an institution whose alumni appeared peculiarly and unfathomably determined to advertise their association with it. In Anthony's case, however, I discovered that this was not for any of the reasons which first occurred to an admittedly slightly chippy outsider – not from social conformity, still less snobbery or exclusiveness, and certainly not as an expression of devotion to Wellington College, or the causes and values for which it stood. It was a disguise, and part of a larger disguise that he has always worn, not for deception but to avoid the appearance of distinctiveness, and with it distraction. He is not only an unassuming man, but one very focused, very consistent, in his own quiet way even ruthless, in following his chosen path. It was ever thus: while others, like all freshmen, expected to talk through the night, Anthony invariably and silently disappeared at his regular bedtime; if the gathering happened to be in his bed-sitter he would retire for his bath and then to bed, while cheerfully bidding the rest of us to carry on for as long as we liked.

The most obvious mark of that independence is that Anthony belongs to no historical school, and can be identified as the student or follower of no great predecessor in seventeenth-century studies. He has no PhD, and once shocked S. T. Bindoff, a notable devotee of academic pomposities, by declining to follow up a professorial intimation that he 'might be allowed' to embark on one. The Merton tutors, R. H. C. Davis, J. R. L. Highfield and J. M. Roberts, formed an outstandingly congenial and talented team, but none of them was especially interested in the seventeenth century. There was, of course, no shortage of great figures in the Oxford of the time. Christopher Hill, Hugh Trevor Roper, Lawrence Stone, John Cooper, were in their prime; Keith Thomas was a rising star; and Conrad Russell, still a graduate student in our first year, taught us Bede's *Ecclesiastical History* (in Latin of course) and often shared our late-night coffee – not that his conversation kept Anthony out of bed. I doubt that any of them influenced Anthony as much as W. G. Hoskins, whose seminar on Tudor economic documents he attended in his third year. Hoskins's *Making of the English Landscape* was among the not particularly impressive (that is, pretentious) collection of books I inspected on my first visit to Anthony's room, along with several volumes of Pevsner's *Buildings of England*, in their original Penguin-sized format, with shabby paper covers and minute soot-and-starch illustrations, and of the works of A. L. Rowse. In short, and with hindsight, his historical curiosity was already formed. It would be hard to think of a historian less like Anthony in personality and temperament than Rowse, but his deep and deeply romantic attachment to the English countryside had found an echo, and more than an echo.

It would be quite wrong to conclude that the road to *A County Community in Peace and War* (1975), *The Outbreak of the English Civil War* (1981), and *Reform in the Provinces* (1986) already lay open, or was mapped out. As an undergraduate Anthony had no thought of making historical research his trade – perhaps because it had long been a hobby for him – and, Hoskins notwithstanding, the sort of history for which he cared did not, in the early 1960s, beckon the ambitious. It was only in his final year that he decided to become a history teacher, and probably only the combination of his scholarly energy and the unusual opportunities created by the sudden and rapid expansion of universities in the wake of the Robbins Report on Higher Education (1963) that made him, after three lively years at Kings College School, Wimbledon, a university rather than a school

teacher. For a short time in the mid 1960s university departments –
especially History departments – recruited rapidly while graduate education – especially in History – remained more or less static. Even so,
a shortlisting on the basis of an article in the *British Journal of Educational Studies* and *Tudor Rebellions* in press (in a series designed mainly for
sixth-formers) must count as a lucky break. It turned out that the luck
was mostly Sheffield's. Expansion had brought to that department as to
many others several enthusiastic and excellent young teachers. Anthony
was remarkable among them not as a glamorous or charismatic figure –
there were plenty of those about in 1968 – but for the transparent sincerity
of his interest both in his subject and in his students. He did not bother
with showmanship, never believed in lecturing *ex cathedra*, and irritated
some of his senior colleagues by his enthusiasm for small group teaching,
an activity then associated, like sex, soft drugs and student demos, with
the 'new' universities at places like York and Sussex. Students were cap-
tivated by his honesty, his perceptiveness and his kindness – especially
to those who lacked the intellectual self-confidence that some of his less
sensitive colleagues were inclined to take for granted: when I mistakenly
supposed that a fresher would be encouraged by advice to put in the
waste paper basket the textbook from which she had carefully compiled
her essay it was on Anthony's shoulder that she retired to weep.

For most of Anthony's time in Sheffield a system of study leave was
a distant dream, and replacement teaching from any source not even
that. Nevertheless, it was in those years, despite heavy teaching loads
so enthusiastically shouldered, growing administrative responsibilities as
his unfailing and unobtrusive efficiency was inevitably exploited, and the
pleasures and distractions of family life, that he laid the foundations of
the three substantial books on which his first reputation was founded, and
published two of them. All were based on extensive research in county
as well as national collections and all appeared to combine an orthodox,
regionally based approach to 'mainstream' preoccupations with traditional, 'national' issues of politics and government and an increasingly
distinctive identification of the issues themselves.

It is fair to suspect that the former quality contributed more than the
latter to his appointment to the Chair at Durham, not at that time generally regarded as a hotbed of the new historiography. Certainly, accession
to the professoriate might have engendered a degree of intellectual com-
placency, a sense that a chair hard won might be comfortably sat upon:
it has been known to happen. That was not Anthony's way. The second half of his career was, by any standards, exceptionally taxing. In a
succession of senior posts, at Durham, at Essex and finally as Director
of the Victoria County History, he has suffered more than his share of

interesting times. The quality of the students he met with at Durham, and the enthusiasm he inspired in them, are attested by the present volume, but he probably found the less traditional ambience and ethos of Essex more congenial. For the Direction of the VCH he was ideally equipped – too well, perhaps, for comfort. During his brief tenure he endowed it with a vision for the twenty-first century to match that of his great predecessors for the nineteenth, founded like theirs on the conviction that his fellow countrymen and women deserved nothing less than the highest standards in scholarship, and scholarship of the highest standard nothing less than exposure to all his fellow countrymen and women by the most accessible means available. Still more remarkably, he communicated that vision to the Heritage Lottery Fund so compellingly as to win for its realisation in his 'England's Past for Everyone' one of the largest endowments that historical scholarship in this country has ever received.

In these years Anthony also became increasingly involved in the affairs of the discipline at national level, in a period when his courteous unflappability, his ability, and concern, to seek every view, and take as many of them as possible on board without losing direction, and to combine flexibility in inessentials with firmness when it mattered, were greatly at a premium. History and historians remain especially in his debt for the skill and determination with which, as chair of the History Benchmarking Group of the Quality Assurance Authority and of HUDG (History at the Universities Defence Group, now History UK), he fought to ensure that national benchmarks in History would define the coherent and adaptable intellectual structure appropriate to the discipline, rather than the quanta of information which the bureaucrats wanted, and succeeded in foisting on other disciplines.

While thus engaged Anthony has found time to redefine his historical interests not once but twice, and each time in ways that required him to come to terms with quite new areas of specialism, and with the modern, as well as the early modern, period of British history. It might seem in retrospect that a move from community to family was a natural one, much as it had been for Lawrence Stone, and certainly it is more likely that Anthony reached it by that route than through the theoretical debates that had been intensified through the 1980s. Theory has never really been his thing, though his ability to make use of it, and to appreciate its capacity to point history in new directions, is fully apparent in the three papers which announced, in 1994, that he had set himself on an entirely new course. The implications and influence of that change are the concern of others in this volume, but it is worth commenting that the qualities which made it possible are those which have marked him out since he was an undergraduate – that he has followed his own path without regard for conventional demarcations of field, intellectual fashion or career advantage, led by his own curiosity, by a flair for spotting what might be done with neglected kinds of documentary evidence, and by his rootedness in certain traditions of English country society. Latterly the same instincts have led him to another and even more dramatic shift. Reggie Chenevix Trench, commemorated on that plaque in Anthony's room at Merton, was his grandfather, and the brother of Cesca, the very remarkable young woman whose papers are leading Anthony himself down a path he had never dreamed of, through the dying days of Anglo-Irish society to the wilder shores of Irish republicanism and the Easter Rising. It seems a long way from Tudor Rebellions. Or perhaps not.

souche). They hypothesised that multi-generational households had been the dominant form of family structure before the impact of the industrial revolution, where kin lived and worked together, producing hierarchical stability under a patriarchal (in this case, meaning paternal) ordering, and social harmony through the provision of care for vulnerable groups such as children and the elderly.[12]

By the mid-twentieth century, early experiments in the use of computer technology offered new techniques for challenging this 'golden age' hypothesis using quantitative data to show the variety of family forms that had existed before the nineteenth century across Europe. Early pioneers of this approach such as Louis Henry and Peter Laslett found a marked difference in the prevalence of extended family structures in the southern Mediterranean countries over the primarily nuclear family formations in northern Europe, including the Low Countries, England and Scandinavia, from at least the sixteenth century.[13] Demography offered (and in many respects still presents) the least parochial approach to the study of the English family, with a strong tradition of quantitative research that demonstrates comparative pan-European and indeed global trends in household size and composition.[14]

Since the 1960s, the Cambridge Group for the History of Population and Social Structure has harnessed evolving computer technologies to develop increasingly sophisticated quantitative techniques to study family history, such as 'back-projection' (the calculation of population size and structure using surviving sources such as parish registers and nineteenth-century censuses, which allows a best-guess of the numbers of people in preceding generations), and 'family reconstitution' (the linking of data concerned with the baptisms, marriages and burials of individual families).[15] For the first time, historians could substantiate some surprising findings about early modern households that exploded the myth of the pre-industrial extended family, and which now are accepted as

---

[12] This debate is usefully summarised in M. Anderson, *Approaches to the History of the Western Family, 1500–1914* (London, 1980), pp. 22–30.

[13] L. Henry, *Anciennes familles genevoises* (Paris, 1956); Peter Laslett, *The World We Have Lost* (London, 1965); see also L. Bonfield, Richard M. Smith and Keith Wrightson (eds.), *The World We Have Gained: Histories of Population and Social Structure* (Oxford, 1986).

[14] See for example P. Laslett, K. Oosterveen and R. M. Smith (eds.), *Bastardy and its Comparative History: Studies in the History of Illegitimacy and Marital Nonconformism in Britain, France, Germany, Sweden, North America, Jamaica and Japan* (London, 1980).

[15] E. A. Wrigley and R. S. Schofield, *The Population History of England, 1541–1871: A Reconstruction* (London, 1981), and E. A. Wrigley et al., *English Population History from Family Reconstitution, 1580–1837* (Cambridge, 1997).

however, been extremely productive, not least in revealing that early modern people did not define the family in the way in which Stone supposed. According to Naomi Tadmor (who examined a range of eighteenth-century diaries and fictional texts), when early modern people referred to their family, they could include members of their household who were unrelated by marriage or blood. Instead of the 'family' there was a concept of the 'household-family'.[19] Furthermore, whereas Stone had no compunction in writing about 'the English family' as though a consensus could be reached about what the family is and has been in history, subsequent historians produced multiple definitions of the subject, insisting upon the contingency of 'families' in various socio-economic and cultural settings. As early as 1980, Michael Anderson insisted upon the diversity of family forms, functions and attitudes, and concluded that a single history of the Western family could not be written.[20] More recently there has also been a recognition that most people experienced family life with more than one family. There was the birth family, the family in which young people might reside if they learned a trade as apprentices or worked as domestic servants, the new family that was formed upon marriage, and further families that could be established when the death of a spouse led to remarriage, step-parents and step-children.[21]

In addition, the spread of postmodern ideas since the 1980s has encouraged historians of the family to attempt to uncover the voices of those who did not represent the majority experience of family life. Berry and Foyster's chapter on childless men in early modern England in this volume is a reminder that not all family lives were conducted in the nuclear family context, but that the pressure to conform could lead to family practices such as surrogate parenting. Previously marginalised or taboo subjects such as marital violence and child abuse are also receiving attention from early modern historians.[22] The revelation of hidden histories is to be welcomed, but the time will no doubt come when current research undertaken in the context of heightened present-day preoccupations with issues such as one-parent families, paedophilia, high divorce rates and gay marriage will in turn be superseded in as-yet unanticipated ways. The family mutates, and the writing of family history must do so too.

---

[19] Naomi Tadmor, 'The concept of the household-family in eighteenth-century England', *Past and Present* 151 (1996), 111–40.

[20] Anderson, *Approaches to the History of the Western Family*, p. 14; the title of Colin Heywood's *A History of Childhood* (Cambridge, 2001) also reflects this attitude.

[21] Will Coster, *Family and Kinship in England 1450–1800* (Harlow, 2001), p. 6.

[22] See Martin Ingram, 'Child sexual abuse in early modern England', in M. Braddick and J. Walter (eds.), *Negotiating Power in Early Modern Society: Order, Hierarchy and Subordination in Britain and Ireland* (Cambridge, 2001), pp. 63–84, 257–62; Elizabeth Foyster, *Marital Violence: An English Family History 1660–1857* (Cambridge, 2005).

During the thirty years since Stone's book was published, contemporary concerns about the family have certainly shifted, and new approaches to the study of history have thus emerged. To fault Stone for not having the prescience to anticipate later historical trends (the field of gender history springs to mind) is, however, fundamentally to misunderstand the novelty of what he achieved in *The Family, Sex and Marriage*, and its importance as one of the canonical works of early modern historiography. In his selective use of sources, Stone was less than a model historian, but his hypothesis about the evolution of the modern family has proved to be 'good to think with'.

Any collection on the theme of the early modern family must simultaneously demonstrate the chronological and thematic breadth which is emblematic of a vibrant field of research, but also the selectivity that comes with specialist focus. All contributors to this volume were asked to reflect upon their research in relation to the landmark contribution of Lawrence Stone to the field, and with this request all have happily concurred. The points of agreement and dissent with Stone's hypothesis summarised at the outset of this introduction are instructive. In general, throughout the collection, there is agreement with Stone that the family in the early modern period was of great political significance, since analysis of contemporary writings has shown that the health and security of the nation was believed to rest on the stability of family life. As one seventeenth-century author declared, 'the family is a seminary of the Church and Commonwealth'; thus, the family was intended to be the testing ground for male authority; 'it is impossible for a man to understand how to govern the Commonwealth, that doth not know how to rule his own house'.[23] The belief that good order in the family depended upon the morality of its members, and that if there was disorder in the family its repercussions would be felt well beyond the walls of the family home, meant that the family was regarded as a public institution. As Joanne Bailey and Tim Stretton show in this volume, individuals outside the family unit, whether servants, employees, neighbours or friends, were rarely reluctant to comment upon or directly intervene in the family lives of others. Families were everybody's business in this period.

Stone's focus upon the social elite meant that, although he paid attention to their property and inheritance considerations, he was not concerned with examining how economic issues affected the majority of

---

[23] William Gouge, *Of Domesticall Duties*, 3rd edn (London, 1634), p. 28; John Dodd and Robert Cleaver, *A Godlie Forme of Householde Government* (London, 1612), p. 16; S. D. Amussen, *An Ordered Society: Gender and Class in Early Modern England* (Oxford, 1988).

early modern families. However, within the rural and proto-industrial economy the family home was the base for economic life, and all family members, whether men, women or children, were expected to be economically productive. Proof that couples were financially independent and self-sufficient before they married, set up their own households, and started families, was routinely required by those in positions of authority. The frequency with which husbands and wives worked alongside one other, performing similar tasks and contributing equally to the household economy, has been the subject of extensive and lengthy debate.[24] A crucial question for historians of women, and (to a lesser extent) children, has been how far their economic input was valued so that it affected the balance of power in early modern households. Historians who regarded the early modern period as a golden age of family life at least partly derived their argument from the conviction that this was a time in which married women were more economically active than in the period that followed.[25] With more recent studies focusing upon women as consumers as well as producers, discussions about these issues seem set to continue.[26] What is undisputed is that, to function as economic producers and consumers, women were required on a regular basis to leave the home. In addition, as John Walter's chapter in this collection shows, women's work and management of family budgets could lead them to assume very public roles as participants and sometimes leaders of popular protests. The presence of children alongside their mothers and fathers on such occasions shows families acting together as economic units. Understanding the economic responsibilities of family members also helps to explain patterns of property crime in early modern England, as Garthine Walker argues here, and in particular highlights the crucial part played by married women in criminal activities.

For the many families that struggled at subsistence levels, day-to-day financial decision-making by family members, rather than just the choices

---

[24] For an overview of this debate see the useful collection of essays in Pamela Sharpe (ed.), *Women's Work: The English Experience 1650–1914* (London, 1998). On the working lives of middling-sort women, see Peter Earle, *The Making of the English Middle Class: Business, Society and Family Life in London, 1660–1730* (London, 1991), and Margaret R. Hunt, *The Middling Sort: Commerce, Gender and the Family in England, 1680–1780* (London, 1996). More recently, see Hannah Barker, *The Business of Women: Female Enterprise and Urban Development in Northern England, 1760–1830* (Oxford, 2006).

[25] An idea first put forward by Alice Clark in *Working Life of Women in the Seventeenth Century* (London, 1919), but since much disputed. See for example, Amanda Vickery, 'Golden age to separate spheres? A review of the categories and chronology of English women's history', *Historical Journal* 36, 2 (1993), 383–414.

[26] For a summary of recent historiography, see H. Berry, 'Women, consumption and taste', in Hannah Barker and Elaine Chalus (eds.), *Women's History: Britain, 1700–1850* (London, 2005), ch. 9.

infinite variety of experiences that individuals encountered when different personalities came into play.

Strikingly, for those currently teaching family history, undergraduate students coming from families of two or three generations of divorce do not necessarily predicate the subject upon any 'golden age' or nuclear family experience, for neither concept may have any critical purchase for them. Devoid of these preconceptions, they refuse to accept *a priori* the myths that Stone's generation were seeking to debunk. The pace of change in family formation and structure in our own time has rendered obsolete the ideals of family life in past societies. We have now reached a situation where it is the 'otherness' of the nuclear family that requires explanation in historical context. Future historians of the family may find this to be one of their greatest challenges.

2 Marriage, separation and the common law in England, 1540–1660

Tim Stretton

King:
Shall I divorce them then? O be it far,
That any hand on earth should dare untie,
The sacred knot knit by Gods majesty;
I would not for my crown disjoin their hands
That are conjoined in holy nuptial bands,
How sayest thou Lacy? Wouldst thou loose thy Rose?

Thomas Dekker, *The Shoemakers Holiday* (1600)[1]

Lawrence Stone believed that from the time of the Reformation, which led to a narrowing of the grounds for annulment, until just prior to the Restoration, when private separation agreements became possible, the bonds of marriage were harder to break than at any other time in English history.[2] Later historians have disagreed with Stone about the precise contours of marriage law and practice during these decades. R. H. Helmholz, for example, has questioned the ease with which the pre-Reformation church granted annulments, while Martin Ingram remains sceptical of Stone's assumptions about the prevalence of desertions after the Reformation. Nevertheless, few historians dispute the legal, ecclesiastical and social strength of the institution of marriage between the mid-sixteenth and mid-seventeenth centuries.[3] Elsewhere in Europe, the Protestant

I would like to thank the Social Science and Humanities Research Council of Canada for funding this project and Andrew Cranmer and Nadia Lewis for their assistance in completing bibliographical searches and document transcriptions. Thanks are also due to Anthony Fletcher and Bernard Capp, for their scholarly generosity in fielding questions about magistrates, and to Lyndan Warner, Helen Berry and Elizabeth Foyster and the members of the Dalhousie University Graduate and Faculty Colloquium and the North Eastern Conference on British Studies for their responses to earlier versions of this chapter.
[1] Thomas Dekker, *The Shoemakers Holiday. Or the Gentle Craft with the Humorous Life of Simon Eyre, Shoemaker and Lord Mayor of London* . . . (London, 1600), Act 5, sc. 5, lines 49–54. Spelling and punctuation in this and all subsequent quotes has been modernised.
[2] Lawrence Stone, *The Family, Sex and Marriage in England 1500–1800* (New York, 1977), pp. 31–2, 37–8.
[3] R. H. Helmholz, *Marriage Litigation in Medieval England* (Cambridge, 1974), pp. 74, 83, 84, 111; Roderick Phillips, *Putting Asunder: A History of Divorce in Western Society*

made at marriage and death examined by Stone, could make all the difference between economic survival, ruin and starvation. Furthermore, Steve Hindle's chapter demonstrates that the experience of poverty, and the likelihood of needing to resort to the parish for relief, was shaped by the family life-cycle. Families with young children, widows, the sick and the elderly were all at vulnerable stages of the life-course when family members could be viewed as more of an economic burden than an asset. Thus the life-cycle approach to the writing of family history has led to more awareness that family experience is contingent upon age as well as status and gender. For example, Walter shows how, depending upon age and gender, contemporaries could either license or condemn the active engagement of family members in popular protests. Instead of Stone's division of the life-course into just two stages of childhood and adulthood, studies of youth and old age have also demonstrated the multiplicity of the 'ages of man', and the inter-generational dynamism that was a feature of early modern family relationships.

As Hindle recognises, early modern families did not operate in splendid isolation, but were embedded in a network of kin, friends and neighbours. The individuals in these networks could provide economic and emotional support, and more negatively, as Tim Stretton argues, become the critics and agents of control and regulation when family life broke down. Stone's theory that kin played less of a role in aristocratic and genteel life as the period progressed has been widely challenged.[27] The contributors to this volume demonstrate that the importance of kin may well have varied across the social scale: Hindle finds that kin were of minor importance to the survival strategies of the poor compared to neighbours, whereas Ingrid Tague's analysis of aristocratic family life demonstrates that kin and family lineage continued to be key concerns among the ruling elite in the eighteenth century.

Since the 1990s, the meaning of friendships to men and women have been explored by historians, especially in the light of their emotional content, but also the extent to which friends could act as substitutes or even competitors for family affections merits further examination.[28] Neighbours made up the communities in which families were located, and

---

[27] See, for example, K. Wrightson, 'Household and kinship in sixteenth-century England', *History Workshop Journal* 12 (1981), 151–8; and D. Cressy, 'Kinship and kin interaction in early modern England', *Past and Present* 113 (1986), 38–69.

[28] For examples of historical studies of friendship see A. Bray, 'Homosexuality and the signs of male friendship in Elizabethan England', *History Workshop Journal* 29 (1990), 1–19; A. Bray and M. Rey, 'The body of the friend: Continuity and change in masculine friendship in the seventeenth century', in T. Hitchcock and M. Cohen (eds.), *English Masculinities 1660–1800* (Harlow, 1999), pp. 65–84; N. Tadmor, *Family and Friends in Eighteenth-Century England: Household, Kinship and Patronage* (Cambridge, 2001); and

published in the 1980s by Martin Ingram, who used the evidence from the church courts to show how popular attitudes towards sex, and actual sexual behaviour, were often at considerable divergence from the injunctions of religious authorities.[31] Historians have since become alert to the possibilities (and problems) that court records can yield. Joanne Bailey's chapter argues that historians of children and parenting should not assume that matrimonial litigation contains material that is only relevant to those interested in marriage, while Stretton, Capp and Walker reveal the pitfalls of an over-reliance upon the most accessible and heavily trawled court records. By no means all marriage difficulties were settled by the church courts, and magisterial interventions into family life were often informal and hence not noted in the official court records. Women's extensive role as 'partners in crime', receiving, selling and consuming stolen goods, is missed if the focus is solely upon formal prosecution records. Historical detective work of the kind shown in these chapters, and a willingness to look beyond the most easily available records, can only further our understanding of family life in the early modern period.

The challenge for any early modern historian remains one of sources, and no historian worth the name can ever present evidence without explicit reference to what is missing: the gaps and silences that echo down the years, as well as the inherent bias of those voices that do survive. These limitations notwithstanding, the past decade has witnessed a revolution in the range of material studied, a result of cross-pollination from other disciplines (particularly in fresh approaches to the use of printed sources, visual and material culture), and the availability of electronic finding aids and online resources for researching family history. In particular, new electronic databases have opened up a vast range of rare and obscure printed material published from the end of the fifteenth through to the nineteenth centuries, and have made it possible to undertake searches on thematic subjects as well as specific names and places. For example, catalogues of family collections containing legal papers, account books, household inventories and personal documents such as diaries and letters that were previously buried in local record offices can now be accessed via the National Register of Archives online.[32] Some important legal documents and court records are now also available electronically; the online version of the *Proceedings of the Old Bailey* is a fine example of the

---

[31] Martin Ingram, 'The reform of popular culture? Sex and marriage in early modern England', in B. Reay (ed.), *Popular Culture in England* (Worcester, 1985), pp. 129–65; see also Ingram, *Church Courts, Sex and Marriage.*
[32] See www.nationalarchives.gov.uk/.

the idea of good neighbourliness was central to family life.[29] For every individual, a unique mix of family, kin, friends and neighbours regulated domestic life, playing a part, as Stretton's chapter illustrates, in separating and ending marriages and household units, as well as establishing them. Crucially, the early modern state was dependent upon the willingness of ordinary people to report and act as witnesses against those who breached the moral codes of acceptable family behaviour. During the strict moral climate of the Interregnum, Bernard Capp finds popular support for the Puritan agenda of a reformation of family life. Thus communities could play an active role in policing families, although the motives for involvement were not always those that would have found approval from the godly elite. Piety, it seems, was tempered by pragmatism.

Historians using legal sources have revealed a wealth of detail about family life. The law governed the rules of family institutions, determining what made a valid marriage, and what could give couples the right to part. Legal documents chart every stage of early modern family life from marriage contracts to wills. It was via the family that estate was transferred from one generation to the next, and for women it was their marital status that at least in theory determined their property rights. Historians have shown how the practice of women's married and family lives differed from this legal theory, and, contrary to Stone, have proved that concerns about family property neither precluded affection between family members, nor were unique to the wealthy.[30] As Tague demonstrates in her chapter, the preservation of family estate could be as high a priority for elite women as for their male kin. Furthermore, as Walker's examination of the offences of forcible entry, detainer and disseisin proves, it was not just the social elite who felt passionately about their property. Across the social scale, the home symbolised family honour and reputation. Legal disputes about household space and property are testimony to the extent to which women and men were prepared to defend that honour.

Since witnesses in the law courts could be drawn from every rank in life, it is court records that have allowed historians to redress the bias towards the family lives of the social elite that Stone's work displayed. One of the earliest and most influential examples of this approach was

---

L. Gowing, M. Hunter and M. Rubin (eds.), *Love, Friendship and Faith in Europe, 1300–1800* (Basingstoke, 2005).

[29] See Keith Wrightson, 'Mutualities and obligations: Changing social relationships in early modern England', British Academy Raleigh Lecture, 2005 (publication forthcoming). *Family and Community History* was launched in November 1998, and focuses on publishing research concerned with the period from the eighteenth to the twentieth century.

[30] Amy Louise Erickson's *Women and Property in Early Modern England* (London, 1993) has been very influential in this field.

vast possibilities which this technology has presented.[33] New resources such as these have made it easier for historians to explore in particular the family histories of those people who were often marginalised in the past – such as the poor, the never-married, the widowed and the elderly.[34]

The development of cultural history has also encouraged family historians to draw upon a much wider variety of sources, in ever more subtle and complex ways. One example of this is the recent advances that have been made in the use of different types of visual evidence, which were central to Philippe Ariès's thesis about the 'invention' of childhood in the eighteenth century, but which Stone regarded mainly as illustrative matter for his theories about family life that he had formulated *a priori* from his interpretation of textual evidence.[35] A new study by Kate Retford has not only shown the limitations of Stone's somewhat cursory foray into art history, but opened up whole new debates about the relationship between artists, sitters and audiences in 'staging' private and public representations of the family.[36]

Another form of evidence that has attracted fresh insights since the 1990s is the material culture relating to family life in the early modern period. This not only promises new information about the context in which family lives were conducted (such as the spatial organisation and construction of homes), but is also pointing to the multiple meanings and use of material goods in, for example, cementing family relationships, and transmitting collective memory between generations.[37] Material objects also played a part in rituals relating to family life, such as the 'love gifts' and tokens that were a crucial component in the making of marriage.[38] Historians now widely recognise that the broadside ballads, chapbooks and other forms of popular print that tell us much about the attitudes and

---

[33] Co-directed by Tim Hitchcock and Robert Shoemaker; see www.oldbaileyonline.or/.

[34] See, for example, J. M. Bennett and Amy Froide (eds.), *Singlewomen in the European Past 1250–1800* (Philadelphia, 1999); S. Cavallo and L. Warner (eds.), *Widowhood in Medieval and Early Modern England* (Harlow, 1999); L. Botelho and P. Thane (eds.), *Women and Ageing in British Society Since 1500* (Harlow, 2001); recent innovations include the ESRC Westminster pauper biographies project headed by Jeremy Boulton and Leonard Schwartz.

[35] P. Ariès, *Centuries of Childhood* (London, 1962); see also P. Ariès, *Western Attitudes Towards Death* (London, 1976).

[36] See, for example, K. Retford, *The Art of Domestic Life: Family Portraiture in England* (New Haven and London, 2006).

[37] See for example A. Vickery, 'Women and the world of goods: A Lancashire woman and her possessions', in J. Brewer and R. Porter (eds.), *Consumption and the World of Goods* (London, 1993), pp. 274–301; see also Raffaella Sarti, *Europe at Home: Family and Material Culture 1500–1800* (New Haven and London, 2002).

[38] Gillis, *For Better, For Worse*; John R. Gillis, *A World of Their Own Making: A History of Myth and Ritual in Family Life* (Oxford, 1997).

values of ordinary people towards family life are in themselves cultural artefacts.[39]

Given the diversity of primary sources now being handled by historians of the family, it is disappointing that there remains so little interaction and collaboration both within the field and across the historical discipline. Although family historians continue to be indebted to other academic disciplines, such as anthropology and sociology, there is a hesitancy about which methods are most appropriate for historical research. This is particularly the case for 'psycho-history'. Lloyd de Mause's attempt to apply psychoanalytic terms to a historical chronology of parent–child relations, in which he argued for a progression from the 'infanticidal mode' of antiquity, to the 'ambivalent mode' of the early modern period, and finally to the idealised 'helping mode' of the mid-twentieth century, has cast a long shadow of doubt about the application of psychoanalysis to historical evidence. De Mause's conclusion that 'the further back in history one goes, the lower the level of child care, and the more likely children are to be killed, abandoned, beaten, terrorized and sexually abused' had close parallels with Stone's depiction of parent–child relations in the early modern period, and has unsurprisingly attracted much criticism.[40] Subsequent historians such as Michael Macdonald (whose brilliant study of madness in early modern England is based upon the notebooks of the seventeenth-century astrological physician Richard Napier) have demonstrated the value of investigating the impact of family stresses upon the mental and emotional lives of our predecessors.[41] There are certainly other models of historical writing that deploy psychology as a tool of analysis, notably in the work of Lyndal Roper, but these remain relatively scarce in English historiography.[42]

It is a surprising feature of much recent work on the subject that many historians working in fields that might be thought to have much in common, particularly women's and gender history, can remain distanced from family history.[43] Although women's history has had a significant impact

[39] See, for example, M. Spufford, *Small Books and Pleasant Histories: Popular Fiction and its Readership in Seventeenth-Century England* (London, 1981); and J. A. Sharpe, 'Plebeian marriage in Stuart England: Some evidence from popular literature', *Transactions of the Royal Historical Society*, 5th series, 36 (1986), 69–90.

[40] Lloyd de Mause, 'The evolution of childhood', in Lloyd de Mause (ed.), *The History of Childhood* (London, 1976), pp. 1–73.

[41] Michael Macdonald, *Mystical Bedlam: Madness, Anxiety, and Healing in Seventeenth Century England* (Cambridge, 1981).

[42] Lyndal Roper, *Oedipus and the Devil: Witchcraft, Sexuality and Religion in Early Modern Europe* (London, 1994); for a good overview of the debates concerning this historical method, see Garthine Walker, 'Psychoanalysis and history', in S. Berger, H. Feldner and K. Passmore (eds.), *Writing History: Theory and Practice* (London, 2003), pp. 141–60.

[43] For suggested explanations, see L. A. Tilly, 'Women's history and family history: Fruitful collaboration or missed connection?', *Journal of Family History* 12, 1–3 (1987),

of such a fundamental unit of social organisation demands new research and fresh critical approaches.

Overall, was Stone right? In brief, the answer must be no, as the contributors and editors of this volume agree overall. There were strands to the weave of his argument that were helpful in illuminating the texture of early modern family life. As Ingrid Tague demonstrates, for example, there were dynastic preoccupations that surmounted other factors (such as grandparent–grandchild affection) in aristocratic families, but this continued right up to 1800 – and beyond. Stone recognised that the family was a crucial site of power relations, but, as a number of our contributors argue, the pattern of gender relations was neither as straightforward as he suggested, nor the sole axis of power at play between family members. Age, economic self-sufficiency, marital status, the ability to have children and to raise them in ways that met with societal approval, were all crucial in determining experiences of family life.

Perhaps, though, Stone *was* correct to identify the eighteenth century as a pivotal moment in the history of family life. Whereas few historians would go so far as to agree with his over-arching view of 'massive shifts in world views and value systems', or in the 'basic personality change' that he believed allowed for an unprecedented tide of familial affection in the eighteenth century, this does not mean that they are content to settle for histories of continuity in family life.[47] As Joanne Bailey shows, for example, the eighteenth century did bring new expectations of the role that fathers should play in the upbringing of their children, and other studies suggest that, during a period of considerable economic and social upheaval, the meanings and representations of the family were subject to alteration.[48]

Stone was emphatically wrong, however, to suggest that the history of the family was one of progression, in which the eighteenth century marked the arrival of a more civilised, loving and recognisably 'modern' family.[49] This is not just a fault that results from his attempt to reduce family history to a model in which there was a succession of family forms or types. Numerous case studies of families have inevitably revealed the

---

[47] Stone, *Family, Sex and Marriage*, pp. 3, 268.

[48] See, for example, Ruth Perry, *Novel Relations: The Transformation of Kinship in English Literature and Culture, 1748–1818* (Cambridge, 2004).

[49] Stone may have rejected modernisation theory in *Family, Sex and Marriage*, pp. 658–60, but like his contemporary, Edward Shorter, in *The Making of the Modern Family* (London, 1976), his approach to family history did much to support it. See also Garthine Walker, 'Modernization', in Garthine Walker (ed.), *Writing Early Modern History* (London, 2005), pp. 31–3, 39–40.

upon family history, and has done much to challenge Stone's view of the early modern family as a site of unmitigated female oppression, family historians struggle to demonstrate the relevance of their subject to the wider academic and general readership. Too often histories of the family are still conflated simply with those of women and children, but the reverse is also true: that studies of these 'categories' of family members can still lack a broader family context. The analysis of early modern families that incorporates the experiences of fatherhood (as the work of Anthony Fletcher on gender and childhood, and John Walter and Joanne Bailey's chapters in this volume demonstrate) is one way of redressing this imbalance.

As Tamara Haraven argued over a decade ago, if family historians could demonstrate that the family was a force *for* change, rather than just an institution that passively responded *to* change, as Stone proposed, surely they would present a history that demanded attention.[44] The vitality of future research in family history may also depend upon relating evidence of family life to the 'bigger picture' of historical change and continuity. Historians of twentieth-century family life, for example, have attempted to link family history to world history, with a recent issue of the *Journal of Social History* examining 'Globalization and the History of Childhood'.[45] Whereas pioneers in the history of eighteenth-century imperialism, such as Linda Colley and Kathleen Wilson, have identified gender as a key component of the experience, it is noticeable that the family is largely absent from their accounts.[46] That family relationships and businesses could operate across continents, and ideas about what defined the English family were forged during encounters with peoples of different race and religion, needs to be recognised by early modern as well as modern historians.

Family history provides the historian with the opportunity to pursue new avenues of enquiry while resorting to a wide range of evidence and developing methodologies that have a relevance to the historical discipline as a whole. Of course, problems and challenges remain for the future. Many of our contributors point to specific aspects of family life that now need to be investigated or reassessed; it is still the case that the study

---

303–15; and M. Doolittle, 'Close relations? Bringing together gender and family in English history', *Gender and History* 11, 3 (1999), 542–54.

[44] T. K. Haraven, 'The history of the family and the complexity of social change', *American Historical Review* 96, 1 (1991), 95–124.

[45] *Journal of Social History* 38, 4 (2005).

[46] L. Colley, *Britons: Forging the Nation 1707–1837* (New Haven and London, 1992); K. Wilson, *The Sense of the People: Politics, Culture and Imperialism in England, 1715–1785* (London, 1995), and *The Island Race: Englishness, Empire and Gender in the Eighteenth Century* (London, 2003).

reforms that removed marriage from its sacramental pedestal also ushered in the possibility of divorce, but in England divorce in the modern sense – the legal dissolution of a valid marriage allowing parties to remarry – remained unobtainable for most couples until 1857.[4] According to conventional wisdom, the only options available to individuals caught in failing marriages, apart from grinning and bearing it, were formal church court separations, which were difficult and expensive to obtain and hard to enforce, or informal (and illegal) practices such as desertion or wife sale.[5] Or were they? This chapter seeks to break this scholarly consensus by exploring other avenues open to English men and women in failing marriages prior to 1660, examining possibilities that Stone and his critics have ignored or downplayed as a result of their concentration on the records of the church courts. In doing so, it questions the extent of the church's monopoly over marriage and separation by highlighting the roles played by alternative jurisdictions, in particular the common law, and examines the prehistory of private separations, agreements that Stone believed emerged in the 1650s from the chaos of the Interregnum.[6]

In theory the division of responsibility for the administration of marriage in pre-modern England was clearly defined. The church claimed sole right to determine whether a marriage was valid, and sole responsibility (with the help of prying neighbours) for policing married couples and ensuring that individuals kept their marital vows. In cases where husbands or wives failed to live up to prescribed norms, churchwardens could 'present' them to the church courts for sinful behaviour including violence, sexual infidelity and living apart, although in most jurisdictions such presentments remained relatively rare.[7] If marriages broke down, couples could approach ecclesiastical authorities to gain a *divortium a vinculo matrimonii* (divorce from the bond of marriage) on such grounds as bigamy, pre-contract, impotence, consanguinity or affinity. However, few applications were successful and these were effectively annulments rather than divorces: declarations that marriages had never amounted

---

(Cambridge, 1988), p. 9; Martin Ingram, *Church Courts, Sex and Marriage in England, 1570–1640* (Cambridge, 1987), pp. 148–9.

[4] The wealthy could divorce by private act of parliament, but this cumbersome and expensive option only became available after 1670; Lawrence Stone, *The Road to Divorce: England 1530–1987* (Oxford, 1990), pp. 368–82; Phillips, *Putting Asunder*, p. 231.

[5] Wife sale, a ritual form of divorce, appears to have been rare before the eighteenth century; Samuel Menefee, *Wives for Sale: An Ethnographic Study of British Popular Divorce* (Oxford, 1981); E. P. Thompson, *Customs in Common* (Oxford, 1988).

[6] Stone, *Road to Divorce*, pp. 149–51.

[7] Ingram, *Church Courts*, p. 180; Carl Bridenbaugh, *Vexed and Troubled Englishmen 1590–1642* (Oxford, 1968), pp. 39, 41. For examples of presentments for these sins, see Paul Blair, *Before the Bawdy Court . . .* (London, 1972), pp. 40, 61, 79, 82, 102, 107, 111, 115, 130, 145–6, 155, 172, 185–6, 197.

to valid unions under ecclesiastical rules. The most famous examples are Henry VIII's 'divorces' from Katherine of Aragon and Anne of Cleves and the annulment of his marriage to Anne Boleyn. In each case, rather than authorising a divorce, church authorities declared the unions invalid *ab initio* because of pre-existing impediments.[8] Where marriages were valid, the best that most spouses could hope for was a separation (*divortium a mensa et thoro*, divorce from bed and board) on the grounds of cruelty or adultery. If successful, a separation *a mensa et thoro* would allow a husband and wife to live apart, but neither could remarry while the other remained alive.[9]

The common law had no jurisdiction over the validity of marriages, and the effects of coverture (the collective term for the common law rules affecting married women) prevented married women or men from entering suit against each other.[10] Nevertheless, the common law governed most aspects of marital property, especially real or immovable property such as land, and provided two key legal options for spouses caught in disintegrating marriages. The first was the ability of victims of domestic assault to approach a magistrate and seek to have their spouses 'bound over' by recognisance to keep the peace or to good behaviour.[11] The second was the ability to enforce the terms contained in church court separation and maintenance orders where these were made conditions attached to penal or conditional bonds. The chief ecclesiastical methods of enforcement – penance and the threat of excommunication – often proved ineffective in these cases, but conditional bonds provided real and often significant financial penalties for broken promises.[12]

The devastating irony for married women was that the church courts claimed jurisdiction over the dissolution of marriage, but faced troubles policing it, while the common law courts, which had fewer problems enforcing their will, proved reluctant to interfere in these circumstances, largely for fear of undermining a husband's legal authority over his wife. A married woman might gain a separation from her husband in the church courts, allowing her to leave the marital home, but in the eyes of the

---

[8] Phillips, *Putting Asunder*, pp. 71–7.

[9] For the complexities glossed over in this briefest of summaries, see Ingram, *Church Courts*, pp. 69–319; Helmholz, *Marriage Litigation*; R. H. Helmholz, *The Oxford History of the Laws of England*, vol. I, *The Canon Law and Ecclesiastical Jurisdiction from 597 to the 1640s* (Oxford, 2004).

[10] For rare exceptions where the common law did consider the validity of forced marriages see Sir John Baker, *The Oxford History of the Laws of England*, vol. VI, 1483–1558 (Oxford, 2003), pp. 620–1.

[11] Michael Dalton, *The Countrey Justice, Containing the Practice of the Justices of the Peace Out of Their Sessions* (London, 1622; repr. New York, 1972), pp. 146–7.

[12] See, for example, *Joyce Asbye* v. *Ralph Worlsey*, The National Archives (hereafter TNA), Public Record Office (hereafter PRO), Court of Chancery (hereafter C) 1/1326/38.

common law the couple's marriage remained valid and the rules of coverture still applied. This meant that if she earned wages, inherited money or goods, or was given gifts, her husband could claim them as his own, and she was defenceless at common law to stop him. The strictures of coverture also meant that she herself could not enter into a bond to ensure that her separated husband paid her alimony, but had to rely on someone else – father, brother, trustee – to do so on her behalf, a reliance that could create problems of enforcement in the future if her husband became recalcitrant.

Equity, the set of legal principles administered in Chancery, Requests and a number of other prerogative courts, supplied a third source of legal options relating to marriage. It is well known that these courts helped to develop and enforce devices such as trusts that allowed married women to maintain some control over their property during and after marriage. They also proved willing, on occasions, to ignore the rules of coverture and to hear cases fought between husbands and wives who had gained separations in the church courts. It was to equity courts that a wife could turn if her estranged husband attempted to claim her wages as his own.[13]

This then, in a highly simplified form, was the theory, but, as this chapter seeks to establish, reality could be more complex for wives and husbands caught in crumbling marriages in the century before the outbreak of the civil wars. A number of alternative options can be observed in the marital fortunes (or misfortunes) of a single couple, Marion and Griffin Jones, a pair of Londoners from the parish of St Alban's near Holborn whose lives spanned the latter two-thirds of the sixteenth century. After many years of apparent contentment, or at least calm, the couple's marriage began to disintegrate as they approached old age. As might be expected, church officials led attempts to restore harmony, as the following interrogatory directed to their local minister makes clear:[14]

Item, what variances and debates hath there been between the party plaintiff and Marion his wife, and in whom is the fault, and how often have you taken pains of your self to set them at unity, and how often did your curate Mr Burton set them at unity, besides what pains took you and the churchwardens in the vestry and others of the worshipful of the parish of St Albans to set them at unity and could not do it, and by reason thereof did not the plaintiff, her husband, say before you all [that] he would once again venture his life and go home to her, that your pains should not be lost, & did it and was commended for it, and how long continued they together?[14]

---

[13] See, for example, *Johane Spraggen* v. *Martyn Spraggen et al.*, TNA: PRO, Court of Requests (hereafter REQ), 2/273/67.

[14] *Griffin Jones* v. *Marion Jones et al.*, TNA: PRO, REQ 2/229/25, m. 19.

The church's role in the Jones case at the parish level was considerable, but a long list of other individuals and bodies showed their desire to see the couple reconcile, or else to part on fair terms, beginning with neighbours and friends. Allan Egerton, a forty-seven-year-old cordwainer, deposed that he 'did take pains between the said Jones and his wife and did make them friends at that time' at which point Marion supposedly said to her husband: 'Jones, if thou wilt forgive me now, we will put up all injuries and all shall be well.'[15] Ralph Crewe, a fifty-six-year-old mercer from St Michael's, Basingshaw in London, also deposed that he did 'take pains to make' Griffin and Marion friends 'and he did think they were friends' for 'being together at his, this deponent's, house' Marion 'did then swear, and very vehemently, that she would continue friends' with Griffin, and the pair went home together.[16]

When relations soured, other neighbours intervened more directly. As Griffin complained in a later court action, he

the said complainant could not at any time rebuke her the said Marion for her evil dealings towards this complainant, her said husband, but straight [a]way the said complainants house should be full of the said defendants, ready to revile & abuse the said complainant & beating the complainant in his house as was not meet for neighbours or honest men to do, and raising of people about the street & door not decent to be seen among Christians.[17]

According to Marion's friends, Griffin's violent behaviour led her to 'take the peace' against him before the local magistrate. Griffin had to find sureties ensuring his good behaviour and enter a bond with a money penalty, and when he defaulted he was imprisoned.[18]

The next intervention came from the lord mayor of London, Sir William Rowe, after Marion appeared before him complaining of her mistreatment at Griffin's hands and 'craving to be quit' of her violent husband. Rowe summoned Griffin from prison to answer to Marion's accusations, and asked him 'whether he would be rid and quit of his wife and take such weekly stipend as two honest men would think sufficient for him'. When Griffin answered yes, Rowe referred the matter to two men, Mr Martin and Mr Tidcastle, with the minister of the parish, Mr Harvey, acting as umpire, to negotiate a separation agreement and to determine maintenance payments for Griffin. Husbands paying alimony to wives was not uncommon, but a wife paying an allowance to her husband was highly unusual, a reflection of Griffin's diminished capacities in his old age. According to Griffin the arbitrators asked him and his wife to sign bonds agreeing to abide by an arbitrated settlement, but Marion

---

[15] TNA: PRO, REQ 2/229/25, m. 3.   [16] TNA: PRO, REQ 2/229/25, m. 15.
[17] TNA: PRO, REQ 2/226/66, m. 1.   [18] TNA: PRO, REQ 2/226/66, m. 12.

refused. Unperturbed, Mr Martin and Mr Harvey remained 'most willing and desirous to set unity between them' and 'entreated by fair means to bring her to make any offer that she would part from willingly'. They presented Marion with three further options, each of which she refused, so the mediation ended in failure, although the mayor intervened on at least one further occasion, doing his best to settle a difference over the correct appraisal of property connected with a common law suit over a bond.[19] The lord mayor enjoyed considerable power, but lacked any official jurisdiction over separation, and no record of this case survives in the archives of the various London mayoral courts. Presumably in this case he was acting in his capacity as a magistrate, but the brokering of what amounted to a private separation without recourse to the church courts is nevertheless remarkable.

The next body to take an interest in Griffin's and Marion's marital woes was the court of the Clothworkers' Guild, held before the master and wardens of the Clothworkers in their hall on 20 February 1592.[20] The couple aired their differences 'in the presence of Mr Crayne & others, a merchant dwelling at Bassings hall in London who traveled & took pains with them both to set them at unity (and did it)'.[21] The next intervention came at the local wardmote inquest, an annual meeting of the aldermen from the city ward to hear complaints and to make presentments about unsatisfactory behaviour within their community. The couple appeared after Griffin accused Marion of attempting to murder him by leaving sharpened knives in his bed. Marion answered that she or one of her maids had 'accidentally' mislaid the knives while preparing dinner for Griffin in his lodgings. Whichever account of this episode is correct, it is interesting that Evan Thomas, an alderman of the ward, later deposed that he and the other members of the wardmote inquest had summoned Marion and Griffin before them 'with intention to make them friends'.[22]

Griffin and Marion finally agreed to separate and live apart – whether through the mediation of friends or through their own negotiations is unclear – with Marion paying her aging husband an allowance for his living expenses. This arrangement continued until Marion's failing health led her to cease making payments. In response, Griffin sued her in the

---

[19] TNA: PRO, REQ 2/226/66, m. 2.

[20] Griffin was a skinner, but Marion's first husband had been a clothworker, and it appears that her entitlements as the widow of a member of the Clothworkers' Guild may have extended to subsidised accommodation, and perhaps to a paternal concern for the protection of her interests; TNA: PRO, REQ 2/226/66, m. 2.

[21] TNA: PRO, REQ 2/226/66, m. 1.

[22] Griffin also accused Marion's friends of 'plucking of his beard', a clear slight to his manhood and patriarchal authority; TNA: PRO, REQ 2/229/25, mm. 9, 19. The minute books for this wardmote inquest do not appear in the Guildhall's collections.

court of Requests for maintenance, seeking to have the flow of money restored. This court action, the source for all of the preceding information, demonstrates how far practice could diverge from the legal theory outlined at the beginning of this essay. Griffin and Marion lived apart, yet parish officials never presented them. Then Griffin sued his own wife without first seeking a separation in the church courts and sought to claim money from her that under the rules of coverture was technically already his. The masters of Requests agreed to hear the case and it progressed to the taking of depositions, but when Griffin failed to proceed with the suit they dismissed it from their court and ordered him to pay ten shillings in costs.[23]

The first puzzle that springs from this case is why Griffin or Marion did not approach the church courts with their problems. The surviving records provide no conclusive answer to this question, but make it possible to speculate that the remedy the church courts could supply was not the sort that Griffin, or indeed Marion, desired. A separation *a mensa et thoro* might have brought peace and legitimacy in the eyes of the church, but it cost money and provided few further benefits and there was no guarantee that ecclesiastical officials would grant one. In fact it was likely that they would seek to reconcile the couple, or even to present them for living apart. The frustration that some discontented spouses experienced in their dealings with ecclesiastical authorities can be seen in a case from earlier in the century. In a Chancery pleading from 1532 or 1533 Edith Mathew described how she had been married to her husband Robert about thirteen years, and had born him nine children, when 'by reason of the other children he had by another wife' disagreements arose between the two and 'she durst not abide' with him. She put in a bill of supplication to the archbishop of Canterbury, William Warham, seeking relief from her violent and unhappy marriage. Warham called the couple before him and then commanded Edith to return home with her husband, who was to be bound by recognisances with sureties to treat her well. Her response to the archbishop was that while he might compel her to go home, she had been so mistreated by Robert that she was not content to live with him 'as man and wife should do', and that therefore it would be better if his lordship required her husband to give her a competent living out of his lands 'whereby she might maintain herself'. The archbishop denied her request and ordered her home, where by her account she endured a further nine years of misery. Finally, after twenty-four years of marriage, and apparently without recourse to the ecclesiastical authorities, in 1531 or 1532 her husband assigned her an annuity of £22 out of his lands, on

[23] TNA: PRO, REQ 1/18, p. 303.

pain of £100 for forfeiture, to maintain her until her death, or his death when she could claim her jointure.[24]

For whatever reasons, Griffin and Marion Jones preferred to tackle their problems away from the scrutiny of ecclesiastical authorities, and while their case is particularly rich in detail, the interventions it describes were not unique and a similar array of groups, officials and private individuals intervened in other marital disputes. The master and wardens of the Clothworkers' Company, for example, heard a complaint in 1602 from Joan Bowre that her husband John, one of the company's beadles, had beaten her 'so that her face, arms and divers parts of her body are black and blue'. Mrs Pilsworth, wife of the company's master, and Mrs Gaylor, wife of a junior assistant, confirmed the extent of Joan's wounds and the company's court warned John that if he beat or misused Joan again they would dismiss him as beadle and he would lose the house that came with the job.[25] Few minute books or other records from London wardmote inquests survive from this period, and none appears to record efforts to reconcile or separate incompatible couples. However, these inquests actively policed married individuals they suspected of illicit behaviour and regularly bound married couples to keep the peace for disorderly behaviour or sexual infidelity.[26]

Dozens of unhappy spouses sued each other in the court of Requests between 1540 and 1640 and, in common with Griffin Jones, many of them appear to have bypassed the church courts altogether. Dame Margery Acton sought relief in the court of Requests in 1540 without having secured a separation *a mensa et thoro*, and, rather than contest her suit, her husband sent word to the court that he would accept any reasonable arrangements for maintenance payments the masters might order. Elizabeth Eggington did not wait to gain a church court separation before suing her husband Francis and her father-in-law John Eggington in Requests in 1619, probably because of the physical harm she alleged she had suffered at both men's hands. According to her bill of complaint her husband, 'by the wicked persuasions of the said John Egginton the father, did beat, hurt, wound and maim your said subject in divers places of her body, whereby your said subject is made unable to labor and work for her maintenance'. She also alleged that the two men had contrived to kidnap her and take her in a cart to John Eggington's house against her will. When

[24] *Edith Mathew* v. *John Mathew*, TNA: PRO, C1/851/17.
[25] Archives of the Clothworkers' Company (Dunster Court, Mincing Lane, London) court book 1602, fol. 212. I would like to thank Dr Alexandrina Buchanan, archivist for the company, for this reference.
[26] See, for example, Guildhall MS 4069; MS 1500; MS 1501; MS 1502; MS 2050, fol. 1r–v.

called to answer these allegations Francis denied hurting Elizabeth, but admitted forcibly taking her by cart to his father's house.[27]

An even greater number of unhappy wives and husbands sought relief in Chancery, both before and after the Reformation. In the 1530s Anne Burwell of Little Munden in Hertfordshire sued her husband William seeking maintenance. She argued that she had brought £200 in money and plate to the marriage but that William, who was supposedly now 104 years old and deaf and blind, 'hath given and distributed all his substance amongst his children' leaving himself 'nothing towards the maintenance of the living of him and your said oratrix'. She asked the chancellor to induce William and his children to 'make and assure to your said oratrix of some competent living during her natural life so that she be not compelled to beg in her old days'.[28] In the same decade Margaret Killyow (using her former surname of Cowling) accused her husband John Killyow of repeatedly assaulting her and then ejecting her from the couple's home, and sought to have him answer for his behaviour in Chancery. In the meantime she asked the chancellor 'to suffer your lordship's said oratrix peaceably to have, receive and enjoy to her own use for the maintenance of herself and her five children' all the rents and profits from the lands and tenements her husband held 'in the right and behalf of your said oratrix'.[29] Anne Brown sued her husband Andrew in Chancery during the reign of Mary I, alleging that 'of his unkind, devilish and ungodly inclination and disposition' he had 'most shamefully and unlawfully' ejected Anne from his house, despite her being 'a young woman and quick with child', and refused to maintain her. He now planned to 'fly the realm' and leave her destitute, 'to the pernicious and evil example of all such like devilish, wicked and evil disposed persons minding and intending to do and practice the like wicked and ungodly doings'. She requested that the chancellor order Andrew to provide her with adequate maintenance.[30] In the dozens of cases where the chancellor and masters in Chancery decided to comply with requests like Anne's they issued injunctions or used conditional bonds or covenants supported by sureties to enforce their orders. If defendants refused to comply, complainants had the option of returning

---

[27] *Dame Margery Acton v. Sir Robert Acton*, TNA: PRO, REQ 2/14/53; REQ 1/9, fols. 157–8; *Elizabeth Eggington v. Frauncis Eggington & John Eggington*, TNA: PRO, REQ 2/414/40, mm. 2, 3; for these and other examples see Tim Stretton, *Marital Litigation in the Court of Requests 1542–1642* (Camden Series: Cambridge, forthcoming).

[28] *Anne Burwell v. William Burwell*, TNA: PRO, C1/736/32.

[29] *Margaret Cowling v. John Killyow*, TNA: PRO, C1/970/63.

[30] Andrew responded by denying almost all of Anne's allegations and making some of his own; *Anne Brown v. Charles Brown*, TNA: PRO, C1/1408/68; C1/1408/69.

to the court, but the expectation was that they would put their bonds in suit at common law to claim the money penalty.

Other courts also heard grievances from unhappy spouses. In 1596 John Edmonds sought a judicial separation from his wife Bridget in the Cambridge University's vice chancellor's court on the grounds of adultery.[31] Earlier in the century Meryell Everyngham entered suit against her estranged husband Henry in the council of the north, arguing that he had sold the lands and tenements that funded her alimony stipend of £6 a year, and requesting a subpoena to help her gain relief in Chancery.[32] In the late 1530s, 'by the motion' of Sir William Fitzwilliam earl of Southampton 'and divers other worshipful men', Sir Thomas and Elizabeth Butler of Bewsey, Lancashire separated 'by their own free wills consent'. It is not immediately clear in which of his many capacities Fitzwilliam was operating. However, he and his colleagues oversaw the drawing up of written instruments that bound Thomas to cede to Elizabeth control over the lands and tenements she held from her late husband, 'in the name of her jointer and dower', for her maintenance, 'as though that no such marriage between them had be[en] made and solemnized'.[33]

A number of wealthier married couples appeared in Star Chamber. To take three examples from the later years of the reign of Henry VIII, Katherine Rocheford from Lincolnshire sued her husband John in the court, alleging that he had kept her imprisoned in chains for sixteen days in a tower until she agreed to release lands enfeoffed to trustees on her behalf.[34] Anne Banestre sued her husband John seeking maintenance, describing how he had deserted her and left her without sustenance for four years. During that time she and her friends had complained to John, and to his master Sir Nicholas Carew, until finally he agreed to pay her an annual allowance. However, when it came time to secure this agreement in indentures to be made with Anne's uncle Edward Boughton, John 'would never come to conclude and make an end' for the allowance.[35] Finally, Alice Bellnappe of Warwickshire sued her husband John, claiming that he 'useth and ordereth your said oratrice in most cruel and

---

[31] Subha Mukherji, '*Edmonds* v. *Edmonds*, 1596', *Queens' College Record* (Cambridge, 2004), pp. 14–17.

[32] *Meryell Everyngham* v. *Henry Everyngham & Sir Thomas Johnson*, TNA: PRO, State Papers (hereafter SP) 46/184/188.

[33] *Elizabeth Butler* v. *John Wyllowes*, TNA: PRO, C1/1105/49; internal evidence suggests that the separation took place between 1536, after Fitzwilliam had ended his term as chancellor of the duchy of Lancaster, and 1540, when he was appointed lord privy seal.

[34] *Katherine Rocheford* v. *John Rocheford*, TNA: PRO, Star Chamber (hereafter STAC), 2/17/202.

[35] *Anne Banestre* v. *John Banestre*, TNA: PRO, STAC 2/3 fols. 62–4. The case refers to Sir Nicholas Carew as master of the horse, a post he held from 1522 until 1539.

ungentle fashion' and 'not only wasteth, consumeth and spendeth' the goods and substance she brought to the marriage but failed to provide her with 'convenient or sufficient goods to maintain her' according to her degree, causing her to 'live in penury and misery'. It was Alice's hope that 'for a quietness and rest' to be had between her and her husband, the king and members of his council would 'limit and appoint unto the said John Bridges such parcel of the yearly profits and rents of the lands and tenements' and the goods and chattels she had brought to marriage 'as by your grace and your said council shall be thought mete and convenient'. The residue could then be 'assigned and appointed to your said oratrice to do therewith her will and pleasure, without any meddling therein to be had by the said John Bridges'. She also asked the council to command John Bridges never to 'resort nor come unto the company' of her or her friends and kinsfolk and to have him bound over to good behaviour.[36]

It is well known that the privy council and other arms of the crown also intervened directly in a number of messy separations and annulments among the aristocracy. To take just two examples, on 11 August 1541 Lord Audley and other members of the king's council bound Sir Oswald Wylsthorpe by recognisance 'in the sum of 100 pounds to be paid to the king our sovereign lord's use' upon condition that if Oswald paid his wife Anne an annuity of £10 and brought in sureties to ensure his performance, then the said recognisance would be void. He was to pay the annuity until such time 'as he could find in his heart to use and accept the said Anne as his wife', but in the first two years he paid her only £7 10s and she sought Audley's assistance again, this time in Chancery.[37] The fracturing of the marriage of Sir Edward Powell and Dame Mary Powell in the 1630s caught the attention of an even larger array of officials. The marriage entered stormy waters after Dame Mary came into a substantial inheritance, in her capacity as executor of her late mother's estate. When Sir Edward attempted to take control of this new wealth for himself, Mary complained to the church courts and secured a separation order that included arrangements for alimony. The ineffectiveness of this solution, however, can be gauged from the veritable *Who's Who* of members of the Stuart court and legal establishment who subsequently intervened in this marital dispute as referees, directed, as one order put it, to 'discover him to be a very beast or her a notable queen, or both' and to negotiate a lasting settlement. They included, at different times, the lord privy seal, the lord treasurer, the lord keeper, the lord chancellor, the barons

---

[36] *Alice Bellnappe* v. *John Bridges*, TNA: PRO, STAC 2/4, fol. 180.
[37] *Lady Anne Wylsthorpe* v. *Sir Oswald Wylsthorpe*, TNA: PRO, C1/1083/49; The act books of the privy council do not survive for the period 22 July 1543–10 May 1545.

the peace appeared in ecclesiastical disputes or were themselves ministers or diocesan chancellors, and many exercised considerable discretion in dealing with minor offenders informally or through arbitration.[43] It is not difficult to imagine that in carrying out their duties, in particular the binding over of violent husbands (or more rarely wives), justices indulged in some discreet marriage guidance, or the brokering of separations of the kind already described.

Further examples exist of high-profile officials acting in private, even further away from the glare of public surveillance and the public record. Sir Julius Caesar, master of the court of Requests, appears to have mediated or negotiated a number of separations, not in the white hall where the court of Requests sat, but in his 'private' chambers in Doctors Commons near St Paul's cathedral, details of which survive as much by chance as by design.[44] Similarly, in 1603 Sir Mathew Carew, master of the court of Chancery, oversaw the drawing up of an indenture of agreement between Robert Garth and his wife Elizabeth that amounted to a private separation. Under the terms of the indenture, which was enrolled in Chancery, the couple 'covenanted, agreed and concluded' that Elizabeth would 'live apart by her self . . . without let, trouble or interruption' by her husband Robert, and vice versa, 'and neither to sue [the] other for cohabitation'.[45] More surprising still, in the 1590s Sir John Popham, lord chief justice of Common Pleas, negotiated a settlement between a couple without reference to the church courts which the couple signed in his presence.[46] And so the list of examples goes on.[47]

The vast majority of church court separations and alternative private settlements relied upon conditional bonds, indented deeds, recognisances or other legal instruments that could be enforced in the courts of common

Historical Society, 6th ser., 8 (1998), 71–89; Steve Hindle, 'The keeping of the public peace' in Paul Griffiths *et al.* (eds.), *The Experience of Authority in Early Modern England* (London and New York, 1996); J. H. Gleason, *The Justices of the Peace in England 1558 to 1640* (Oxford, 1969), pp. 10–11; Dalton, *Countrey Justice*, p. 172; William Sheppard, *The Whole Office of the Country Justice of Peace* . . . (London, 1650), pp. 108–9. Parties wishing to enter into marriage contracts sometimes became bound to public officials, such as mayors or burgesses, making marriage by a certain date a condition of the bond; TNA: PRO, REQ 1/18, pp. 583–4.

[43] Ingram, *Church Courts*, pp. 34, 60, 210.

[44] See, for example, TNA: PRO, REQ 2/234/61 and Lamar Hill, *Mistress Bourne's Complaint* (forthcoming), as well as Caesar's letter books in the British Library (hereafter BL) Lansdowne collection of manuscripts.

[45] *Robert Garth* v. *Sir Benjamin Tichborne & Elizabeth Garth*, TNA: PRO, REQ 2/210/17.

[46] *Anne Lloyde* v. *Humfrey Lloyde & John Bradshaw*, TNA: PRO, REQ 1/19, pp. 19, 104, 116, 224.

[47] See, for example, *John Gascoigne* v. *Jane Gascoigne* from 1605 and *William Dunford* v. *Elianor Dunford* from 1631; TNA: PRO, REQ 2/300/47; TNA: PRO, REQ 1/34, pp. 183–4.

having another husband or wife living, to the great dishonour of God, and utter undoing of divers honest men's children and others'.[67] As the author of *The Lawes Resolutions of Womens Rights* reflected, 'in pursuing of divorce the strict order of judicial proceedings is not always severely kept'.[68]

High profile and often politically motivated 'divorces' also did little to shore up the sanctity of the marriage bond or the reputations of the religious bodies empowered to defend it. In an infamous example from 1605, William Laud presided over the secret marriage of Penelope Rich to her lover, Sir Charles Blount, just six weeks after Rich and her husband secured a separation from bed and board. Blount wrote an elaborate and confidently argued twenty-eight-page defence of this marriage, drawing on Erasmus, the laws of Moses and interpretations of the same biblical passages favoured by the authors of tracts advocating remarriage after divorce.[69] Rich was banished from court and her children by Blount suffered the stigma and legal incapacities of illegitimacy, but this union, described by one contemporary as a 'most dishonorable and both unlawful and ungodly match', did not result in a prosecution for bigamy.[70] It was difficult for the watching public not to become cynical, or further confused, as they observed the divorce of Frances Howard, countess of Suffolk, from Robert Devereux, 3rd earl of Essex, in 1613 on the grounds of impotence. Frances succeeded in having her marriage annulled after claiming that her husband was impotent with her, but not with other women.[71] The intimate details of this case were not immediately made public, but the apparent ease with which elite couples could sever marriage ties did not escape popular notice. When John Strype reflected in the seventeenth century how in Thomas Cranmer's lifetime 'adulteries and divorces increased much; yea, and marrying again without divorce' he was guilty of exaggeration, but not of outright fiction.[72]

---

[67] 1 Jas I cap 11. As quoted in Bridenbaugh, *Vexed and Troubled Englishmen*, p. 41.

[68] T[homas] E[dgar] (ed.), *The Lawes Resolutions of Womens Rights: Or, The Lawes Provision for Woemen* . . . (London, 1632), pp. 67–8; in *Matrimonial Honour*, published in 1642, Daniel Rogers complained of couples 'of all sorts . . . abandoning each other by law or lawless divorce'; Capp, *When Gossips Meet*, p. 114.

[69] BL Additional MS 4149, fols. 306–19v.

[70] Stone, *Road to Divorce*, p. 307; Pearl Hogrefe, *Tudor Women: Commoners and Queens* (Ames, Iowa, 1975), p. 89; David Lindley, *The Trials of Frances Howard: Fact and Fiction at the Court of King James* (London and New York, 1993), p. 87.

[71] BL MS Lansdowne 132, fols. 95–7.

[72] John Strype, *Memorials of the Most Reverend Father in God Thomas Cranmer* . . . (London, 1694), pp. 80, 205–6; in the mid-sixteenth century the marquess of Northampton and Sir John Stawell both remarried after separating from their wives for adultery; Ingram, *Church Courts*, p. 147.

Royal or parliamentary pressure brought to bear on ecclesiastical assessments of the validity of particular marriages, either directly or through politicised bodies such as the high commission for ecclesiastical causes, might also encourage a level of scepticism or cynicism in observers. As Clement VII wrote to Henry VIII as he sought to escape the first of his many marriages, 'you ought not to give cause for scandal nor to set a bad example . . . for the deeds of princes, and above all of one so illustrious as you, stand forth as an example for the imitation of all men'.[73] In the reigns of Henry VIII and Edward VI, parliaments passed acts in Parr's case and Sadler's case recognising dubious unions as lawful and legitimating the offspring they produced, in defiance of existing canon law.[74] In the Essex case, mentioned above, the archbishop of Canterbury strongly objected to the granting of an annulment, but when he made his position clear in a letter to James I, the king replied with a four-page point by point dismissal or rebuttal of the archbishop's arguments.[75]

Finally, there was the confusion created by the word 'divorce' itself. The chief culprit here was ecclesiastical law, and its use of the labels divorce *a vinculo* to describe an annulment and divorce *a mensa et thoro* to describe a separation. As this essay has explained, the first allowed remarriage, the second did not. Is it any wonder that a number of ordinary citizens conflated the two and believed, or at least pretended to believe, that remarriage was possible after a 'divorce' on the grounds of adultery or cruelty? Katherine Willoughby from Middlesex remarried while her first husband was still alive, and when the second match failed she sued both her husbands in a single action in the court of Requests in 1601. If her pleadings are to be believed, she had no inkling that remarriage after a church court separation was illegal (and could result in a bigamy charge) until her lawyers informed her. The masters of Requests seemed undisturbed by this state of events and let her proceed with her case.[76] According to the complainants in another Requests case, Mary Goodricke not only remarried after a separation *a mensa et thoro*, but also continued to collect alimony from her first husband, guaranteed under an indenture of obligation enforceable at the common law that her father put in suit in the court of Queen's Bench.[77] When Hercules Fuljambe defended himself

---

[73] As quoted in Thompson, *Marriage and its Dissolution*, vol. I, p. xiv.

[74] Dibdin and Healey, *English Church Law* , pp. 63–9; BL Harleian MS 7089, fols. 453–7v.

[75] BL Add. MS 34218, fols. 143–5v.

[76] *Katherine Willoughby* v. *Kenelm Willoughby & Henry Fenner*, TNA: PRO, REQ 2/31/3. For further examples of bigamous marriages, see Ingram, *Church Courts*, p. 179; Michael Macdonald, *Mystical Bedlam: Madness, Anxiety, and Healing in Seventeenth-Century England* (Cambridge, 1981), p. 101.

[77] TNA: PRO, REQ 2/231/43; for a similar case see REQ 2/402/39.

in Star Chamber in 1602 against accusations of bigamy, he alleged that he had sought the counsel of 'divers divines and civilians [doctors of civil law] of great account and learning' who confirmed to him that he had properly divorced his two former wives and therefore 'might by the laws of God and this realm, as he was informed by the said divines and civilians, lawfully marry again'.[78] Some were confused about the law of divorce, some feigned confusion and others knew exactly what they were doing. In a Chancery case from the late 1530s or early 1540s Joyce Lambe alleged that her husband Thomas ap Harry had 'relinquished, forsaken and cast off your said oratrice, feigning a void and untrue divorce by him to be sued and had between him and your said oratrice of the said matrimony, but also of his most evil conscience' had married again while Joyce was still living.[79] The uncertainty that made possible each of these examples is clearly apparent in another case from Chancery, where a woman who gained a separation from her husband *a mensa et thoro* described herself as 'lawfully divorced and separated by the holy church'.[80]

In the century following Henry VIII's break with Rome the church courts were not the corrupt 'stinking ditch' of Puritan polemic, but neither were they held in universally high regard.[81] During this period, these courts witnessed a decline in levels of litigation over matrimonial causes, and historians have read this as a sign of 'a growing acceptance among the laity of the church's rules about marriage'.[82] It seems undeniable that marriage as an idea, as an ideal and as an institution remained strong throughout this period, as evidenced by the energy that neighbours, friends and high officials expended trying to keep couples together. Yet at the same time the willingness of a small but significant minority of individuals to bypass the church courts' monopoly and look elsewhere for solutions to their marital difficulties suggests that respect for these courts may have been waning rather than growing.[83] Some ignored the church courts out of ignorance or confusion, but others appear to have done so knowingly. They either doubted the ecclesiastical authorities' ability

---

[78] As quoted in Dibdin and Healey, *English Church Law*, p. 58.

[79] *Joyce Lambe* v. *Thomas ap Harry*, TNA: PRO, C1/1016/74.

[80] *Margaret Molde* v. *The mayor & sheriffs of London*, TNA: PRO, C1/852/57.

[81] Martin Ingram, 'Puritans and the church courts, 1560–1640', in Christopher Durston and Jacqueline Eales (eds.), *The Culture of English Puritanism, 1560–1700* (New York, 1996), p. 58.

[82] Helmholz, *Canon Law and Ecclesiastical Jurisdiction*, p. 564.

[83] The court of Requests heard spouse against spouse suits in every decade for which the relevant records survive, except perhaps for the 1630s; Stretton, *Marital Litigation*, Introduction; Tim Stretton, 'The legal identity of married women in England and Europe 1500–1700', in Andreas Bauer and Karl. H. L. Welker (eds.), *Europa und seine Regionen: 2000 Jahre Europäisches Rechsgeschichte* (Cologne and Vienna, Weimar, 2006), pp. 309–21.

to ensure personal safety or to protect property interests, or wished to avoid the financial costs, the unwelcome publicity or the meddling with broken marriages that formal separation proceedings might bring. The precise number who trod this path may never be known, given the legacy of silence and discretion in the sources, yet it remains intriguing that, when particular marriages went awry, an array of lay officials and bodies chose to let pragmatism trump dogmatic adherence to the rules of the church.

If the options for warring couples appear to have been broader than a focus on church court archives suggests, so too was the cast of people who busied themselves with the formal and informal regulation of marriage. Diana O'Hara has characterised the making of marriage in early modern England as a process of 'courtship *and* constraint' in which family members, kin, neighbours, friends, colleagues and even public officials did their best to scrutinise and influence the free choices of prospective marriage partners.[84] What seems clear from the examples in this essay is that the complex web of consultation, negotiation and compromise, and the consent and approval (willing, tacit or begrudging) of different members of the community, that preceded marriage did not suddenly evaporate once a couple became husband and wife. This rich mix of family, neighbourly and political surveillance continued to play a key role in maintaining (or where necessary in breaking) marital bonds throughout the duration of marriage.[85]

Statutes, pulpits and prescriptive literature presented a unified voice extolling in the strictest terms the strength and permanence of the bonds of marriage. Marriage was the agreed entry point into adulthood, a prerequisite for holding municipal and political office, and the key building block of the nation in countless patriarchal metaphors that fused biblical with political thought. Neither church nor state could afford to admit publicly that spouses could break their vows, for the whole political, and much of the spiritual, edifice relied for its authority on the rigid solidity of marriage.[86] Yet neither church nor state benefited from forcing miserable or incompatible or violent spouses to cohabit once their marital

---

[84] Diana O'Hara, *Courtship and Constraint: Rethinking the Making of Marriage in Tudor England* (Manchester, 2000); and see Catherine Frances, 'Making marriages in early modern England: Rethinking the roles of family and friends', in Maria Ågren and Amy Louise Erickson, eds., *The Marital Economy in Scandinavia and Britain* (Aldershot, 2005), pp. 39–55.

[85] For examples from a later period, see Joanne Bailey, *Unquiet Lives: Marriage and Marriage Breakdown in England, 1660–1800* (Cambridge, 2003), esp. ch. 3, and Elizabeth Foyster, *Marital Violence: An English Family History 1660–1857* (Cambridge, 2005), esp. ch. 4.

[86] Mary Lyndon Shanley, 'Marriage contract and social contract in seventeenth century English political thought', *Western Political Quarterly* 32 (1979), 79–91.

relations had soured or disintegrated. As the examples in this essay show, in individual marriages where the ideological vision that embodied the values of those in power was proving unworkable, exceptions could be made and practical solutions achieved. The ability of the law of marriage to bend helped to ensure that the ideology of marriage did not break.

These cases also suggest that the date of the origin of private separations needs to be pushed back before the 1650s. It is undeniable that in that decade, when the jurisdiction of the church court was abolished with no immediate thought given to its replacement, estranged spouses had to seek alternative ways to separate. Their industrious lawyers quickly turned to private settlements by deed or conditional bond, but in doing so they were not acting as radical mavericks inventing a new secular, contractual way to end unhappy marriages. Instead they were drawing upon a tried and tested mechanism familiar since at least the time of Queen Elizabeth.

3   Republican reformation: Family, community and the state in Interregnum Middlesex, 1649–60

Bernard Capp

On 18 June 1658 a Middlesex justice bound over Priscilla Frotheringham:

for being a notorious strumpet, a common field walker and one that hath undone several men by giving them the foul disease, for keeping the husband of Susan Slaughter from her ever since December last and hath utterly undone that family, and also for threatening to stab the said Susan Slaughter when ever she can meet her, the woman being a very civil woman, and also for several other notorious wickednesses which is not fit to be named among the heathen.[1]

'Binding over' was a common legal procedure, making the subject financially liable for any further misconduct before the next meeting of the relevant court. But the emotional language of the issuing magistrate, Thomas Hubbert, was far removed from the dry formulae usual in such documents, and betrays his deep disgust at Priscilla's alleged behaviour. For men such as Hubbert, 'godly reformation' meant not Lawrence Stone's repressive package of 'anti-pleasure principles' but a crusade against vices that were destroying families and poisoning society.[2] An Independent lay preacher, Hubbert had already penned a diatribe attacking those who paid merely lip-service to piety while failing to act against vice and profanity.[3] But if Hubbert embodies godly reformation, Priscilla Frotheringham, a victualler's wife, personifies the challenge it faced. She and her husband Edmund appear repeatedly in the sessions records for gaming, tippling, disorder, and running a suspected bawdy-house. Parish officers entering their house in March 1652 had found her 'sitting between two Dutchmen with her breasts naked to the waist and without stockings, drinking and singing in a very uncivil manner'. Incorrigible, she survived a spell in Newgate to achieve notoriety after the Restoration as one of the

---

[1] London Metropolitan Archives, MJ/SR/1183/70. All manuscripts cited are from this archive. (Spelling has been modernised throughout.)

[2] L. Stone, *The Family, Sex and Marriage in England 1500–1800* (London, 1977), p. 627.

[3] T. Hubbert, *Pilula ad expurgandam Hypocrisin* (1650). For Hubbert as preacher see MJ/SR/1102/131, and MJ/SR/1158/201 (requesting Thomas Walley to stand in for him). On Walley's church see K. Lindley, 'Whitechapel Independents and the English Revolution', *Historical Journal* 41 (1998), 283–91.

most scandalous bawds in London.[4] Hubbert and the Frotheringhams embodied utterly irreconcilable cultures.

The campaign for godly reformation in the 1650s thrust the state into the everyday lives of thousands of ordinary families. The reformers targeted a range of abuses such as disorderly alehouses, sexual immorality, blasphemy, and profanation of the Sabbath. While these had been concerns for generations, the Puritans had now at last secured control of central government, and had installed hundreds of like-minded ministers and magistrates to spearhead the work of reformation at local level. Almost all their concerns impinged directly on family life. The alehouse, they complained, encouraged men to neglect their domestic responsibilities and squander family resources, and drew younger folk into the vices of illicit sex, gambling or violence. Even blasphemy, an offence against God, undermined family values by leading the young astray. The influential minister William Gouge warned bluntly that blaspheming parents set their children a fatal example, 'and lead them on forward to hell'. Many shared his concern, and observers frequently commented on the foul language of children playing in the street.[5]

Most historians have regarded the reforming campaign of the 1650s as doomed to failure. Lawrence Stone judged it 'Draconian' but ultimately counter-productive, provoking a cultural backlash after 1660.[6] Others have seen even its short-term achievements as negligible. Derek Hirst speaks bluntly of 'the failure of godly rule', a view shared by Christopher Durston and by Jean Mather, who undertook a preliminary trawl of the Middlesex records. By contrast Keith Wrightson identified some tangible achievements in his pioneering exploration of reform in Essex and Lancashire. Anthony Fletcher, surveying campaigns for reform across the century, also pointed to temporary successes and noted that godly magistrates found a measure of support among the respectable 'middling sort'.[7] The reformation of morals and manners involved local communities as well as zealots and sinners. It brought together, however uneasily, the concerns of state, neighbourhood, families and individuals.

---

[4] MJ/SR/1081/136; (G. Garfield), *The Wandering Whore* (1660), part I, p. 6.
[5] W. Gouge, *Of Domesticall Duties* (1622), p. 523; and see, e.g., R. Flecknoe, *The Diarium* (1656), p. 8.
[6] Stone, *Family, Sex and Marriage*, pp. 627–8.
[7] D. Hirst, 'The failure of godly rule in the English Republic', *Past and Present* 132 (1991), 33–66; C. Durston, 'Puritan rule and the failure of cultural revolution, 1645–1660', in C. Durston and J. Eales (eds.), *The Culture of English Puritanism, 1560–1700* (Basingstoke, 1996), pp. 210–33; Durston does note some local successes: pp. 219–20; K. Wrightson, 'The Puritan reformation of manners, with special reference to the counties of Lancashire and Essex' (PhD thesis, Cambridge University, 1973); A. Fletcher, *Reform in the Provinces: The Government of Stuart England* (New Haven, 1986), e.g., pp. 240–4, 250–1, 281.

This chapter revisits the debate. Where did godly reformers focus their energies? What resources lay at their disposal? What degree of popular co-operation, evasion or resistance did they encounter? And how far did their efforts affect family life? Middlesex provides a useful case study, not least because its judicial records have survived well, unlike those of Interregnum London. The county was compact, with a supportive central government close by. Many of the parish churches, such as Stepney, were in the hands of committed Puritan ministers and vestries. Reformers could also call, if necessary, on the assistance of the New Model Army, part of it garrisoned nearby. John Barkstead, regicide and Lieutenant of the Tower from 1652, was an active member of the Middlesex bench, and an energetic Major-General for Middlesex in the Cromwellian experiment of quasi-military rule in 1655–6.[8]

At the same time, the reformers faced formidable problems. Some historians, such as Christopher Hill and Christopher Durston, have focused on the disruption that civil war had inflicted on traditional family ties, exacerbated by novel and sometimes libertarian beliefs on personal and social morality. Moderate Puritans saw this as a period of unprecedented threat as well as opportunity.[9] Reformers in Middlesex also faced more specific problems. The London suburbs had been growing at a prodigious rate for decades, and the influx of newcomers, coupled with high mobility, brought an equally high level of social anonymity. Most of the petty crime and disorder in Middlesex occurred, predictably, within the London suburbs. Moreover, the structures of local government had failed to keep pace with the demographic explosion. Where London had an efficient corporate government reinforced by the city guilds and the Bridewell governors, Middlesex still relied on justices of the peace, meeting in 'quarter' sessions (in practice roughly every six weeks) and smaller, local petty sessions.[10] Beyond that, government rested on unpaid parish officers: petty constables, headboroughs, and the watch, alongside the churchwardens. The Long Parliament had abolished the ecclesiastical courts without establishing any machinery to replace them, leaving the enforcement of godly discipline to secular officials. And while Middlesex had numerous Puritan ministers, by no means all were committed to co-operation with

---

[8] On Barkstead see *The Oxford Dictionary of National Biography* (Oxford, 2005; henceforth ODNB); C. Durston, *Cromwell's Major-Generals. Godly Government During the English Revolution* (Manchester, 2001), *passim*.

[9] C. Hill, *The World Turned Upside Down* (Harmondsworth, 1975), ch. 15; C. Durston, *The Family in the English Revolution* (Oxford, 1989), esp. ch. 7; A. Hughes, *Gangraena and the Struggle for the English Revolution* (Oxford, 2004).

[10] For criminal justice in Middlesex see R. B. Shoemaker, *Prosecution and Punishment. Petty Crime and the Law in London and Rural Middlesex, c.1660–1725* (Cambridge, 1991).

reforming magistrates. Many had fiercely opposed the execution of the king and deeply resented the Interregnum regimes. Justice Hubbert complained bitterly in 1649 that Presbyterian ministers and magistrates chose to harry separatists while ignoring bawdy-houses, 'though they have power in their hands to suppress them, yea and could have done it with a word from their mouths, or line from their hands'.[11] Some Middlesex clergy were not Puritans of any kind. Edward Sparke, ejected from his parish in London, found a new berth as vicar of St James, Clerkenwell and in 1652 published a pugnacious defence of the old church and its festivals. After the Restoration he was to become a chaplain to Charles II.[12] So even in Clerkenwell, where the justices met in sessions, reformers did not control all the levers of power and influence.

Much therefore depended on the magistrates' bench. It included a group of energetic reformers in the same mould as Hubbert, men such as the redoubtable John Waterton of Stepney, a naval contractor, and Josias Berners, a republican Baptist. Solomon Smith, a radical Independent in Tower Hamlets, Richard Loton, a lay preacher in Whitechapel, and John Biscoe, active in both Westminster and the county, were all stalwarts, while William Goffe and Thomas Pride, like Barkstead, were religious and political radicals as well as army officers. But there were fissures even among the radicals. William Rainborough was removed for alleged Ranter sympathies, while Loton was outraged by Cromwell's forcible dissolution of the Long Parliament in April 1653.[13] And many justices fell short of the reformers' zeal, as Hubbert remarked pointedly to his fellow magistrates; greatness and godliness rarely coincided, he observed, and religion was 'almost out of fashion'.[14] The elderly lawyer Laurence Whitaker, though now a Puritan Rump MP, had once been known as a courtier and monopolist. Other justices were easy-going, or venal. One victualler, threatened with suppression in 1658, could retort that 'if he were suppressed one day he would have a licence the next'.[15]

The parish officers, inevitably, were still more diverse. Some were energetic and committed, whether Puritans themselves or sharing a more general 'middling-sort' aversion to a sub-culture associated with drunken violence, illegitimacy and crime. They were reinforced by two other

---

[11] Hubbert, *Pilula*, p. 38.
[12] E. Sparke, *Scintillula Altaris. Or a Pious Reflection on Primitive Devotion* (1652); A. G. Matthews (ed.), *Walker Revised* (Oxford, 1948), p. 57; *ODNB*, Sparke.
[13] For Smith, Loton and Biscoe see K. Lindley, *Popular Politics and Religion in Civil War London* (Aldershot, 1997); Lindley, 'Whitechapel Independents'; *The Humble Petition and Representation of Several Aldermen* (1653), p. 7. For Berners and Rainborough see *ODNB*.
[14] Hubbert, *Pilula*, sig. a2v.   [15] *ODNB*, Whitaker; MJ/SR/1183/88.

important groups. The provost-marshal and his men helped to detect and suppress disorder in and around the capital, while semi-professional informers reported numerous alehouse and other offences, claiming half the fines that accrued. But we can also find plenty of lax or dishonest parish officers while informers, as we will see, were frequently accused of corruption.

In Middlesex the forces of both reformation and resistance were unusually strong and concentrated. Instead of struggling in isolation, godly magistrates constituted a powerful bloc. But their enemies could rally much greater numbers, and the cultural war sometimes exploded into violence. When Justice Hubbert examined two men arrested for alehouse drinking on the Sabbath, in March 1647, an angry mob stormed and ransacked his house. An alehouse-keeper told two young rioters that victuallers and apprentices should stand together against religious zealots, and drank a defiant health to the king.[16] While reformers controlled many of the levers of power, they remained an embattled and sometimes despised minority.

The reforming agenda itself had taken shape long before 1649. A substantial body of pre-war legislation already existed on most of the alleged abuses, with statutes on blasphemy (1624), the Lord's Day (1624, 1628), and alehouses and drunkenness (1604/6, 1624, 1628). In the 1640s the Long Parliament closed the theatres and banned Christmas, and further measures in the 1650s tightened the laws on blasphemy, the Sabbath, and sexual offences. It would be wrong, though, to see the 'cultural wars' as a straightforward struggle between zealots and the profane. Nor were they a clash between 'elite' and 'popular' culture, to use Peter Burke's formulation.[17] Rather, they represent an attempt to impose a religiously inspired 'reformed' culture by a Puritan minority, whose concerns and ideals overlapped in some measure with those of a much wider body of the respectable 'middling sorts'.[18] Puritan reformers wanted to go much further than most of the 'middling sort', but they could assume a bedrock of shared concerns and values. The pre-war legislation underlines the breadth and depth of such concerns. Similarly, at local level, reformers targeting sin might enjoy the co-operation of householders exasperated by the disruptive behaviour of anti-social neighbours. In Interregnum Middlesex, as elsewhere, disorderly alehouses often came to the attention

---

[16] *Strange and Terrible News from Moorfields* (1647); *A Brief Relation of the Great Disorders and Riot Attempted Upon the House and Goods of Thomas Hubbert* (1647); MJ/SBB/69/32.
[17] P. Burke, *Popular Culture in Early Modern Europe* (1978).
[18] J. Barry and C. Brooks (eds.), *The Middling Sort of People: Culture, Society and Politics in England, 1550–1800* (Basingstoke and London, 1994); K. Wrightson and D. Levine, *Poverty and Piety in an English Village: Terling 1525–1700* (Oxford, second edition 1995).

of parish officers and magistrates when violent brawls drove respectable neighbours to summon the watch. Neighbours reported bawdy-houses when they felt provoked by disturbances or women touting for custom in doorways. Respectable citizens might thus co-operate with reformers through self-interest rather than zeal, while others, some far from respectable, were looking to pursue private feuds. Squabbling individuals who accused each other of sexual promiscuity, attempting to manipulate the godly agenda for their own ends, were playing directly into the magistrates' hands. Similarly Alice Jervis, who charged a neighbour with assault and curried favour by adding that he allowed his children 'to play at stool-ball on the Lord's day', was serving the magistrate as much as herself.[19]

Assessing the nature, scale and success of the reforming campaign presents several methodological problems. Most studies have focused on the records of the assize courts and quarter sessions, counting indictments and convictions. Such methods, applied to the 1650s, suggest an increased but hardly dramatic level of prosecutions for moral offences.[20] The Middlesex sessions papers yield a crop of prosecutions for adultery, but they give little indication of a vigorous campaign against other sexual offences, swearing or breach of the Sabbath.[21] But we may have been looking in the wrong place. The reformers wanted to alter behaviour, not fill prisons or swamp the sessions, and they generally preferred to work through informal warnings, summary punishments and recognisances. The Middlesex recognisances of the period, unlike most, spell out in some detail the nature and circumstances of alleged offences, and they furnish both quantitative and qualitative evidence of the impact of godly reformation. The figures tell a striking story (see Table 3.1).

By the later years of the Cromwellian Protectorate, recognisances had recovered from the disruption of the war years and were running at roughly twice the level of the late 1630s, the last years of Personal Rule. And much of this increased business concerned moral offences. The recognisance was in many ways an ideal weapon for reformers. Offenders were arrested, questioned by a justice, and detained until they found sureties for their good behaviour and appearance at the next sessions. The sureties had a strong personal interest in seeing the conditions honoured. At the sessions the justices might cancel the recognisance, extend it, or indict serious and unrepentant offenders.

[19] MJ/SR/1156/90–2; MJ/SR/1167/190.
[20] Fletcher, *Reform*; Wrightson, 'Puritan reformation'.
[21] See the Middlesex Sessions Books (MJ/SBB) and Gaol Delivery Registers (MJ/GB/R/005-6).

Table 3.1: *Recognisances to keep the peace/ be of good behaviour:*

1637	1,221	1653	1,694
1638	1,098	1654	1,753
1644	979	1655	2,111
1646	998	1656	2,143
1647	1,206	1657	2,376
1651	1,599	1658	2,265
1652	1,894	1662	1,321

Source: Sessions Rolls and Books, Middlesex: MJ/SR and MJ/SBB, *passim.*

Recognisances themselves, moreover, were often employed only when more informal methods had failed, or seemed likely to fail. Most parish officers relied initially on persuasion and warnings. Late-night revellers were simply told to go home, and usually only defiant and abusive drinkers were arrested. Similarly, most 'incontinent' couples were dismissed with a warning, sometimes repeatedly, before officers proceeded to more formal action. Summary punishments also played an important role, often overlooked by modern scholars. Sessions records tell us almost nothing about the punishments that magistrates and officers could, and frequently did, impose on their own authority. We are familiar with the 'dark figure' of unrecorded crime, but we need to be aware of the equally important 'dark figure' of unrecorded punishments. Justices were authorised to deal with many minor offences either individually or acting in pairs. A single justice could hear and determine cases of drunkenness, swearing, Sabbath-breach and unlawful games, for example, and impose fines; those who failed to pay he could order to be distrained (i.e., have their goods seized to an equivalent value) or set in the stocks. Justices acting in pairs could suppress disorderly alehouses, and punish bastard-bearers.[22] Such punishments generally went unrecorded, and we can only guess at their scale. But two justices' notebooks that survive from the 1650s, from Coventry and Yorkshire, suggest that a local community might well feel the impact of an active justice far more heavily through his work out of sessions than in court.[23]

---

[22] M. Dalton, *The Country Justice* (1655); C. H. Firth and R. S. Rait (eds.), *Acts and Ordinances of the Interregnum, 1642–1660* (1911); Fletcher, *Reform*, pp. 148–58.

[23] L. Fox (ed.), 'Diary of Robert Beake, Mayor of Coventry, 1655–1656', in R. Bearman (ed.), *Miscellany I* (Dugdale Soc., 31, 1977) pp. 111–37; G. D. Lumb (ed.), 'Justice's Notebook of Captain John Pickering', *Miscellanea IV* (Thoresby Soc., 11, 1904), pp. 69–100 and *Miscellanea V* (Thoresby Soc., 15, 1909), pp. 71–80.

How does the picture of godly discipline change when we widen our approach to the evidence? The issue of swearing (which generally meant blasphemy, not obscenities) was only loosely connected to the family, but it offers a striking example. Taken in isolation, the Middlesex sessions books would not suggest this was a high priority for magistrates. Clerks noted details of sixteen cases, with fines handed down, generally at the standard rate of 3s 4d for each offence. William Lidgould was fined 30s for nine oaths in 1650. A Sabbath brawler was fined 13s 4d for two oaths in 1654, levied at a higher rate 'he being a gentleman as he saith', and another man paid £5 for thirty oaths in 1655.[24] One egregious offender was held in Newgate and then sent to the house of correction for six months in December 1652 as 'an infernal curser and swearer'. Another man, detained in 1655, turned the tables by accusing the arresting bailiff of swearing several oaths, and had the satisfaction of seeing his captor prosecuted and fined 33s 4d.[25] The sessions evidence, taken alone, would suggest a law enforced only sporadically, mainly in extreme or exceptional circumstances.

Casting our net more widely, however, we find a very different picture. Swearing was also punished under a range of other headings. It was one of the charges often cited against alleged scolds and barrators, both frequently prosecuted, and against those charged with keeping disorderly alehouses, numbering many hundreds. Petty sessions also dealt with blasphemy; the minutes of the Brentford sessions, the only ones to survive, add another nine indictments.[26] More important, the sessions rolls include recognisances against roughly a hundred people specifically for swearing, sometimes alongside other offences. It is clear, moreover, that most of these were bound over because they had failed to pay summary fines, were contesting the charge, or were particularly flagrant offenders. The hundred recognisances represent, in other words, only the tip of an iceberg of punishments by individual magistrates acting on their own authority. Occasionally we can still glimpse traces of this activity, such as two certificates which Richard Loton, a Whitechapel justice (and religious radical) returned to sessions in 1653 and 1655. They give particulars of twenty-two men and women he had convicted of sixty-eight separate oaths over the preceding few weeks.[27] It is likely that Loton and many other justices routinely convicted blasphemers in this way throughout the period, while binding over the more flagrant offenders. Justice Waterton bound

---

[24] MJ/SBB/91/36; MJ/SBB/130/51; MJ/SBB/140/33.
[25] MJ/SR/1095/47; MJ/SBB/140/33.
[26] MJ/SP/xx/508: Brentford Petty Sessions Minute Book 1651–1714.
[27] MJ/SR/1108/41a; MJ/SR/1136/84.

over a Wapping victualler in 1650 for swearing twenty oaths after being summarily convicted for a similar offence not long before; a disorderly carpenter in 1654 for swearing forty; and an unruly waterman in 1659 for swearing 'above fifty'.[28] Richard Loton similarly judged a recognisance more appropriate than the usual summary fine for a recalcitrant weaver accused of swearing seventy oaths.[29] Others were bound over after refusing to pay, like the drunken mathematician Nathaniel Moorcock, taken by the watch in May 1653. Railing at them as rogues and knaves, Moorcock had rapped out 'ten several oaths', 'for which drunkenness and swearing . . . he refused to pay the full sum', as Justice Swalowe's recognisance explains.[30]

Moorcock's combination of obstinacy, foul language and other offences reflected a common pattern. A recognisance in April 1653 against a gentleman of New Inn for assault and wounding bears the additional clerical note, 'And to pay xxs [20 shillings] to the poor for swearing'.[31] Mary Hill, bound over by Barkstead in July 1652 for keeping a suspected bawdy-house, responded with a blasphemous tirade which triggered a fine, prompting in turn further angry words and threats. Barkstead thereupon amended the recognisance to include Hill's 'threatening to bring her children and leave them with me because I execute the law against her for swearing'. Similarly when a blasphemous Ratcliff blacksmith threatened the headborough who had reported him, the justice who bound him over to good behaviour added a note that he was to be discharged only on paying 6s 8d for his two oaths.[32] In each of these cases the offender had been summarily convicted by a justice acting alone, and we know of these punishments only because those involved were bound over to answer further offences. Not all those summarily convicted proved able or willing to pay their fines. We have no way of knowing how many were distrained or placed in the stocks, but such punishments were probably not uncommon. We find two sailors in Horsey Down bound over in December 1653 after rescuing a friend placed in the stocks for swearing, while a court in 1656 sentenced a woman to sit in the stocks for six hours, though she later submitted and paid a fine.[33] And when a drunken cordwainer of Rosemary Lane swore several oaths in the presence of the examining magistrate, in March 1657, the justice noted that he was binding the man over only because the parish had no stocks in which to place him for summary punishment.[34] Reforming justices were still proceeding against swearers as late as March 1660.[35] This was

---

[28] MJ/SR/1060/152; MJ/SR/1071/2210; MJ/SR/1204/119.   [29] MJ/SR/1127/248.
[30] MJ/SR/1104/169.   [31] MJ/SR/1104/101.   [32] MJ/SR/1093/36; MJ/SR/1169/356.
[33] MJ/SR/1132/55–6; MJ/SBB/155/30.   [34] MJ/SR/1121/172.
[35] MJ/SR/1209/34, 106.

a campaign waged with energy and determination throughout the Interregnum.

Historians have paid far more attention to the Puritan obsession with sexual promiscuity, where the concerns of the state, local communities and individual families intersected more directly. Puritan resolve was embodied in the notorious Act of 1650, which imposed the death penalty for female adulterers and their male partners, and imprisonment for fornication.[36] The severity of this measure triggered considerable debate, and it is clear that in practice the death penalty was rarely imposed. Keith Thomas concluded that its importance was primarily symbolic, and that the Act never formed 'an effective part of the criminal code'. J. C. Jeaffreson's pioneering research in the Middlesex judicial records, over a century ago, found only one conviction for adultery, with juries thereafter consistently acquitting the accused. Stephen Roberts, studying the Act's operation in Devon, found a group of Puritan magistrates eager to implement it but thwarted by juries invariably acquitting those charged.[37] So what significance, if any, did the Adultery Act have for reformers, communities and families in 1650s Middlesex?

A re-examination of the Gaol Delivery and related papers shows twenty-four women and twelve men tried for adultery in Middlesex. At least one other woman confessed before trial; four other persons were indicted but evaded arrest; and several more were named as partners in indictments but never indicted themselves. Jeaffreson noted the condemnation of Ursula Powell in 1652, later reprieved on grounds of pregnancy, but he missed the trial, condemnation and reprieve of Ellen Farre in 1655. All but five of the thirty-six trials occurred under the Protectorate, not Commonwealth, which indicates that magistrates and grand juries, at least, were ready to act under this law for as long as it remained on the statute-book.[38] It is generally agreed that most contemporaries recoiled from the harshness of the Act, an attitude reflected in jury verdicts, but evidential problems also played an important part. Conviction required a voluntary confession, or direct witnesses. Both were unlikely, and one frustrated critic called for circumstantial evidence to be allowed.[39] In

[36] Firth and Rait, *Acts and Ordinances*, vol. II, pp. 387–9.
[37] K. Thomas, 'The Puritans and adultery: The Act of 1650 reconsidered', in D. H. Pennington and K. Thomas (eds.), *Puritans and Revolutionaries: Essays in Seventeenth-Century History presented to Christopher Hill* (Oxford, 1978), pp. 257–82; F. A. Inderwick, *The Interregnum* (1891), pp. 33–8; J. C. Jeaffreson (ed.), *Middlesex County Records* (1888), vol. III, pp. xxii–xxiii and *passim*; S. Roberts, 'Fornication and bastardy in mid-seventeenth century Devon: How was the Act of 1650 enforced?', in J. Rule, (ed.), *Outside the Law: Studies in Crime and Order 1650–1850* (Exeter, 1992).
[38] MJ/GB/R/005–6. For Farre see MJ/GB/R/005, fols. 256, 258.
[39] Thomas, 'Puritans and adultery', pp. 278–80.

practice, as we would expect, couples generally had time to separate before suspicious neighbours or parish officers could enter the room. Repeatedly we hear of couples found in highly incriminating circumstances, but not quite *in flagrante*. One member of the watch, returning home early, found his wife lying in bed and a stranger hiding beneath it.[40] Some suspects contrived to hide or flee, while others proved defiant. When officers raided a bawdy-house in Clerkenwell in April 1654, the alleged bawd hid her client in a cupboard and then rounded on the constable, threatening to abandon her children to the parish. As the reprobate were well aware, the most godly zeal might falter at the prospect of imposing an additional burden on the community.[41] Many indictments were thrown out by grand juries which recognised that the evidence was insufficient to secure conviction, and many of the acquittals at trial should probably be seen as 'not proven' verdicts. On several occasions the justices indeed responded by sending the accused to the house of correction, or remanding them until they found sureties for good behaviour.

But indictments and trials again tell only part of the story. The Act, and the impulses behind it, helped trigger a flood of recognisances binding alleged adulterers to appear at quarter sessions. Their wording often suggests that the justices, though conscious that the evidence would be insufficient to sustain an indictment, were determined to bring pressure to bear on suspected offenders. Thus George Flamstead, bound over in December 1654 after being taken late at night with Margaret Dickinson of Clerkenwell, both being married, was said to be 'vehemently suspected to live feloniously in an adulterous manner' with her.[42] Many recognisances used formulae such as 'living in adultery' or 'living incontinently'.[43] Most of those accused were never brought to trial. Ellen Dobson proved less fortunate. John Baylie, a ropemaker accused in 1651 of 'living incontinently' with her, was able to prove they had been married for eight years; but further investigations showed that Ellen had earlier married another man, still living. She was thereupon charged with bigamy (not adultery), convicted, and sentenced to be hanged.[44] Contemporaries were often unsure of their neighbours' marital status, especially in areas of high mobility and in the aftermath of a civil war that had torn apart many families. As Lawrence Stone observed, the law of marriage

---

[40] MJ/SR/1140/297; cf. MJ/SR/1140/350; MJ/SR/1144/158.

[41] MJ/SR/1123/127. The bawd, Hester Furmer, employed three aliases.

[42] MJ/SR/1132/83; cf. MJ/SR/1085/48.

[43] E.g., MJ/SR/1126/303; MJ/SR/1129/247–8; MJ/SR/1132/44.

[44] MJ/GB/R/004, fol. 181; MJ/SR/1067/41; MJ/SR/1068/9, 40. Seven witnesses testified against her.

was confused throughout the Interregnum and marriage registers were often poorly kept. The situation was exacerbated in 1653 by an Act prohibiting church marriages; henceforth marriages were to be conducted by justices, though many couples preferred to find a minister willing to perform a clandestine ceremony.[45] Suspicions about neighbours might therefore crystallise as accusations of either adultery or bigamy. The latter remained generally easier to prove, despite the shortcomings of the records. Three people were condemned to death for bigamy, and several others indicted, in 1651 alone; one man had remarried under a false name, a ruse that failed to save him from the gallows.[46] But deep uncertainty about the marital status of alleged offenders is reflected in the decision in 1656 to make Joan Davies stand trial for both adultery and bigamy.[47]

If the 1650 Act brought few convictions for adultery, it triggered a stream of binding-over orders against suspected offenders throughout the decade. Recognisances were rarely used for this purpose before 1650, or after the Restoration. During the Interregnum, many contemporaries were clearly willing to report alleged offenders, even if we assume that few wished to see them hanged. That suggests a considerable degree of co-operation with the Puritan agenda, or a readiness to manipulate it for private ends. Who brought these allegations to official notice, and why?

A few cases were exposed by zealous clergymen, or the newly appointed 'Registers'. Isaac Harding, minister, reported that Cornelius Lowers and John Jennings's wife had been living together for years as husband and wife, and had christened several children in the church of St Giles-in-the-Fields. We can only guess what chance had exposed their secret.[48] Far more often we find charges brought by the parish officers, usually after being tipped off by disgruntled neighbours. Some informants had doubtless been scandalised by behaviour flouting the norms of respectable society and damaging to the social fabric and good name of the neighbourhood. The Act could be used against notorious prostitutes and their clients as well as against cohabiting couples. Thus in the case of Margaret Dickinson, noted above, the magistrate commented that 'she hath often been admonished for her wicked life before and she will not reclaim'. Indeed, she had been bound over only two months earlier, along with three other men taken in her bawdy-house. Neighbours, exasperated by its 'great disorders', had sent for the constable telling him she was

---

[45] L. Stone, *The Road to Divorce. England 1530–1987* (Oxford, 1990), p. 149; Durston, *Family*, pp. 66–86.
[46] MJ/SR/1070/33; MJ/SR/1075/38; MJ/GB/R/005, fos. 181, 191.
[47] MJ/GB/R/006, fols. 2, 12v, 14, 16.
[48] MJ/SR/1138/21, 78–9; for Registers see, e.g., MJ/SR/1136/288.

'but a whore and a bawd'.[49] Thomas Barker, a surgeon and 'haunter of whorehouses', was another such, consorting with a 'noted [and married] whore'; the pair had been seen in bed together, and Barker was accused of beating and publicly cursing his own wife.[50] In cases like these, neighbours could hardly miss illicit behaviour and its social repercussions. Cohabiting couples, by contrast, may well have gone undetected or unreported as long as they lived quietly, though disruptive behaviour would quickly attract attention. Katherine and Joan Lovegrove, bound over in April 1651, were accused of 'continually fighting when they meet about one husband challenged by them both'. Neighbours viewed the disputed husband, a horse-courser and 'nightwalker', as equally undesirable, and we need hardly invoke Puritan zeal to explain their complaints.[51]

Other allegations appear to have been triggered by family feuds rather than concern for the community. When two women denounced a Shadwell seaman and another sailor's wife in 1651 for living incontinently 'for the space of eight years together, at times', private quarrels look a more likely explanation than moral outrage.[52] Elizabeth Alford (or Allfleet), one of the very few Middlesex women to be prosecuted for fornication under the 1650 Act, had been denounced by her lover's widow, who claimed Alford had given him the pox, from which he had died.[53] And the informant who revived old allegations of bigamy or adultery against Oliver Langdon of Wapping in 1654 proved to be no Puritan zealot but one of a criminal gang, languishing in Newgate, whom Langdon had charged with burgling his house and stealing over £200. The man was probably clutching at straws to discredit the charges against him.[54] Even the ungodly might make common cause with Puritan reformers, however different their agendas.

Far outnumbering all these categories, however, are the hundreds of allegations brought by resentful spouses. The Adultery Act provided a weapon for family members as well as disapproving neighbours, and was indeed their only legal recourse following the abolition of the ecclesiastical courts. Angry husbands denounced men for illicit affairs with their wives, while embittered wives accused 'the other woman' with whom their husbands were 'living incontinently' – which might mean cohabitation, consorting with prostitutes, or simply socialising in an alehouse. Wives often complained of being left without maintenance, and sometimes of violent assaults by the husband or his mistress. Other cases were inevitably

[49] MJ/SR/1131/165–6, 169–70, 173; above, p. 50.
[50] MJ/SR/1176/218; cf. MJ/SR/1056/40; MJ/SR/1079/97.   [51] MJ/SR/1067/52–3, 79.
[52] MJ/SR/1076/231.   [53] MJ/SR/1089/29; MJ/GB/R/005, fol. 211.
[54] MJ/SR/1090/30; MJ/SR/1115/210; MJ/SR/1129/34, 47. Langdon's alleged sexual partner was one of the gang held in Newgate.

more complex. In April 1651 Edward Meggs, a former Newgate poulterer now serving in Cromwell's own regiment of horse, accused Sir Edward Norton, Bt, of Sibsey, Lincs, of conducting a prolonged adulterous relationship with his wife Mary. Norton, bound over, denied the allegation and was never indicted. But two years later Norton was accused of having married Mary, who was thereupon indicted and tried for bigamy. This may at last have broken the liaison, but Meggs failed if he was hoping to rescue his marriage; in 1656 Mary stood trial again, this time for adultery with another man. Though cleared, she was packed off to the house of correction, and then back to Newgate, as a 'lewd woman, night-walker'.[55] The law seems to have broken Mary's adulterous relationship with Norton, only to push her into prostitution. In other cases it is clear that a marriage had failed and that one partner had embarked on a new, committed relationship – the modern option of divorce and remarriage being of course unavailable in the seventeenth century. The protracted case of William Goffe, a Whitechapel sawyer charged with bigamy in 1653, suggests a scenario of this kind. Goffe eventually confessed, claimed benefit of clergy, and escaped with his life. Though ordered to return to his first wife, Anne, he continued to consort with his second wife Mary, and in 1655 she was bound over after being spotted leaving Goffe's house at 4 a.m., and 'though it cannot be proved (yet suspected) to live incontinently together'. On the same day Anne accused Mary of giving out that she was still William's lawful wife.[56]

In about thirty cases we find victims denouncing the offending spouse rather than the alleged lover. The cases cover a wide range of situations, a reminder that marital breakdown among ordinary folk could take as many forms as among the elite, whose travails Lawrence Stone documented in loving detail.[57] Some individuals had been driven beyond endurance. Susan Ward complained in 1651 that her husband had not only fathered an illegitimate child but had brought his mistress home one night and into the marital bed, 'having carnal copulation with her whilst his wife was in the bed with them'.[58] His callous contempt appears to have goaded Susan into a response of which he had perhaps deemed her incapable. Robert Pegg also demanded retribution when he came home late one night in 1655 to find his wife in bed and her lover sitting upon it, hastily

---

[55] Jeaffreson, *Middlesex County Records*, vol. III, pp. 202–3, 293–4; MJ/GB/R/005, fols. 182, 185, 236v; MJ/GB/R/006, fols. 12v, 14v, 15, 17v; MJ/SR/1115/47; MJ/SR/1118/5.

[56] MJ/SR/1106/15; MJ/SR/1114/16; MJ/SR/1138/184; MJ/SR/1140/250.

[57] Stone, *Road to Divorce*; L. Stone, *Uncertain Unions: Marriage in England 1660–1753* (Oxford, 1992); L. Stone, *Broken Lives: Separation and Divorce in England 1660–1857* (Oxford, 1993).

[58] MJ/SR/1076/221.

'pulling on his drawers'; Pegg promptly laid charges against them both.[59] It is possible that in such circumstances an angry spouse might want to see the offending partner suffer the rigour of the law. But in other cases the offender had left home long ago and established a *de facto* second marriage. In 1653 Mary Reade, a butcher's wife, said her husband had left several months earlier to live with another woman, 'whereby he is suspected to be married to her'. Dorothy Biggins similarly accused her husband of living 'in adultery with another woman as his second wife and to have had a child by her'.[60] Allegations like these were not triggered by the shock of sudden discovery. The complainants were more probably hoping for financial redress, or using desperate measures to break a long-standing liaison; some may have been ready to settle for either outcome. By contrast John Goodheart, a Wapping victualler, was clearly looking for vengeance when his unfaithful wife gave birth to twins in January 1652; not content with denouncing the alleged father, Goodheart threatened to kill him. Elizabeth Goodheart, the erring wife, was committed to Newgate by Justice Waterton, and admitted both her adultery and an earlier liaison, which rendered a trial unnecessary. Surprisingly, perhaps, her frank confession and remorse secured her discharge at the Old Bailey in February.[61] That suggests the bench itself, though determined to root out sin, was more concerned with reform than savage retribution. Magistrates as well as plaintiffs were ready to use the Adultery Act to pursue their own agendas.

Traditional views of the 1650 Act are thus only partially correct. Though the death penalty was rarely imposed, the 1650s witnessed a vigorous and sustained campaign in Middlesex against alleged adulterers. While prosecutions in Devon were dependent on zealous magistrates, the Middlesex campaign enjoyed the active co-operation of both resentful neighbours and embittered husbands and wives. Only in a relatively small number of flagrant cases did accusations lead to trials. Mary Meggs appears to have been a high-class prostitute, as well as having a bitter and estranged husband; Ellen Farre may have been embroiled in a case of sexual extortion; while Elizabeth Burke, probably another prostitute, had also been named as the sexual partner of a man indicted for buggery, and may well have shocked even non-Puritan sensibilities.[62] The magistrates themselves appear to have behaved with a somewhat pragmatic zeal.

[59] MJ/SR/1144/158.   [60] MJ/SR/1112/246; MJ/SR/1126/157.
[61] MJ/SR/1079/98, 108; *A True and Perfect List of . . . Prisoners in Newgate* [tried at the Old Bailey, 18 Feb. 1652] (1652), p. 6.
[62] Farre may have been the consort/accomplice of Richard Farr: *The Cheating Solliciter Cheated* (1665), p. 7. For Burke: MJ/GB/B/004/89–91; Jeaffreson, *Middlesex County Records*, vol. III, p. 290.

Thomas Hubbert had been scandalised in 1646 by a notorious bawdy-house in Bunhill Fields kept by one Bridget Calthrop, who offered her customers 'women dancing naked'. Hubbert bound her over, but when she gave bond to leave the parish the clerk scribbled a note, 'therefore no prosecution'. Even Hubbert was content to see the problem resolved informally.[63] Magistrates also proved reluctant to indict alleged fornicators under the 1650 Act, perhaps fearing the prisons would be swamped. Once again, they preferred to work through recognisances.

Most bastardy cases were dealt with out of sessions, so evidence is patchy, but while single mothers were sometimes committed to the house of correction or even Newgate, this does not appear to have been standard practice. Puritan magistrates, like their predecessors, focused primarily on financial aspects, determined to prevent the child's maintenance burdening the parish. When Sarah Stone gave birth in 1650, after her sailor-husband had been away in the East for two years, her adultery was obvious; she laid the child to a bodice-maker in Golding Lane, who was ordered to take financial responsibility, but there is no record of any further action.[64] By contrast Elizabeth Ratcliffe, a single mother, was committed to Newgate and charged under the Act in 1652. But when she appeared in court, the magistrates decided to discharge her, noting that she appeared 'very penitent', that the child was still living, and that she had co-operated by naming the father.[65] Even the fiery Justice Waterton could show restraint. He made Mary Pilkington identify the father of her unborn child, binding the man over to appear after its birth; but he then applied (we surmise) some vigorous persuasion, and was soon able to annotate the recognisance, with evident self-satisfaction: 'he is since married to the said Mary Pilkington by me'. Further action was rendered unnecessary.[66] And the most zealous reformers might also display compassion. Joan Holmes, sent to the house of correction by the Westminster bench in 1646 for bearing an illegitimate child, was ordered to be released when she was reported to be very sick. In the same year Justice Hubbert committed a woman for living with a married man, only to order her release on learning that she had a young child at home likely to perish for want of relief.[67] Puritan zeal was not necessarily blind.

Another traditional Puritan concern was the suppression of disorderly ale-houses, long associated with drunkenness, crime, promiscuity, gambling and violence. The Middlesex magistrates took energetic action against unlicensed and disorderly houses. At each sessions informers reported

[63] MJ/SR/989/244.   [64] MJ/SR/1058/224.   [65] *A True and Perfect List*, p. 6.
[66] MJ/SR/1160/88.   [67] MJ/SBB/57/83; MJ/SR/985/119.

offenders, who were obliged to attend and compound the heavy fines incurred. At the October 1653 sessions alone informers reported thirty-seven offenders for permitting unlawful gaming.[68] Offending alehouse-keepers were generally bound over to the next sessions, where they might be discharged, indicted and fined, or suppressed. Most of the routine work of awarding and withdrawing licences was handled in petty sessions, and the Brentford minutes suggest that justices took the task seriously. While only a handful of JPs attended most petty sessions, the clerk noted that 'more Justices than the book can hold' had appeared at the licensing sessions in March 1653. The campaign was stepped up when Barkstead became Major-General for Middlesex. In February 1656 he and twenty-eight other justices issued an order for the strict regulation of alehouses; their numbers were to be reduced, with disorderly houses suppressed for at least three years, and no licence was to be issued henceforth except by a majority of justices in open session.[69]

Like sexual immorality, disorderly alehouses were a significant issue for local communities as well as Puritan reformers. Popular resentment of anti-social behaviour marched hand in hand with godly reformation, and parish officers reporting drink-related offences had frequently been summoned to the scene by exasperated or frightened neighbours. A Whitechapel headborough, called to a general fracas late one night in 1655, described finding the alehouse-keeper, George Morgan, 'all bloody about the face'. Binding him over, Justice Swalowe observed that the house was known to harbour felons and ought to be suppressed, as was duly ordered at the next sessions.[70] At Poplar, neighbours complained after being disturbed early on Christmas morning 1656 by drunkards spilling out of an unlicensed alehouse, fighting, and shouting 'Murder!'[71] Sometimes neighbours complained directly to the magistrate. Several denounced Hugh Floid, a Whitechapel tobacco-cutter who kept an unlicensed and disorderly alehouse, after he had spurned their informal complaints and threatened to kill them. And in 1657 several women obtained a recognisance against Sara Corbett, a sailor's wife in Stepney, exasperated by the drunken brawls in her alehouse, and by Corbett herself. She had been seen lying on the floor, they complained, 'with her hair about her ears, stinking of strong waters, and not able to speak'.[72] For respectable neighbours, Corbett's alehouse was a social nuisance, not a bastion of Merry England.

---

[68] MJ/SR/1112/7–12, 22–63; MJ/SP/xx/508, p. 15.
[69] *Publick Intelligencer* 22 (19–26 Feb. 1656), 359–62.
[70] MJ/SR/1140/103; cf. MJ/SR/1147/147.   [71] MJ/SR/1160/106.
[72] MJ/SR/1162/130; MJ/SR/1167/140; cf. MJ/SR/1077/91.

Many of these alehouse brawls had originated in quarrels over gaming. While cards, bowls and other games were central features of alehouse culture, tempers often flared over unpaid debts and alleged cheating. Some offenders appear to have been semi-professional; Charles Weale, arrested in a gaming-house in July 1654, was 'suspected to live only by gaming and cheating'.[73] Quarrels over gambling debts posed an obvious threat to public order, and they sometimes escalated to dangerous brawls involving knives and even swords.[74]

Disorderly alehouses might thus generate a pragmatic alliance between reforming magistrates and respectable neighbours. But drunkenness and gambling affected family life too, creating tensions that could add a third strand to this alliance. We often find family members utilising the law to curb the folly or exploitation of a spouse or child addicted to alehouse pleasures. Thus in August 1651 Lydia Harrison of Poplar denounced a victualler for keeping her husband 'tippling all Saturday night and most part of the sabbath day', and running a disorderly house. Lydia's personal mission to reclaim her husband had the side-effect of bringing a crop of alehouse offences to the notice of the zealous Justice Waterton.[75] Another woman complained to Justice Swalowe in 1659 that Charles Warren of Rosemary Lane, Whitechapel, allowed unlawful games, 'encouraging poor women's husbands to spend and consume their monies there for his lucre and gain'; when she came one night to demand her husband, she reported, Warren had abused her as 'bitch and whore'. Her complaint was thus prompted by a combination of domestic tensions, defamation, and public concern.[76] Others were triggered by parental worries. George Dashwood, himself a brewer, was willing to report a widow for keeping his son tippling in her house on the Sabbath 'and helping him to the company of a lewd woman'. Similarly John Stevenson denounced a woman and an alehouse-keeper who, together, had enticed his son to spend 55s in the space of a few hours.[77] It seems likely that most parents resorted to such measures only when informal pleas and warnings had proved fruitless. Katherine Wilson had tried to stop her son frequenting an alehouse where young folk would spend nights 'ranting, singing and roaring'. Thwarted, she called in the watch to raid the house, and three women arrested at the scene were bound over to answer for disturbing the neighbourhood. But Katherine's own agenda was personal, and on reaching a private agreement with the chastened

---

[73] MJ/SR/1127/261.
[74] See, e.g., MJ/SR/1032/200; MJ/SR/1038/134; MJ/SR/1076/272; MJ/SR/1140/345; MJ/SR/1165/98–9; MJ/SR/1174/403.
[75] MJ/SR/1071/188.   [76] MJ/SR/1198/265.
[77] MJ/SR/1090/135; MJ/SR/1191/117, 148; cf. MJ/SR/1154/63.

offenders she dropped the charges.[78] By contrast another woman, savagely beaten when she called at a victualling-house one night in 1657 to enquire for her son, probably felt she had little option but to turn to the magistrate.[79]

We can find employers similarly using the law to prevent their servants wasting time and money in alehouses, and running themselves into debt. A Gray's Inn gentleman complained that a victualler and his two female lodgers had, between them, soaked up most of his servant's modest estate.[80] Francis Stevens, a bookseller, had more immediate concerns: his young servant, sent out one day in 1654 to collect debts amounting to £36, had been quickly surrounded by fawning women who 'kept him company night and day' until the money was almost gone. Stevens and the lad's father both laid charges against the women who had led him astray.[81] Servants had little money of their own, and employers understandably feared they might squander their masters' possessions as well as their own.[82] And drunken servants could pose a more direct threat to household discipline. A farrier complained in 1657 that his servant regularly came home drunk and violent on Sundays, and that on one occasion he had assaulted his mistress and threatened to knock out her brains.[83]

No reformers imagined for one moment that they had won the war against illicit and disorderly drinking. But their campaign is impressive, not only for its scale and determination but for the degree of co-operation it secured. And the records of neighbouring Westminster (which shared many of the same justices) show that offending alehouse-keepers were pursued, sometimes for several years, until they submitted and paid their fines.[84]

The campaign against disorderly alehouses was related to a much wider issue of cultural conflict, the last to be considered here: people's freedom to spend leisure-time as they wished. The most familiar battleground was enforcement of the Sabbath, a long-standing bone of contention between reformers and people determined to enjoy their only regular day of leisure. Magistrates regularly ordered 'privy searches' during the hours of church service, and often drew a rich haul of offenders tippling in private houses and alehouses, or skulking in suspected bawdy-houses.

---

[78] MJ/SR/1174/126–9.   [79] MJ/SR/1165/142.

[80] MJ/SR/1112/129; cf. MJ/SR/11081/245.   [81] MJ/SR/1129/207, 261.

[82] See, e.g., MJ/SR/1144/233; MJ/SR/1152/395; MJ/SR/1183/206.

[83] MJ/SR/1163/229.

[84] E.g., WJ/SR/1072, 1077, 1083, 1087. For some account of social regulation in Westminster see J. F. Merritt, *The Social World of Early Modern Westminster* (Manchester, 2005), ch. 7.

Hundreds of offenders were bound over on such charges. In the first six months of 1650 Col. Pride, commanding a garrison quartered in St. James's, supplemented magisterial efforts by launching a personal crusade against all forms of Sabbath-breach, despatching his soldiers each week to crack down on pleasure-seekers in Islington, Moorfields and elsewhere.[85] In 1656 Major-General Barkstead and the Middlesex justices launched a new campaign for the strict enforcement of the Sabbath, and appointed informers in each parish to report offenders.[86]

Alehouse drinking was by no means the only contentious leisure activity. Music and dancing were also sites of cultural conflict, especially when they 'profaned' the Sabbath. Puritans were not hostile to music as such. Genteel, domestic music-making was perfectly acceptable, as were professional performances at civic functions. But singing and playing in disorderly alehouses were very different matters, and recognisances repeatedly complained of alehouse patrons 'singing, roaring and roistering'. Bawdy songs were doubly offensive; by celebrating or making light of sexual promiscuity, they undermined the moral values broadcast each week from the pulpit. Defamatory or seditious ballads, also common, could easily trigger quarrels and violence.[87] Even instrumental music might carry a deliberately subversive message. At Christmas 1659, for example, a young gentleman named Leonard Langsdale was accused of striding into Norton Folgate 'with a fiddle playing before him, going into a suspected bawdy-house, and afterwards coming out again with a fiddle playing before him'.[88] Langsdale had been making a public gesture of cultural defiance, as well as awarding himself an illicit Christmas present.

Instrumental music was often found in alehouses, usually to accompany dancing, and such venues provided a precarious livelihood for professional musicians throughout the Interregnum. Christopher Waters, 'musitioner', was bound over in 1657 by the Puritan Justice Swalowe for living 'loosely and idly, going up and down from alehouse to alehouse, and from tavern to tavern, to play upon organs and virginals which are prepared in sundry such houses to delight persons that live loosely and ungodlily'. A few months later another musician, Thomas Gibbs, was bound over for living 'now here, now there, spending freely' in taverns in

[85] *The Man in the Moon* 44 (20–7 Feb. 1650), 349; 45 (27 Feb.–6 March 1650), 360; 49 (20–9 March 1650), 342; *Mercurius Pragmaticus* 2, 44 (26 Feb.–5 March 1650); *The Royall Diurnall* 6 (26 March–3 April 1650); *A Perfect Diurnall* 24 (20–7 May 1650), 259; *The Impartial Scout* 53 (21–8 June 1650), 222.

[86] *Publick Intelligencer* 28 (1–14 April 1656), 468–9; Durston, *Cromwell's Major-Generals*, pp. 156–7.

[87] E.g., MJ/SR/1079/104.   [88] MJ/SR/1205/56.

Smithfield, 'playing upon the organs to all manner of people . . . where there is dancing and too much drinking'.[89]

Music might seem an area where ordinary people would harbour little sympathy for the Puritan reformers. Yet even here the authorities found a measure of co-operation, with irritated neighbours frequently complaining about noise and commotion in alehouses and bawdy-houses.[90] And we sometimes find support from more unexpected quarters. Thus in January 1651 Helen Aspinall, a musician's wife, was bound over at the request of 'the inhabitants of Cow Cross for singing of ballads which is the cause of many tumults and uproars at Smithfield Bars, the butchers complaining that their meat is stolen off their stalls there by pilfering people that do accompany and follow the said Helen Aspinall'.[91] Even family members might report offenders to the authorities. John Lambert's parents had apprenticed him to a Stepney musician, Walter Trotter, but they were vexed to find their son sent out every day 'to play fiddle and make music in alehouses and taverns', touting for custom. As they realised, he was at risk of being arrested as a vagrant and, alarmed for his safety, they eventually prosecuted Trotter.[92]

For godly magistrates, music and dancing were objectionable mainly because of predictable concerns about illicit sexual activity and disorder. Again we can sometimes find neighbours siding with the 'killjoy' authorities. Thus in September 1649 Justice Hubbert bound over three young women taken late at night 'revelling and dancing in a pretended dancing school', where noisy fights had left neighbours allegedly 'much affrighted and disquieted'.[93] In January 1650 Col. John Okey, justice and regicide, bound over Philip Maynard for entertaining sixty people 'revelling and dancing with lewd and idle women in the night time'. Here too the neighbours had complained, repeatedly, and Maynard was bound over only after ignoring earlier warnings.[94] Alehouse dancing persisted throughout the period, though its scale is hard to judge. Neighbours probably complained only when levels of noise, drunkenness or violence became a public nuisance. Magistrates became seriously concerned when they found aggravating circumstances, as with the man bound over in 1653 'for being found with a woman dancing naked supposed to be Ranters'.[95] Thomas Hyho of Staines, playing his fiddle at a dance in May 1655, was bound over after brazenly claiming to have been authorised by Oliver Cromwell

---

[89] MJ/SR/1165/190; Jeaffreson, *Middlesex County Records*, vol. III, pp. 258–9; MJ/SR/1171/26; cf. MJ/SR/1174/92.
[90] E.g., MJ/SR/1081/136.   [91] MJ/SR/1062/126.   [92] MJ/SR/1175/28.
[93] MJ/SR/1036/76.   [94] MJ/SR/1043/70.   [95] MJ/SR/1103/79.

himself.[96] Magistrates also disapproved of dancing at rowdy seasonal festivities, which might easily pose a threat to public and Puritan order. We
occasionally hear of victuallers hanging up summer garlands, and drawing
large crowds to dance for them as prizes. Mary Miller of St Katherine's-
by-the-Tower, a maidservant, bore her garland triumphantly through the
streets at midnight in June 1659 amidst a huge crowd, but she soon paid
for her hour of fame.[97]

It was not dancing, however, but sport that triggered the most serious
confrontations of the period. Sunday sports had long aroused deep passions, which James I's *Book of Sports* (reissued by Charles I in 1633) had
merely exacerbated. For Puritans the Sabbath was to be kept as God's
holy day in its entirety; many less pious people, however, especially in
large towns, viewed it simply as a day of recreation and stayed away
from church altogether. Despite parliament's victory, crowds continued
to gather for sport in Moorfields and other open spaces on Sundays and
festival days. As well as posing a threat to public order, they represented
a blatant repudiation of Puritan beliefs and values, encouraging young
people to escape both religious instruction and domestic discipline.[98]
One entrepreneur defiantly set up pigeon-holes in Lincoln's Inn fields
on a parliamentary fast day in May 1649, and attracted large crowds.[99]
Large numbers also assembled in Clerkenwell fields on summer Sundays
in 1649, to play games and then bathe in the New River pond. On 1 July
a group of parish officers tried to drive them away but were themselves
chased away by a crowd of some 200 to 300, 'hooting and hallowing' and
hurling stones. Several officers were caught and badly beaten. The following week the officers tried again, reinforced by the provost-marshal and
his men, but were again beaten and driven away.[100] There were further
large-scale and violent clashes in both Lincoln's Inn fields and Clerkenwell on Sundays in April 1650, and in 1652 we find the Council of State
itself attempting to suppress weekly cudgel-fights being staged in Moorfields.[101] There are few such reports thereafter, but it remains unclear

---

[96] MJ/SR/1138/113. He was later in trouble for drinking a health to Charles II:
MJ/SR/1148/285.
[97] MJ/SR/1198/182; Jeaffreson, *Middlesex County Records*, vol. III, pp. 280–1. Miller was
bound over but on the same day obtained a recognisance against a Whitechapel ropemaker for calling her a whore and raising tumults against her, through which she had
lost her place: MJ/SR/1198/193. For similar episodes see MJ/SR/1049/96 (May 1651);
MJ/SR/1140/100 (June 1655).
[98] R. Hutton, *The Rise and Fall of Merry England* (Oxford, 1994).
[99] MJ/SR/1029/48; cf. MJ/SR/1030/47. [100] MJ/SR/1032/203–4.
[101] MJ/SR/1046/253; MJ/SR/1051/32; *Calendar of State Papers, Domestic, 1651–2*, pp. 303,
316.

which side had abandoned the struggle. We hear of a wrestling match in Well Close, Stepney, one Sunday afternoon in 1657 which had attracted 'a multitude of people'.[102]

The clash between the cultures of recreation and godliness surfaced in many other contexts. Though the London playhouses had been closed, entertainments of various kinds continued sporadically. Bear-baiting, a traditional feature of London life repeatedly condemned by parliament in the 1640s, continued until February 1656 when Col. Pride had most of the animals shot at the Bankside bear-garden. Even then the 'sport' survived, precariously, in the Middlesex suburbs. A cordwainer was bound over in April 1658 'for keeping a bear which was baited in the ducking pond at Clerkenwell', and baiting continued there to the Restoration.[103] Cock-fighting proved still more resilient, despite numerous attempts to suppress it. Seven men were bound over for attending a cock-fight at Well Close in March 1656, 'contrary to the Ordinance'. Many others probably escaped notice, though one gentleman invited trouble by publicly advertising a cock-fight at his house in Shoe Lane, in May 1654.[104] And we hear of entertainers of various kinds: two foreigners arrested in 1650 for showing 'unlawful sights'; a Gray's Inn gentleman showing tricks in a tavern till midnight; and Andrew Perry, an impoverished gentleman, performing tricks and jests on a scaffold on Tower Hill in January 1652, 'pretending himself to be a fool, clothing himself in unseemly apparel'. His audience, a magistrate noted, had included both servants and pickpockets, an observation reflecting the authorities' perennial sensitivity to any threat to family order.[105] We also hear of crowds attending 'shows' at fairs in the final months of the Interregnum. By far the largest was reported in May 1659, when Anne Smith allegedly drew a crowd of some 4,000 to a show outside her house in Moorfields, which degenerated into brawls. Anthony Denoe from Bermuda, presenting another show the same day, was arrested when it too ended in violence.[106]

More significant was the struggle over traditional calendar festivities, another long-standing battleground in England's cultural wars.[107] The abolition of Christmas was generally hated, and most families continued to celebrate the day at home or with friends. Most people were probably content to see alehouses doing brisk business at Christmas, provided the merry-making did not end in rowdy disturbances.[108] Another old

---

[102] MJ/SR/1172/170.
[103] L. Hotson, *The Commonwealth and Restoration Stage* (New York, 1962), pp. 59–81; MJ/SR/1181/148.
[104] MJ/SR/1148/210–13, 215–17; MJ/SR/1123/72; cf. MJ/SR/1136/295.
[105] MJ/SR/1050/106, 160; MJ/SR/1079/71–2.   [106] MJ/SR/1198/207, 266–7.
[107] Hutton, *Rise and Fall*.   [108] MJ/SR/1081/57; MJ/SR/1121/157; MJ/SR/1160/53, 106.

calendar custom, Shrove-Tuesday 'cock-throwing' (throwing stones at cocks tethered to a stake), also proved impossible to eradicate. In February 1657 Barkstead and the justices issued strict orders for constables to prevent crowds from assembling to bait bulls and throw at cocks, and pursue 'other dissolute games more becoming heathens than Christians'. Despite the order a large crowd gathered at Bethnal Green, assaulting the constable and his men who attempted to disperse them, and a similar disturbance was reported at Stepney.[109] Magistrates were readier to allow bonfires on 5 November, Gunpowder Treason day, but intervened if revelry degenerated into violence.[110] Many law-abiding citizens probably held ambivalent feelings about seasonal festivities. Justice Waterton may well have appeared over-zealous in binding over a Stepney man on May Day 1655, 'for suffering poor labourers to play at nine pins a whole day together'.[111] But respectable folk would have sided with the authorities on May Day 1656 when a crowd rampaged through St Giles-in-the-Fields, at night, smashing windows and attacking property, and when young men paraded through Whitechapel in June 1657, sporting willow garlands on their heads, beating the watch with clubs, and threatening to fire the town. Alcohol could rapidly transform celebration into frightening violence, and popular sympathies might be reversed with equal speed.[112]

How, then, can we sum up the impact of godly reformation on the lives of families and communities in Interregnum Middlesex? The evidence surveyed in this essay demonstrates the energy and drive of the Puritan reformers, sustained throughout the Interregnum, and the co-operation they secured from many ordinary citizens. But equally striking is the scale of the challenge they confronted. Justices were part-time officials, burdened with many other public and professional commitments. However committed to moral reformation, they recognised an equally pressing need to fight crime and maintain the security of the regime. And, severely hampered by the rudimentary structure of local government, they depended heavily on the parish officers, many of whom doubtless remained wedded to more traditional and relaxed concepts of 'good order'.

Less familiar to historians, perhaps, is that the new culture of godly discipline brought with it new opportunities and temptations for the unscrupulous. John Bond, for example, was accused of visiting

[109] *Publick Intelligencer* 69 (2–9 Feb. 1657), 1179–80; MJ/SR/162/60–3; Durston, *Cromwell's Major-Generals*, p. 157.
[110] MJ/SR/11131/233. A hundred butchers' men attacked the watch on 7 Nov. 1657: MJ/SR/1174/389; cf. MJ/SR/1096/171–2, 181.
[111] MJ/SR/1138/122.   [112] MJ/SR/1150/45; MJ/SR/1167/179, 185.

suppressed alehouses in 1654, taking money to secure new licences and promising to protect the proprietors from charges of gaming, claiming to have a warrant from the Protector.[113] Informers were frequently accused of taking bribes to secure alehouse licences, and one had allegedly offered to teach a victualler 'a way how to keep gaming in his house and that none should question him for it'.[114] The Sabbath laws encouraged similar frauds. Humphrey Bateman, a tailor, was exposed in 1657 as one of a gang 'who pretend to be very much afflicted in spirit for the profanation of the Lord's Day'; securing warrants from several justices to arrest offenders, Bateman and his friends would then demand bribes to drop the charges against them.[115] Other rogues exploited the gullible by issuing forged licences, or posing as officials.[116] While not unique to this period, such frauds appear far more numerous than before 1640 or after 1660. Their effect was not only to undermine the drive for godly reformation, but to discredit it. Other rogues exploited the new environment in still more nefarious ways, and it was in the 1650s that the new word 'trepan' entered the language. A trepan was a conspiracy to entrap often innocent victims and extort money by threatening public disgrace or prosecution. Most featured sexual allegations, such as fathering an illegitimate child, adultery, rape, or sodomy, while one group attempted to extort £60 from Major William Rainborough (a former justice) in 1657 by accusing him of drinking a health to Charles II.[117] The newspapers were full of outrageous stories, and one promised to publish a weekly update. Contemporaries agreed that these scams often succeeded, though naturally we know only of attempts that backfired. In one such case, Gilbert Mabbott, a former licenser of the press, was accused of fathering a child by a married woman; in the event it was his alleged paramour, Hester Griffin, who found herself on trial for adultery and conspiracy in 1656.[118]

The Middlesex evidence also reveals the huge scale of popular hostility, defiance and resistance from the ranks of the unregenerate. Parish officers repeatedly met with abuse, threats and assault and, while such defiance was by no means confined to the Interregnum, the volume of recorded incidents suggests both a sharp increase in the level of enforcement and a corresponding surge of resentment. The justices too, especially the most

---

[113] MJ/SR/1123/86; cf. MJ/SR/1143/292.   [114] MJ/SR/1088/114.

[115] MJ/SR/1171/179; cf. MJ/SR/1088/88; MJ/SR/1126/50, 261; MJ/SR/1187/177.

[116] MJ/SR/1102/255; MJ/SR/1152/108; MJ/SR/1163/128; MJ/SR/1169/255.

[117] *Oxford English Dictionary*, 'trepan'; Jeaffreson, *Middlesex County Records*, vol. III, pp. 221, 256, 263, 273; MJ/SR/1172/56, 162; MJ/SR/1119/55 (rape); MJ/SR/1172/233 (sodomy).

[118] *Mercurius Democritus* 64 (13–20 July 1653), 505–6, 509–10; MJ/SR/1135/24; MJ/GB/R/004, fos. 276v–277; for Mabbott see *ODNB*.

zealous, provoked an astonishing level of hatred and scorn.[119] A Shoreditch joiner railed at Thomas Hubbert as a preaching 'Justass', rogue and rascal.[120] John Waterton, mocked in the royalist press as a 'bawdy-court justice', faced repeated abuse and jeers in enforcing godly discipline. A vicious squib, published on his death in January 1660, heaped scurrilous abuse on his memory. His harshness towards female sexual offenders, it claimed, was rooted in the clap he had once contracted; he 'never favoured woman or wench,/ 'Tis said they formerly gave him a wrench/. . . Instead of Peace he was a Justice of Jar'.[121] While the sexual sneer was a conventional jibe at Puritan hypocrisy, Waterton's provocative assiduity is a matter of record. The sessions rolls show him issuing 117 recognisances in the space of only a few weeks in 1654, and on dozens of recorded occasions his victims responded with verbal abuse or physical threats.[122] Calvinist magistrates probably expected, of course, to find the reprobate impervious to godly discipline, or indeed authority of any sort. A firkinman brought before John Barkstead, lieutenant of the Tower, in April 1652 simply laughed in his face, while a woman hauled before Waterton bade him 'commit her to gaol if he durst'. On 4 July 1653, the day the so-called 'Parliament of Saints' assembled, Elizabeth Smith could retort when charged with running a brothel that 'she did not care a fart for never a Justice in England'.[123]

But such outbursts are not proof of failure; indeed their ubiquity testifies to the impact of the magisterial campaign. Godly magistrates reciprocated the contempt of the worldly and profane, and they remained determined to curb offenders even if they could not reform them. The strength of that determination, sustained throughout the 1650s, is reflected less in indictments than in summary fines and over 18,000 surviving recognisances, testimony not only to magisterial zeal but to the degree of co-operation magistrates received from the public. Puritan reformation, like most early modern policies and programmes, stood the best chance of success when it coincided with the values and objectives of a wider public. What revellers viewed as merry-making and Puritans as sin, many respectable householders might well deplore as anti-social behaviour posing a direct threat to the stability and tranquillity of their own families. Husbands and wives angry at a feckless or unfaithful spouse, householders alarmed when their children or servants succumbed to the dangerous temptations of the alehouse, had their own good reasons for turning to a

[119] MJ/SR/1076/321; MJ/SR/1127/341; MJ/SR/1152/169.   [120] MJ/SR/1102/131.
[121] *The Man in the Moon* 27 (24–31 Oct. 1649), 223; MJ/SR/1058/233; MJ/SR/1110/166; *Room for a Justice* (1659), broadside.
[122] MJ/SR/1142/99–216.   [123] MJ/SR/1084/50; MJ/SR/1108/192, 160.

justice for help. Manipulating the regime's public concerns for their own private advantage, they simultaneously assisted the campaign for reformation by bringing 'sin' to the magistrates' attention. So did squabbling neighbours who sought to exploit Puritan sensibilities by accusing their adversaries of Sabbath offences or swearing.

The Middlesex magistrates never expected to eradicate sin or convert the unregenerate masses. Nor did they. The poet Richard Flecknoe, travelling round London's environs in 1656, found manners as rough as ever, not least the salty language of the bargemen: 'Rude rogues have nought but "shit" and "turd",/And "kiss my arse" at every word.' But Flecknoe noted changes too: no more Sunday dancing on village greens, for example.[124] The Puritan reformers secured significant results, however short-lived, in curbing at least the public manifestation of 'profanity' and disorder. Their resources were too meagre, the regime itself too unsettled, to achieve much more, and there are indications of Puritan discipline weakening by 1659. Even so, those who experienced the Restoration, whatever their sympathies, had no doubt that it signalled the end of a cultural as well as political revolution. The 1660s saw the pendulum swing far away from Puritan cultural values now widely viewed as dangerous and fanatical. But those values lived on in the Nonconformists, a significant presence in the political and religious life of the capital. And when the Revolution of 1688 ushered in another sober, strongly Protestant, government, we find many of the aspirations of the 1650s revived in the Societies for the Reformation of Manners, even if the new reformers judged it unwise to acknowledge the parallels.[125]

[124] Flecknoe, *Diarium*, pp. 25, 50–1 and *passim*.
[125] Fletcher, *Reform in the Provinces*, pp. 273–7; R. B. Shoemaker, 'Reforming the city: The reformation of manners campaign in London, 1690–1738', in L. Davison *et al.*, eds., *Stilling the Grumbling Hive* (Stroud, 1992), pp. 99–120.

4 Keeping it in the family: Crime and the early modern household

Garthine Walker

Historians of the early modern family and of early modern crime have underestimated the relationship between the family and crime.[1] Histories of the family usually limit consideration of crime to two areas: what we would now term domestic violence, especially wife-battering and child abuse, and unlawful sexual activities such as adultery, pre-marital sex and bastardy. Within the social history of crime, one might expect the family to have a higher profile given that the household is acknowledged to have been the very foundation of early modern social order. Yet here too the family takes centre stage only when the household is a site of internal conflict. Violence looms large in such studies: the family is populated by battered wives, petty traitors, infanticidal mothers, and abused servants and apprentices. Crime historians also recognise conflict within the household in the theft of goods by servants and employees and sometimes by husbands or wives during bitter separations. In both historiographies, then, crime is presented overwhelmingly in narrow terms as a disruptive force that damaged the cohesion of an 'ideal' family unit. Indeed, for Lawrence Stone in *The Family, Sex and Marriage*, crime – whether directed against family members or not – demonstrated the absence of close emotional ties. Confronted with evidence that suggested that sixteenth-century people far more frequently used violence outside the family than within it he suggested that 'familial emotive ties were so weak that they did not generate the passions which lead to intra-familial murder and mayhem'. Family members were united not by positive affective relationships (which in his view were 'modern' attributes) but by negative habits of distrust and hostility towards outsiders. It was, Stone mused, 'tempting to argue that the family that slayed together, stayed together' – but not, one might add, in a 'good' way.[2]

[1] I am grateful to Kevin Passmore, Lloyd Bowen, and the editors, for their comments on this chapter.
[2] Lawrence Stone, *The Family, Sex and Marriage in England 1500–1800* (London, 1977), p. 95.

Stone in fact paid scant attention to crime *per se* in *The Family, Sex and Marriage*. Nonetheless, he revealed throughout the book assumptions about the nature of and motivations for unlawful activities – especially those involving violence – that were consonant with views he had articulated in previous works, notably *The Crisis of the Aristocracy* (1965), and which he would again in a series of articles in the mid-1980s and in his tripartite work on marriage and divorce in the 1990s.[3] This is relevant for our present purpose, for while *The Family, Sex and Marriage* shaped the subsequent historiography of English family life, historians of crime have engaged more with Stone's arguments about levels of violence in early modern society. Yet neither Stone nor other crime historians were alive to the family dynamic of much violence in early modern England. The focus of the debate about 'interpersonal' violence was the actions of individuals. This was partly the consequence of assumptions about the period's nascent modernity: family feuds and the violence of household retainers were viewed as 'traditional' vestiges of feudal life that were gradually superseded after 1500 by the development of an altogether more 'modern', individually motivated aggression.[4] In early modern England, criminality was conceptualised as 'a flaw within the individual, and not society'.[5]

Contemporaries and historians were nonetheless aware that the consequences of crime extended beyond individual victims: criminal acts threatened the peace of the community and the commonwealth. Without a formal police force or Crown Prosecution Service, the onus lay upon private individuals – usually the victims of crime – to initiate and pursue proceedings in the criminal courts. The inhabitants of early modern England invested considerable energy in resolving or furthering disputes with others through criminal and civil litigation.[6] The harm caused by crime did not stop with the community. The king's or queen's peace had been

---

[3] Lawrence Stone, 'Interpersonal violence in English society 1300–1980', *Past and Present* 101 (1983), 22–33; Lawrence Stone, 'The history of violence in England: Some observations: a rejoinder', *Past and Present* 108 (1985), 216–24; Lawrence Stone, *The Past and the Present Revisited* (London, 1987), pp. 295–310; Lawrence Stone, *The Road to Divorce: England 1530–1987* (Oxford, 1990); Lawrence Stone, *Uncertain Unions: Marriage in England 1660–1753* (Oxford, 1992); Lawrence Stone, *Broken Lives: Separation and Divorce in England 1660–1857* (Oxford, 1993).

[4] Stone first presented this argument in *The Crisis of the Aristocracy 1558–1641* (Oxford, 1965). Other influential accounts along similar lines include G. R. Elton, *The Tudor Revolution in Government: Administrative Changes in the Reign of Henry VIII* (Cambridge, 1953) and Mervyn James, *Society, Politics and Culture: Studies in Early Modern England* (Cambridge, 1986), esp. ch. 8.

[5] Cynthia B. Herrup, *The Common Peace: Participation and the Criminal Law in Seventeenth-Century England* (Cambridge, 1987), p. 4.

[6] J. A. Sharpe, '"Such disagreements betwyx neighbours": Litigation and human relations in early modern England', in John Bossy (ed.), *Disputes and Settlements: Law and Human*

broken. The monarch was the symbolic victim of all crimes; it was he or she whom the criminal justice system ultimately avenged.[7] Historians of crime thus considered the role of and impact on both the local community and the state in the execution of criminal justice. The questions they asked in the 1970s and the 1980s also reflected the broader concerns and categories of the discipline in that they were particularly interested in the relative involvement in crime and treatment before the courts of different classes. While historians repeated the maxim that the household was conceptually a microcosm of the state, and that order in it was therefore of critical importance, and while they acknowledged that criminal acts and their prosecution involved households and families as much as they did individuals, communities, or classes, they rarely explored in detail what this meant for the family in practical terms.

The focus upon individuals as the perpetrators of crime contributed to the family dynamic of much criminal activity being overlooked in another way too: it encouraged a male-centred analysis that was blind to women's positive involvement in unlawful enterprises. The quantitative methods favoured by so many historians of early modern criminality revealed that women formed a minority of persons who were officially prosecuted for most categories of offence. Stone was thus able to assert in *The Family, Sex and Marriage* that married and unmarried women alike 'had a minimal share in crimes of theft, commercial fraud and violence, and when violence took place they were usually aiding their menfolk'. Whereas '[m]en in want stole, women turned to men – husbands or sexual clients – or to public charity; men brawled, women slandered; men took direct action against the law when they felt aggrieved, women only in accordance with a higher moral code'. Early modern women, he concluded, were 'as submissive and as dependent as the conduct books suggested that they ought to be'.[8]

Feminist scholarship and work influenced by it has since challenged the view that early modern women simply internalised patriarchal codes, stressing instead that women exercised greater or lesser amounts of agency in negotiating their position both in and outside the household. But even here the emphasis is frequently upon the household as a site of conflict, as the titles of influential works such as *Dangerous Familiars*

Relations in the West (Cambridge, 1983), pp. 167–87; James Sharpe, 'The people and the law', in Barry Reay (ed.), *Popular Culture in Seventeenth-Century England* (London, 1985), pp. 244–70.

[7] Herrup, *Common Peace*, pp. 1–10.

[8] Stone, *Family, Sex and Marriage*, p. 201; he is drawing heavily on Carol Z. Wiener, 'Sex roles and crime in late Elizabethan Hertfordshire', *Journal of Social History* 8, 4 (1975), 38–60.

and *Domestic Dangers* imply.[9] Moreover, the subjective positions available to women sometimes appear limited to a simple dichotomy: internalisation or resistance. Feminist scholarship, and work influenced by it, has tended to focus upon the indisputable disadvantages that women faced in a patriarchal society. Women who were burned at the stake as petty traitors for killing abusive husbands, for instance, were doubly damned: their suffering at the hands of patriarchy was all the greater *because* they resisted it. Feminist studies focus on such crimes as evidence of the costs for women of a system of female subordination. Yet many writers seem to have internalised the very messages about women that they attribute to early modern folk: even in the twenty-first century, one comes across erroneous comments such as that women fought with words not deeds and 'it was as a scold rather than a brawler that a woman was more likely to come to the attention of the authorities'.[10] In fact, women prosecuted for petty treason, and other supposedly 'feminine' crimes such as infanticide and scolding, constituted a tiny proportion of women who were brought before the courts. Figures for early modern Cheshire are instructive. Petty treason, for example, accounted for less than 2 per cent of homicides, while for every ten women suspected to have murdered their husbands, almost 500 were prosecuted for various sorts of theft, 600 for assault, and 1,500 were bound over by recognisance to keep the peace or to be of good behaviour towards their neighbours. The same general point applies to indictments for infanticide and scolding, even though prosecutions were more numerous than for husband-killing.[11] In sum, far greater numbers of women were prosecuted for common offences that were not especially associated with women than there were for those that conventionally have been identified as peculiarly feminine.

In this chapter, I shall argue that historians' failure to appreciate the proper nature of female criminality is both a cause and consequence of their failure to acknowledge the manifold ways in which family and household provide crucial context for crimes committed by women *and* by men. I have shifted the focus away from the usual issues of domestic abuse and sexual immorality that dominate discussions of the family and crime

---

[9] Frances E. Dolan, *Dangerous Familiars: Representations of Domestic Crime in England 1550–1700* (Ithaca, N.Y., 1994); Laura Gowing, *Domestic Dangers: Women, Words and Sex in Early Modern London* (Oxford, 1996).

[10] Christine Peters, *Women in Early Modern Britain 1450–1640* (Basingstoke, 2004), p. 100.

[11] These figures are based on an extensive study of Cheshire quarter sessions and great sessions (assizes) prosecutions, with quantitative evidence drawn from the 1590s, 1620s, 1640s, 1650s and 1660s. See Garthine Walker, *Crime, Gender and Social Order in Early Modern England* (Cambridge, 2003) for the Cheshire figures and references to those for other counties: *passim*, and esp. pp. 138–48 (petty treason), 148–58 (infanticide), 100–11 (scolding).

towards property offences, which were far more commonly prosecuted at the criminal courts. First, I shall discuss some of the ways in which the family had an at once mundane and profound impact upon the nature and treatment of theft in both conceptual and practical terms. In doing so, I pay particular attention to the implications of coverture for verdicts and sentences of married couples. I argue that in practice its effects were far more varied than many historians have previously believed. In the subsequent section of the chapter, I explore the family dynamic in categories of offence that have received very little attention by historians, namely forcible entry, detainer and disseisin. These criminal misdemeanours in which family members used force to protect and retain property – primarily land – for the benefit of their households have been subject to scarcely any analysis even in social histories of crime. A consideration of such offences is apposite in the present volume, for quarrels over property peppered the pages of Stone's work. Examining them invites us to re-appraise some of Stone's assumptions about both the family and violence in early modern England that have been accepted in, and to varying degrees have shaped, the subsequent historiographies of these subjects. I propose that crime, violence and disorder are not usefully consigned to categories such as 'traditional' or 'modern'; they do not represent in any simple way the 'spirit of the age'. Nor were they, either from our or the early modern perspective, necessarily the unfortunate consequences of patriarchal extremes. Unlawful acts could reinforce familial bonds in what were perceived to be constructive ways.

Partners in crime

One of the most significant features of early modern criminality is the extent to which family members were involved in or affected by each other's unlawful activities. This was reflected in the concerns of moralists as well as in prosecutions for criminal acts. Authors of moral treatises viewed families who harboured those 'attainted with open crimes' as analogous with pigsties, those 'stinking' places that were figuratively associated with 'pillories, privy-houses, whipping-posts . . . and bawdy-houses'.[12] In contrast, law-abiding, godly households were likened to churches.[13] Disorder within the household was contaminating. Robert Cleaver observed that people were like 'the company . . . they keep';

---

[12] 'B. Ste.', *Counsel to the Husband: to the Wife Instruction a Short and Pithy Treatise of Seuerall and Joynt Duties, Belonging unto Man and Wife* (London, 1608), p. 10; Pierre du Moulin, *The Accomplishment of the Prophecies* (London, 1613), p. 234; Edmund Gayton, *Pleasant Notes upon Don Quixot* (London, 1654), p. 85.

[13] Du Moulin, *Accomplishment of the Prophecies*, p. 234.

'if man may be known by nothing else then he may be known by his companions: for like will to like, as Solomon saith, "thieves call one another"'. In a household economy, people might spend the greatest part of their time in the company of those with whom they lived as well as worked. Husbands and wives were particularly implicated in each other's criminality. There was, after all, 'no greater society or company than is held between a man and his wife', who shared in common their house, goods, children and 'all good and evil success, of prosperity and adversity'.[14] Coverture, in its fiction that man and wife (the *feme covert*) were one person and that person was the husband, was one expression of this 'sharing in common'. The extent to which married women's legal existence was subsumed into and negated by that of their husbands, however, has frequently been exaggerated by historians in assertions such as the one that wives 'had no rights or existence apart from their husbands', or that under common law 'no female had any rights at all'. Even the more circumspect interpretation that '[u]nder the doctrine of coverture, the husband became legally responsible for his wife's actions' is inaccurate.[15]

Common law did not wholly deny married women a legal identity of their own. This was true with regard to property-holding, with which coverture was largely concerned; it was especially so apropos of criminal prosecution and not only with regard to murder, treason and brothel-keeping as some scholars have believed.[16] The author of *The Lawes Resolutions of Womens Rights* (1632) acknowledged that, as a *feme covert*, a married woman might indeed wonder whether 'she be either none or no more than half a person', but he urged her to 'be of good cheer', for in nature (that is, her physical form and her character), in God's eyes, and 'in criminal [law] and other special causes', wives were of course whole and separate individuals independently of their husbands (although how much comfort a woman might have taken from the latter is debatable). Put more simply, marital unity was a perplexing puzzle 'whereof two persons become but one, which still are two'.[17] At common law,

---

[14] Robert Cleaver, *A Godly Forme of Houshold Government for the Ordering of Private Families, according to the Direction of Gods Word* (London, 1621), sigs. G5v, K4r.

[15] Susan Kingsley Kent, *Sex and Suffrage in Britain 1860–1914* (Princeton, 1987), p. 27; Antonia Fraser, *The Weaker Vessel: Woman's Lot in Seventeenth-Century England* (London, 1984), p. 51; Susan A. Lentz, 'Revisiting the rule of thumb: An overview of the history of wife abuse', in Lynette Feder (ed.), *Women and Domestic Violence: An Interdisciplinary Approach* (Binghamton, N.Y., 1999), p. 11.

[16] E.g., Susan Chaplin, *Law, Sensibility, and the Sublime in Eighteenth-Century Women's Fiction: Speaking of the Dead* (Aldershot, 2004), p. 35.

[17] Thomas Edgar, *The Lawes Resolutions of Womens Rights: or, the Lawes Provision for Woemen* (London, 1632), p. 4; 'B. Ste.', *Counsel to the Husband*, p. 215.

husbands were accountable for their wives' criminal activities *only in specific circumstances*. For non-felonious crimes of violence, for instance, marital coercion was immaterial, so much so that the index of a recent monograph about gender and petty violence in the late seventeenth and early eighteenth centuries has no entry for coverture at all.[18] For felonious property crime, a woman's marital status was legally relevant, but how it fell out depended on context. If a woman stole 'by the compulsion or constraint of her husband' and if the pair 'jointly together do steal goods', the felony was imputed only to the husband. But if she stole something 'without any constraint', even if it was 'by the commandment or procurement of her husband', she was the principal offender and her husband merely an accessory.[19] In other words, coverture afforded wives no protection if they committed a theft in their husband's absence even if the act was done as a result of his instruction, bullying or threats. In practice, this meant that many early modern wives prosecuted for felony could expect to face the full force of the law.[20]

Granted, not everyone – neither the hacks who wrote up reports of trials for popular consumption nor even the authors of certain legal manuals – was sure of the law's provision in this respect. In 1740, for instance, the printed Old Bailey *Proceedings* strongly implied that Martha White was acquitted of robbery while her supposed husband, Arthur Bethell, hanged because she had benefited from 'the law supposing every wife to be under the coercion of her husband'.[21] In 1782, *The London Chronicle*'s account of the trial of John and Jane Graham for forging bank notes, which was also a capital offence, reported that married women who committed crimes other than murder and treason with their husbands could not be convicted because of this legal presumption. This was somewhat disingenuous because the prosecution had discussed the extent of coverture in open court and had pointed out that 'if the married woman was the active person, and acted without the control or interference of the husband' or if she 'was not in the presence of the husband but distinct from him', she 'has no privilege whatever' that 'will protect her from the guilt of which she is charged'.[22] Similar inaccuracies even appeared in a popular guide to women's legal status: *The Laws Respecting Women* of

[18] Jennine Hurl-Eamon, *Gender and Petty Violence in London 1680–1720* (Columbus, 2005).
[19] Dalton, *The Country Justice* (1619; London, 1705 edn), p. 374.
[20] Walker, *Crime, Gender and Social Order*, p. 76.
[21] *Old Bailey Proceedings Online* (www.oldbaileyonline.org, 10 August 2006), May 1740, trial of Arthur Bethell, alias Bethwell, alias Barwin, and Martha White (t17400522–9).
[22] *The London Chronicle*, 14/17 September 1782, cited in Deirdre Palk, *Gender, Crime and Judicial Discretion 1780–1830* (Woodbridge, Suffolk, 2006), pp. 30–1; *Old Bailey Proceedings Online*, September 1782, trial of John Graham and Jane Graham (t17820911–12).

1777 stated unequivocally that 'a *feme covert* shall not be punished for committing any felony in company with her husband, the law supposing she did it by the coercion of her husband'.[23]

In practice, the principle of married women's diminished accountability was not routinely applied by early modern courts. Whatever the view of the newspapers, Jane Graham's marital status afforded her no formal advantage: she was held to be fully culpable for her role in planning the forgeries during John's recent spell in prison, and although John might have altered the notes, it was she who had put them into circulation in London and Southampton. Both John and Jane were convicted and sentenced to death.[24] The fact that the jury afterwards recommended that Jane's execution be mitigated underscores the extent to which coverture could not be applied indiscriminately to married women who were indicted with their husbands. We must not fall into the error of supposing the doctrine of coverture to exemplify 'traditional' attitudes towards women that were swept away by a rational 'modern' worldview that extended to women the rights of man. On the contrary, the idea that the law presumed that a wife who committed an offence in the presence of her husband did so under compulsion might have been more commonly believed in the nineteenth century than it had been in the preceding centuries. It was not, as modern historians have argued, '[o]nly at the end of the nineteenth century' that it was 'admitted that "no presumption shall be made that a married woman committing an offence does so under compulsion only because she commits it in the presence of her husband"'.[25] Although it is true that the *limited* principle of marital coercion was abolished by the 1925 Criminal Justice Act, when it was replaced with a statutory defence based on actual coercion by a husband, I have shown here that sixteenth- and seventeenth-century legal manuals presumed no such absolute thing.

Throughout the early modern period and well into the nineteenth century, coverture constituted both a resource upon which women drew in attempts to avoid conviction and punishment, and a means by which juries could acquit women of crimes for which they were not convinced that they should hang. It was in this respect similar to other legal 'fictions' by which the administration of criminal justice might be mitigated, such as the 'benefit of clergy' which presumed literacy where there

---

[23] [J. Johnson,] *The Laws Respecting Women, as They Regard their Natural Rights, or Their Connections and Conduct* (London, 1777), pp. 70–1.

[24] *Old Bailey Proceedings Online*, September 1782, trial of John and Jane Graham.

[25] Palk, *Gender, Crime and Judicial Discretion*, p. 32.

very often was none.[26] In Martha White's case in 1740, it was her husband Bethell who planned to follow and rob the victim after declaring 'money I want, and money I will have'; it was he who violently knocked the victim to the ground and took his watch from him; it was he who afterwards considered that he 'had as good be hanged for an old sheep, as a young lamb' and so followed and knocked down the victim again, this time taking his cash. Martha had by all accounts merely accepted and carried the watch in her apron pocket, and had exchanged its green ribbon for one she had on her hat.[27] Studies of judicial decision-making suggest that her minor role compared to Bethell's leading one was likely to have produced a verdict of 'not guilty' even if she had not invoked coverture.[28]

Receiving stolen goods as Martha White did, as well as selling stolen items, and, in the case of foodstuffs, in preparing them for the table were all common ways in which wives were implicated in thefts committed by their husbands. While it is instructive that the great majority of women who were suspected of receiving thieves or stolen goods were married, these behaviours were almost certainly under-represented in the criminal records as a result of the familial and household relationships between the protagonists. There are a number of reasons why this was so with regard to wives receiving things that their husbands had stolen, for instance. The first of these was coverture. Technically, a woman who relieved, received or kept company with her husband, 'knowing him to be a felon, . . . is no accessory thereby . . . for she ought to relieve him, not to discover his counsel'. When the roles were reversed, however, husbands were accountable. Only if 'the wife shall procure, counsel or conspire with her husband to commit any felony, and the husband thereupon shall execute the same, although the wife be not present thereat, yet [she] may seem to be accessory to her husband'.[29] Second, receiving stolen goods was not itself a felony until 1691. Details about who received stolen goods were therefore legally relevant only when they constituted circumstantial evidence that identified the thief.[30] Moreover, the clerks who recorded pre-trial depositions were required to summarise in writing only 'as much thereof as shall be material to prove the felony', and they could

---

[26] 'Benefit of belly' whereby convicted women might be temporarily reprieved due to pregnancy was less beneficial and usually only postponed execution: Walker, *Crime, Gender and Social Order*, pp. 197–201.

[27] *Old Bailey Proceedings Online*, May 1740, trial of Arthur Bethell, alias Bethwell, alias Barwin, and Martha White.

[28] Walker, *Crime, Gender and Social Order*, pp. 201–6.

[29] Dalton, *Country Justice*, p. 398; Sir Matthew Hale, *Pleas of the Crown: or, a Methodical Summary of the Principal Matters Relating to that Subject* (London, 1707), p. 65.

[30] Statute 3 & 4 William & Mary, c. 9 (1692).

do so up to two days after the examination had taken place. Concern to gain information that was materially relevant to the case obviously structured the magistrates' questions, too.[31] Third, the indictment – the formal record of the offence – had to state the specific offence that allegedly had been committed; any additional information that deviated from the requisite formulaic Latin phrases merely increased the possibility of errors of spelling or form being introduced that could result in the case being thrown out on a technicality. Taken together, such evidence strongly suggests that the involvement of thieves' wives was very likely to have been excluded from the formal documentation of the legal process.

This was true not only of wives who took into their custody or sold on the things their husbands had stolen but also of all women in the household – including mothers, sisters and maidservants – who prepared and served stolen foodstuff for the family's consumption. Neither indictments nor pre-trial depositions routinely include details about what happened to the meat, fowl or fish – staple foods for those who could afford them but otherwise luxuries – that thieves or poachers brought home. But we know enough about the gendered nature of domestic labour to be confident that women were active in converting such commodities into tasty dishes for the family. Several geese that were 'put upon the spit in [Richard] Ward's house to roast' in 1560 were pilfered by Ward, his wife and three of their friends, but it was almost certainly Ward's wife or a maidservant who plucked and dressed the geese and turned the spit.[32] Similarly, Katherine Crosse roasted a shoulder of venison that her butcher husband had received in return for 'breaking up' a deer poached from Vale Royal in 1669.[33] The part played by other members of a thief's household, particularly the household's women, is thus largely hidden in the official record.

Household organisation and the gendered division of labour also affected what women and men stole and what they could sell on without attracting suspicion. The basic work of most early modern women was the production of food, drink, clothing and other household items for their families.[34] Women thus had a high profile in the legitimate acquisition, exchange and sale of these things, whether they were bought by

---

[31] Statute 2 & 3 Philip & Mary, c. 10 (1555); Dalton, *Country Justice*, pp. 406, 72.

[32] Karen Jones, *Gender and Petty Crime in Late Medieval England 1460–1560* (Woodbridge, Suffolk, 2006), p. 48; Larry J. Hoefling, *Chasing the Frontier: Scots-Irish in Early America* (New York, 2005), p. 47.

[33] Cheshire and Chester Archives and Local Services [CCALS]: QJF 51/2, fol. 40. For other examples, see Walker, *Crime, Gender and Social Order*, pp. 169–70.

[34] For an overview, see Sara H. Mendelson and Patricia Crawford, *Women in Early Modern England* (Oxford, 1998), pp. 303–12.

or exchanged with individuals or, in the case of clothes and household items, pawned in alehouses as part of their routine contributions to the household's wellbeing. It is not surprising, therefore, to find that women were disproportionately likely to steal clothes and household linens. Not only did clothes and linens constitute a far greater proportion of women's thefts, but women were also prominent among the receivers of such goods.[35] Similarly, women played an important part in selling on small livestock and fowl, stolen by themselves, their husbands or other members of their families, for again the lawful marketing of such commodities came within the usual confines of their work. Thus after George Abraham stole a sheep from a certain field, which he apparently did on a weekly basis until he was caught, it was his wife who was apprehended with a basket of mutton in the town, presumably on her way to sell it.[36]

Household organisation and the gendered division of labour explain the predominance of men in certain crimes too. Horse-theft and the sale of stolen horses mirrored the lawful exchanges and sales at horse-fairs made by itinerant horse-dealers. Both were predominantly male, peripatetic activities, in which fathers and sons, brothers, or even uncles and nephews acquired horses in one county and sold them on in another. Roving did not necessarily mean being rootless. Horse-theft was rarely opportunistic but almost always planned. In fact, dealers sometimes engaged in a mixture of legitimate and illegitimate dealings. The wives of such men, and other family members, were likely to have been well aware of the nature of the family 'business' even when their participation was less direct. While their menfolk travelled away from home, the wives of regular horse thieves remained at home to maintain the household. The work of drovers and stockmen, who covered sometimes considerable distances driving cattle and sheep for sale at markets far from home, was similarly men's employment. It followed that men could easily assume the part of an innocent trader with livestock to sell. An itinerant woman selling cattle would, in contrast, immediately arouse suspicion. Women instead tended to steal the sorts of things they could sell without difficulty, namely the commodities that they were normally responsible for marketing.[37]

---

[35] Walker, *Crime, Gender and Social Order*, pp. 162–7; Garthine Walker, 'Women, theft and the world of stolen goods', in Jenny Kermode and Garthine Walker (eds.), *Women, Crime and the Courts in Early Modern England* (London and Chapel Hill, N.C., 1994), pp. 81–105; Jones, *Gender and Petty Crime*, pp. 42–5. For the lawful trade, see Beverley Lemire, 'The theft of clothes and popular consumerism in early modern England', *Journal of Social History* 24 (1990).

[36] Jones, *Gender and Petty Crime*, pp. 46–7.

[37] Walker, *Crime, Gender and Social Order*, pp. 167–9. For the lawful trade in horses, see Peter Edwards, *The Horse Trade of Tudor and Stuart England* (Cambridge, 1988); for

Gender roles and organisation of particular household economies informed felonious and lesser property crimes in both the acquisition of goods and their subsequent exchange or disposal. In this way, the family is of critical importance to our understanding of early modern crime.

This was also the case in many types of lesser offence that made up most of the routine business at quarter sessions. Quarrels that resulted in litigation reflected and perpetuated economic and social competition between households. It is perhaps easy for us to view rows over unmended fences, obstructed water supplies, or the damage to pasture that was consumed by someone else's livestock as trivial. But in the sixteenth and seventeenth centuries, matters like these could have far-reaching consequences for families. John Stevenson in 1624 argued bitterly with Joan Pott over the 'great wrong' she and her husband had done to him 'in the tithing of his hay', and proceeded to 'thrust at [her] with a pike-fork'. Her husband, John, hearing them 'so loud in words', offered to accompany Stevenson to view the tithings and promised to right any wrong that had been done. But as they reached the meadow, Stevenson accused John Pott of enmity towards his son and seeking to bring about his death, and again ran at John and Joan with his pitchfork. It had in fact been Stevenson's daughter-in-law (not his son) who had secured the bargain concerning the tithes with the Potts. It was she too who 'desired [Stevenson] to let Pott have them for quietness sake'.[38] In both rural and urban settings, such issues lay at the heart of conflicts that were played out in criminal, civil and ecclesiastical litigation. Suits alleging assault, breach of contract, or defamatory words, for instance, could all arise from disputes between families about similar things.[39] When household resources were at risk, complex and lengthy rivalries could be played out between various members of the families concerned. Married women again played a particularly prominent role due to their household responsibilities.

Spousal relationships were the most common of familial ties in commonplace offences such as assault and trespass and damage. In

drovers, see Joan Thirsk, *The Rural Economy of England: Collected Essays* (London, 1984), pp. 146–7, 176. For women's work, see Mendelson and Crawford, *Women in Early Modern England*, pp. 256–344.

[38] CCALS: QJF 53/3, fols. 73, 92, 74. The courts were also involved in their disputes in QJF 49/2, fols. 59, 61 (1620); QJF 53/3, fols. 48, 100, QJF 53/4, fol. 13 (1624); QJF 55/2, fol. 93 (1626). My sample of Cheshire quarter sessions excludes any cases in the dispute that were prosecuted in odd-numbered years. On tithes, see Laura Brace, *The Idea of Property in Seventeenth-Century England: Tithes and the Individual* (Manchester, 1998).

[39] For criminal, civil and ecclesiastical litigation, see respectively Walker, *Crime, Gender and Social Order*; Craig Muldrew, *The Culture of Obligation: The Culture of Credit and Social Relations in Early Modern England* (Basingstoke, 1998); Gowing, *Domestic Dangers*.

seventeenth-century Cheshire, married couples especially but also parents and children, and other relatives or co-habitants, were involved in as many as *three-quarters* of assaults where there were two or more assailants.[40] Inter-household disputes were frequently played out in clusters of cases brought before the courts – a further characteristic of early modern crime that is obscured in studies that count individuals without taking account of the dynamics of the groups in which people acted and were prosecuted. In April 1622, for instance, Elizabeth Towers, a husbandman's wife, and her son, George, and daughter, Margaret, were prosecuted together for an assault on John Pike.[41] At the same sessions, Pike prosecuted her husband, Henry, separately for assaulting him with a two-edged axe. He also prosecuted Henry and George for obstructing the way to the local mill by pulling down a footbridge over the stream. In addition to these three indictments, each of which concerned a separate incident, Pike and another fellow, Humphrey Mainwaring, had laid others against various members of the Towers family at the previous sessions in January, at which time Elizabeth, Henry, George and Margaret Towers had all been bound to be of their good behaviour; Elizabeth Towers was additionally bound to keep the peace towards John Pike's son Thomas. For their part, the Towers secured recognisances of good behaviour against John and Thomas Pike. The bench at the January sessions had referred the quarrel to Sir Thomas Savage, who was landlord of both households, 'for determining' upon his return to the county. In the meantime, however, Humphrey Mainwaring procured writs of *supersedeas* for himself, John Pike, and Pike's wife and children (which stopped any legal proceedings that otherwise would have been taken against them), while 'plotting' to keep the Towers bound. According to John Savage, Sir Thomas's brother, Mainwaring endeavoured to 'detract all things from the Justices and [the quarter sessions] into the ecclesiastical courts'. Savage warned the clerk of the peace, Peter Mainwaring, that 'although he be Mainwaring of your name believe him not for you shall find of my word his dealings naught'.[42] The courts were involved again in July, when John Pike prosecuted Henry Towers, successfully this time, for ripping up the bridge leading to Barrow mill.[43] Mainwaring's intention to initiate a suit against Towers in the church courts exemplifies a common dynamic: families involved in quarrels frequently sued each other in a number of courts. The limited range of jurisdictions that studies of litigation necessarily focus on obscures

---

[40] Walker, *Crime, Gender and Social Order*, p. 36.
[41] CCALS: QJF 51/1, fol. 99.
[42] CCALS: QJF 51/1, fols. 19, 100, 136; QJB 2/5 fol. 21v; QJB 1/5, fol. 67v.
[43] CCALS: QJF 51/1, fol. 24; QJB 2/5, fol. 24v.

the full dynamic of family and inter-family involvement in legal disputes. Furthermore, the view of some historians, that neighbours resorted to law only when informal sanctions failed, seems to suggest that an easy distinction may be made between disorderly offenders and the orderly neighbours who prosecuted them.[44] In cases such as that between the Towers and the Pikes, who was the good neighbour and who the unlawful rogue was far less clear-cut; it was a matter of perspective.

The same was true of the very activities that could be framed as unlawful. Protecting the household and preserving its resources sometimes demanded that technically laws must be broken. What were presented as criminal acts by plaintiffs were not necessarily understood in negative and destructive terms by defendants who construed their own behaviours as positive and defensive. Indeed, even the law recognised that beating someone in defence of 'a man, his wife, father, mother, or any of his children within age, or to disseise him of his land, or to dispossess him of his goods' was both justifiable and lawful. We see here, too, a legal acknowledgement of the cohesion of the family unit. Such was 'not an intended breach of the peace, but to defend him from violence offered to his person, and injury to his freehold or term'.[45] It is to these matters – forcible entry, detainer and disseisin, and forcible rescues of goods – that we shall now turn.

Holding the house by force: defending and offending families

The often dramatic role of household and family is apparent in disputes over real property (freehold) and leases (which were technically 'real chattels'), such as forcible entry and detainer, and forcible disseisin. These offences involved the use of physical or threatened violence to keep out (hence to detain), or to eject, thereby dispossessing (disseising), whoever lawfully possessed or occupied the lands and tenements in question.[46] Various legal remedies for these existed in civil law and equity as well as in criminal law. The most common was a personal action of trespass (particularly of ejectment) under civil law at the courts of King's Bench, Common Pleas, and Exchequer.[47] But they were also regularly prosecuted as

---

[44] E.g., Robert Bucholz and Newton Key, *Early Modern England: 1485–1714* (Oxford, 2004), p. 174.

[45] Ferdinando Pulton, *De Pace Regis et Regni* (London, 1609), fols. 42r, 6r; Dalton, *Countrey Justice*, p. 189.

[46] William Blackstone, *Commentaries on the Laws of England*, 4 vols. (Oxford, 1765–9), vol. IV, p. 147.

[47] J. H. Baker, *The Oxford History of the Laws of England: Volume VI: 1483–1558* (Oxford, 2003), pp. 720–2; J. H. Baker, *An Introduction to English Legal History*, 3rd edn (London,

criminal misdemeanours at quarter sessions, assizes and the Westminster courts that had a criminal jurisdiction, including King's Bench, as well as before justices of the peace who were empowered to deal with them summarily out of sessions.[48] Here, we are concerned with these criminal cases. A successful conviction at a jury trial resulted in 'speedy redress' by way of a writ of restitution upon which the sheriff's men put the plaintiff back in possession of the property.[49] Writs of restitution did not follow summary convictions by JPs, but as defendants were fined and sometimes imprisoned, and had often departed before the justices arrived, a *de facto* restoration of the ejected party usually followed.[50]

Stone supposed that forcible possession of property was endemic to the least 'civilised' parts of the realm, notably Wales and the far north of England, in which he believed the inhabitants 'still preferred traditional methods of settling disputes to obedience to the law'. His evidence was not particularly convincing for several reasons, not least because the 'early sixteenth-century' Welsh case he cited was in fact an account published in 1770 but written between 1580 and 1616 by an author who merely reported what his uncle had told him many years before about a late fourteenth-century ancestor who 'durst not go to church on a Sunday from his house of Penanmen', which was only a mile away, without leaving it 'guarded with men, and . . . the doors sure barred and bolted', and a watchman standing 'at the Garreg big, during divine service; being a rock whence he might see both the church and the house, and raise the cry, if the house was assaulted'.[51] The northern English example was of advice 'still' being given by a Yorkshire gentleman to his son in the early seventeenth century: be certain that 'the doors at night be surely shut up by some trusty ancient servant, and your men so lodged as they may defend your house'. For Stone, these examples confirmed his suspicions that in the 'remote' highland zones of England and Wales human relationships frequently operated 'quite outside an only partly effective

---

1990), pp. 262–71; Alan Harding, *A Social History of English Law* (Harmondsworth, 1966), pp. 41, 94–9; Sir William Holdsworth, *A History of English Law*, 16 vols. (London, 1922–66), vol. VII, pp. 5–32; S. F. C. Milsom, *Historical Foundations of the Common Law*, 2nd edn (London, 1981), pp. 133–7.

[48] Most early modern cases came under the statute 8 Henry VI, c. 9 (1429) which confirmed and augmented earlier statutes 4 Henry IV, c. 8 (1425), 15 Richard II, c. 2 (1391), 5 Richard II, c. 7 (1381); other relevant statutes were 13 Elizabeth I, c. 11 and 21 James I, c. 15.

[49] Pulton, *De Pace Regis*, fol. 35v.

[50] Statutes 15 Richard II, c. 2 (1391); 8 Henry VI c. 9 (1429). For an example of a summary conviction, see CCLAS: QJF 95/1, fols. 163–5, 46 (1667).

[51] Sir John Wynn, *The History of the Gwydir Family, Now Re-edited with . . . Notes by a Native of the Principality [Angharad Llwyd] . . .* (Ruthin, 1827), pp. 94–5; Wynn's *History* was first published in 1770. Stone, *Crisis of the Aristocracy*, p. 228 cited the 1878 edition.

legal machinery'.[52] In fact, forcible entries, detainers and disseisins were routinely prosecuted in all parts of the realm, not primarily in areas with reputations (among contemporary southerners and historians) for disorder and lawlessness.[53] Nor were such activities necessarily unlawful. The law *permitted* the use of force to regain possession of land in certain circumstances.[54] Conveniently, this did not require Stone to revise his view. In the transitional society that he presumed to exist between the traditional world of violent disorder and the modern one of orderly restraint, both lawlessness and recourse to the law could indicate the latter rather than the former. Thus societies 'being weaned from habits of private revenge always turn to the law with intemperate enthusiasm'.[55]

Stone was nonetheless partially correct in observing that the 'issues men [*sic*] fought over were prestige and property, in that order. What might ostensibly appear as a quarrel over a piece of land or an office, in fact was at bottom a struggle for position and authority.'[56] His insight that honour, reputation and authority were central to the nature of disputes between elite men has been confirmed in many subsequent studies, including Anthony Fletcher's on local office-holding.[57] Less helpful is Stone's attempt to categorise the causes or nature of such quarrels, with some as 'real' or 'primary' and others 'ostensible' and 'secondary'. Concerns about honour, reputation, authority, wealth, inheritance, land, leases, office-holding – succinctly encompassed in Stone's 'prestige and property' – were interconnected in complex ways that impacted upon the circumstances in which criminal prosecutions for forcible entry, detainer and disseisin arose.

Stone was, of course, concerned with elite groups. Most of the people who sued or were sued for these offences at quarter sessions and assizes were humbler. In late sixteenth- and seventeenth-century Cheshire,

---

[52] Stone, *Crisis of the Aristocracy*, p. 228.

[53] For a selection of Essex cases, for example, see F. G. Emmison, *Elizabethan Life: Disorder* (Chelmsford, 1970), pp. 117–31. A brief perusal of calendars of Star Chamber proceedings gives an indication of the geographic diversity of cases.

[54] Holdsworth, *History of English Law*, vol. VII, pp. 5–30; C. F. Kolbert and N. A. M. Mackay, *History of Scots and English Land Law* (Berkhamsted, 1977), pp. 227–34; Milsom, *Historical Foundations*, pp. 133–7; Pulton, *De Pace Regis*, fols. 42r, 6r; Dalton, *Countrey Justice*, p. 189.

[55] Stone, *Crisis of the Aristocracy*, p. 240. This is a typical assumption of modernisation theory which can be seen to have informed Stone's work despite his disclaimers: see Garthine Walker, 'Modernisation' in Garthine Walker (ed.), *Writing Early Modern History* (London, 2005), pp. 25–48, esp. 39–40.

[56] Stone, *Crisis of the Aristocracy*, p. 223.

[57] Anthony Fletcher, 'Honour, reputation and local office-holding in Elizabethan and Stuart England', in Anthony Fletcher and John Stevenson (eds.), *Order and Disorder in Early Modern England* (Cambridge, 1985), pp. 92–115.

husbandmen were the largest group among defendants, followed by yeoman, then artisans and tradesmen. A mere one in six defendants were gentlemen; only labourers were prosecuted less as lead defendants.[58] This did not mean that labourers were not involved. On the contrary, a great many men styled as labourers (sons, servants, apprentices) participated in incidents alongside other members of their households, but not over land of which they themselves claimed legal title. The social status of plaintiffs, on the other hand, roughly corresponds to patterns of landholding.[59] Almost half of plaintiffs were below gentry status, principally yeomen, but with a sizable minority of husbandmen, tradesmen, and even the occasional labourer; the remainder were gentlemen.[60] As plaintiffs, yeomen, husbandmen and artisans all accused people from their own social group more than they did any other.[61] This meant that yeomen were almost equally represented among defendants and plaintiffs. Husbandmen, artisans and tradesmen, however, were three times more likely to be prosecuted than they were themselves to prosecute. When gentlemen sued each other over land, they preferred civil over criminal actions and the central Westminster courts over local quarter sessions and assizes. At the latter courts, gentlemen were most likely to prosecute husbandmen, most probably their tenants who resisted or attempted to reverse eviction in disputes where landlords had racked rents, shortened leases, raised entry fines, or denied customary tenures of copyhold land.[62] The

---

[58] Husbandmen 31%, yeomen 27%, craftsmen and tradesmen 19%, gentlemen 15.8%, labourers 7.2%. Source: status of 524 individuals prosecuted before the Cheshire quarter sessions and great sessions (assizes) prosecutions in alternate years during the 1590s, 1620s, 1640s, 1650s and 1660s.

[59] Disseisin originally applied only to freeholders, but by the end of the sixteenth century copyholders were understood to be seised of tenements 'as of freehold' at the will of the lord, and tenants for years were said to be possessed of land they leased and their landlord to be possessed of the freehold. Holdsworth, *History of English Law*, vol. VII, pp. 24–5.

[60] Non-gentry plaintiffs were 45.5% of the total, comprising yeomen 28%, husbandmen 9.9%, craftsmen and tradesmen 6.1%, labourers 1.5%. Source: Cheshire quarter sessions and great sessions (assizes) prosecutions in the 1590s, 1620s, 1640s, 1650s and 1660s.

[61] Members of lower social groups tended to seek redress against gentlemen in the equity courts or at Star Chamber, which had a particular remit to hear allegations of oppression. E.g., The National Archives (henceforth TNA): Public Records Office (hereafter PRO), STAC 7 13/14, STAC 8 87/11, STAC 8 126/1, STAC 8 136/7, STAC 8 144/17, STAC 8 174/16, STAC 8 201/25, STAC 8 203/32, STAC 8 224/15, STAC 8 228/10, STAC 8 228/31, STAC 8 230/9, STAC 8 274/26, STAC 8 291/1, STAC 9 1/39.

[62] On the gentry as oppressive landlords, see Stone, *Crisis of the Aristocracy*, pp. 129–98, 273–334; William Hunt, *The Puritan Moment: The Coming of Revolution in an English County* (Cambridge, Mass., 1983), ch. 2; Roger B. Manning, *Village Revolts: Social Protest and Popular Disturbances in England 1509–1640* (Oxford, 1988), ch. 6; Felicity Heal and Clive Holmes, *The Gentry in England and Wales 1500–1700* (Basingstoke, 1994), pp. 97–135.

law was constructed to landlords' advantage: even tenants who forcibly resisted and prevented their landlords from distraining for rent in arrears were guilty of 'holding with force' under the statutes.[63]

Writing more than a decade before the publication of *The Family, Sex and Marriage*, Stone underestimated the extent to which entire families rather than chiefly elite male individuals were affected by precisely these issues. This was so not merely in disputes that one might characterise as family affairs, such as in rows between relatives over inheritance, but also in the other contexts in which title to and possession of land was disputed. In addition to conflicts between landlords and tenants, complaints about forcible entries, detainers and disseisin arose from disputes with neighbours over property boundaries, the encroachment on or enclosing of common or waste land and, in the 1640s and 1650s, the sequestration of and compounding for royalist estates. The methods used varied. Some were full-on assaults by large numbers of people arrayed with weapons. Some involved little 'actual' force in gaining entry, such as when deforciants climbed down the chimney of an empty house and then physically prevented the family from coming back in. Still others were cunningly laid plans intended to dupe the occupiers into vacating the premises so that would-be possessors could move in. In a most bizarre case of 1613, Raphe Starkey determined to gain possession of the house that his father had bequeathed to his younger brother Henry after his older brother, the original heir, had died prematurely. Raphe had been disinherited after he had 'greatly displeased, grieved and offended' his father by 'attempting and stirring up diverse and sundry causes, suits and troubles against him'. Raphe's plan was 'by some sudden stratagem of fireworks or strange sight or wonder' to 'draw, entice and inveigle' his sister-in-law and her servants out of the house while his brother, Henry, was absent. To this end, Raphe's friend placed 'a strange beast or serpent called a tortoise' on the green near the gates of the house and then, pretending to be a traveller, told Henry's wife and the others present (her brother and her servants) of the beast's presence. Meanwhile Raphe – attired eccentrically in 'a suit of swine skin with the hairy side outward wherewith to disguise' himself and with a mask over his face for good measure – hid in the barn with some other men armed with rapiers and pistols as well as devices 'to spit fire and other fireworks' to set fire to the house should the need arise. Once everyone had vacated the house in order to view the tortoise (which his sister-in-law ordered a manservant to kill), Raphe made a run for the house. After a violent assault on his sister-in-law and her brother, he gained entry and kept them out.[64]

---

[63] Dalton, *Countrey Justice*, p. 181.   [64] TNA: PRO, STAC 8 256/28, m. 2.

Families, whatever their status and wealth, were profoundly affected by being physically ejected or kept out of property in which they lived or from which they got their living. Even when the detainment was temporary, serious harm could be done to a household. In 1618, for example, at least ten men and women allegedly took 'very near twenty loads' of wheat, rye, barley, peas and oats 'being well worth a hundred pounds of money' that were growing on land they had forcibly entered and from which they kept the household's servants. When one of the latter, Randle Fletcher, resisted them, they allegedly attacked him with pitchforks and did not desist even after he was 'felled to the ground' and 'not able to lift his arms unto his head, who cried out unto them most pitifully to save his life he would yield unto them'.[65] Others spoke of their corn and grass being ruined by the defendants pasturing their cattle there, assaults on their wives and daughters who tried to drive the said cattle off the land, as well as their chests, boxes and cupboards being broken and rifled, and valuable goods and writings being taken away.[66] The binding magistrate in a case of 1622 noted that the detaining of the house was to 'the no small affrightment and discouragement of the family'.[67] These were strong terms. Affrightment indicated intimidation and terror, while discouragement denoted grief and terror as well as disheartenment. As Ferdinando Pulton put it, the force in such cases 'resembled . . . fire, which being abused, may consume the whole house'.[68] The formulaic clauses in which complainants stated that their wives and children as well as themselves were 'undone' in fact communicated an often acute truth.[69]

Household or familial connections also informed the groups in which people carried out these offences – they are indicated in around 80 per cent of cases sued at quarter sessions and assizes.[70] Many cases exemplify both the ties and divisions between and within families and households. A dispute involving three minor gentry siblings, John, Margaret and William Brock, between May 1665 and January 1666 was manifested in eleven indictments – seven for dispossession, three for assault, and one for keeping a common and disorderly lodging-house – and nine recognisances for the peace or good behaviour.[71] The main players on one side were John Brock and Grace his wife, John's unmarried sister Margaret, and four of their servants: spinsters Eleanor Ankers and Mary

[65] TNA: PRO, STAC 8 252/31, m. 2.
[66] E.g., TNA: PRO, STAC 8 225/10, mm. 1, 4, 3 (1610).
[67] CCALS: QJF 97/1, fols. 47–51.   [68] Pulton, *De Pace Regis*, fol. 51r.
[69] E.g., TNA: PRO, STAC 8 268/18, m. 2 (1619), STAC 8 268/25, m. 2 (1621).
[70] Household or family alliances appear to have been present in 79% of cases in the 1590s and 85% in the 1620s in the Cheshire sample.
[71] CCALS: QJF 93/2, fols. 9, 10, 11, 25, 28, 76, 77, 78, 79, 88, 89, 90; QJF 93/3, fols. 9, 10, 11, 55, 56; QJF 93/4, fols. 13, 15.

Catherall, and labourers Edmund Morgan and Randle Jackson. Their adversaries were John and Margaret's brother William, his wife Ann, and their maidservants and servants in husbandry. In all, fourteen individuals associated with the two households became embroiled in legal action as defendants, complainants, and often witnesses too. Servants played out the quarrel between the households independently of, as well as along-side, their master or mistress. For instance, William Brock had his sister Margaret, his sister-in-law Grace, and her servant Eleanor Ankers bound to keep the peace towards him early in May 1665; Eleanor Ankers had William Brock bound to be of his good behaviour towards her at the end of the month on the same day that William's wife, Ann, craved the peace against John Brock and his servant Randle Jackson.[72]

Steve Hindle has argued, convincingly, that binding over by recognisance 'acted as a non-aggression pact, initially precluding any further physical self-assertion, and subsequently allowing a cooling-off period during which negotiation, either "informally" (through mediation) or "quasi-formally" (through arbitration), might restore disputing parties to the condition of charity'.[73] However, because recognisances curtailed an adversary's scope to undertake further direct action (on pain of forfeiting a considerable sum of money), they were equally likely to prolong and aggravate matters. In the Brock dispute, interpersonal, gendered, and inter-household relations were complex. William alleged that the day following (and notwithstanding) their bindings over, Margaret, her sister-in-law Grace, and Eleanor Ankers, along with Grace's husband John (Margaret's brother), their other maidservant Mary Catherall, and their two menservants Edmund Morgan and Randle Jackson, ejected him from a parcel of land in Bunbury (they were later aquitted by the trial jury).[74] Similarly, John Brock alleged that on the day after his brother's wife, Ann, had had him bound over, she and William had expelled him from two butteries in his possession, William and his servant Mary Moody ejected him from 'the little chamber', and Thomas Taylor, one of William's men, assaulted Edmund Morgan, a servant of John's.[75] Matters continued in much the same manner throughout the summer and into autumn, with further accusations that John, Grace and Margaret Brock ejected William from his tenement, and that John and Grace assaulted Ann with staves and knives (the bill was thrown out by

---

[72] CCALS: QJF 93/2, fols. 88, 89, 90, 76, 77, 78.
[73] Steve Hindle, 'The keeping of the public peace', in Paul Griffiths, Adam Fox and Steve Hindle (eds.), *The Experience of Authority in Early Modern England* (Basingstoke, 1996), p. 217.
[74] CCLAS: QJF 93/2, fol. 25, QJB 3/1, fol. 249v.
[75] CCLAS: QJF 93/2, fols. 9, 10, 11.

the grand jury). William, Ann and their servants were charged with detaining John's parlour and kitchen, and later his shop, and the parlour (again), and assaulting John's servants (Randle Jackson and Mary
Catherall). Further recognisances were issued against Ann Brock and
Thomas Taylor. In all of this, William and Ann appear to have come off
worst, being successfully prosecuted by John but having their charges
against him and members of his household dismissed by the grand or
petty juries.[76] The Brock dispute reminds us that family relationships
could be shaken by rivalries that cohered around separate households.
Family was thus simultaneously a cohesive and a divisive force.

A further feature of the Brock case is the number of women who were
actively involved. First and foremost is the involvement of the mistresses
of the competing households. Married women were frequently the victims and perpetrators of forcible possession: wives allegedly took part
in over half of all cases in which two or more deforciants were prosecuted, whereas only one in seven groups of deforciants included unmarried or widowed women (see Table 4.1). Moreover, almost half of all
female defendants were married, which is greater than their representation in the general population, while a third were spinsters and under a
fifth widows. The high profile of wives is easily explained. Coverture did
not eliminate married women's accountability in these offences: Dalton
explicitly advised JPs that a married woman '(by her own act) may commit a forcible entry or detainer' regardless of the presence or absence of
her husband, and that she could be punished independently of him.[77]
The possession of both freehold and leasehold property was the foundation upon which most households subsisted. Married women thus had
as much at stake in disputes over property as their husbands who held
or claimed the legal title to it. Recent studies have shown that, in spite
of coverture, various provisions of equity, customary, canon, and even
common law itself meant that married women's property rights were
far from negligible.[78] Real as well as moveable property that technically
belonged to one spouse belonged for all intents and purposes to both.
Wives were *de facto* owners of their husbands' property, hence its appel-
lation as 'marital', 'household', or 'common'. This was why the written
copy and the verbal notice of ejectment in civil actions could be delivered
to either the tenant-in-possession *or his wife*.[79] And it was why the latter's

[76] CCLAS: QJF 93/3, fols. 9, 35, 56, 10; QJF 93/4, fols. 13, 14.
[77] Dalton, *Countrey Justice*, p. 182.
[78] Amy L. Erickson, *Women and Property in Early Modern England* (London, 1995); Nancy
    E. Wright, Margaret W. Ferguson and A. R. Buck (eds.), *Women, Property, and the Letters
    of the Law in Early Modern England* (Toronto, 2004).
[79] Holdsworth, *History of English Law*, vol. VII, p. 14.

Table 4.1: *Forcible detainer and disseisin: marital status of women defendants and plaintiffs.*[80]

Marital status	Defendants	Plaintiffs/Disseisees
Married	48.8%	27.8%
Single	33.3%	6.1%
Widowed	117.9%	66.7%

feelings ran high.[81] Married women occupied positions of considerable power *vis-à-vis* freehold and leasehold land as well as moveable property pertaining to the household. Women were sometimes particularly concerned about leases that they had brought with them into the marriage despite the status of leases as 'real chattels' that technically became their husbands' property during his life, and which only reverted to them if they had remained intact and unalienated.[82] Losing leases could be devastating for a whole family, not just the man in whose name the lease had been held. In 1661, Edward Birth was hauled before magistrates for saying that 'Sir John Arderne was the cause of his wife's death and the child within her' for 'as soon as Sir John Arderne did pull off the sales of the leases her child died in her belly'; others claimed that Lady Arderne had declared that she 'was very glad of the cancelling of the leases and of the making of the new ones'.[83] Arderne's wife was presumed to have had strong feelings either way.

Changes in women's wealth, household position and loyalty brought about by marriage or death could destabilise the hierarchy of family relationships in distressing ways. A good proportion of forcible entries, detainers and expulsions were connected to such events. No wonder that in some cases a widow purposefully 'resolved not to dispose of herself in marriage to any person whatsoever' precisely because of the potential effects of remarrying on her children's rights and entitlements to land.[84] After their grandmother had died, Richard Massy used the courts against his sisters, Elizabeth and Maud, and direct action in ejecting Elizabeth from the house that she now leased with her husband, during the course of

---

[80] Source: status of 524 individuals prosecuted before the Cheshire quarter sessions and great sessions (assizes) prosecutions in alternate years during the 1590s, 1620s, 1640s, 1650s and 1660s

[81] E.g., CCLAS: QJF 102/4, fol. 91 (1675).

[82] Baker, *Introduction*, p. 552; Pearl Hogrefe, 'Legal rights of Tudor women and their circumvention by men and women', *Sixteenth Century Journal* 3 (1972), 100.

[83] CCLAS: QJF 89/2, fols. 129, 130.   [84] TNA: PRO STAC 8 87/14 (1610).

which he allegedly dumped what he believed to be her dead body (she was unconscious) into a ditch, saying 'then a whore is dead'.[85] Dame Mary Cholmondeley, widowed in 1597 at the age of thirty-four, was involved in lawsuits over property (including disseisins) against her eldest son Robert when he attained his majority in 1610, and against her paternal uncle after her father's death when, as sole heir, she inherited the family home, Holford Hall. (It is, incidentally, a painting of Dame Mary's two daughters, Lettice and Mary, with their infants that graces the cover of *The Family, Sex and Marriage*.)[86] Not all widows were as formidable an adversary as Dame Mary, whom James I called 'the bold Lady of Cheshire'. The fact that widows constituted two-thirds of the women who prosecuted others for casting or keeping them out of their property reflects both widows' legal capacity to launch suits on their own behalf and their vulnerability as victims.

Mistresses of households, whatever the latter's wealth, were responsible for the provision, maintenance and preservation of all manner of household property, 'ordering, accounting, dividing, distributing, spending, and disposing of... both durable and perishable goods'.[87] Robert Cleaver instructed that the housewife 'must lay a diligent eye to her household-stuff in every room, that nothing be embezzled away, nothing spoiled or lost for want of looking to, nothing marred by ill usage, nor nothing worn out by using more than is needful, nothing out of place, for things cast aside, are deemed to be stolen, and then there followeth uncharitable suspicions, which breedeth much disquietness'. The virtuous housewife, Cleaver stated, '*girdeth her loins with strength, and strengtheneth her arms*'. Although he was quick to explain that this meant that she should set 'her self painfully about some work that is profitable', he gave little instruction as to how women should respond if their houses or possessions really were under physical threat.[88] In order to protect her household's resources, both at her husband's side and in his absence, a housewife's role might require courage, strength and active defence. But some conduct books contained more explicit references – which sat somewhat uneasily with the virtue of wifely submission – to how she might be required to behave. An earlier sixteenth-century work suggested that the housewife 'should

---

[85] TNA: PRO STAC 8 228/10, m. 7 (1609).

[86] C. B. Philips and J. H. Smith, *Lancashire and Cheshire from AD1540* (London, 1994), pp. 22–3. John T. Hopkins, '"Such a likeness there was in the pair": An investigation into the painting of the Cholmondley sisters', *Transactions of the Historic Society of Lancashire and Cheshire* 141 (1992), 1–38. The painting, *The Cholmondley Sisters*, c.1600–10, is held by the Tate Gallery, London.

[87] Natasha Korda, *Shakespeare's Domestic Economies: Gender and Property in Early Modern England* (Philadelphia, 2002), p. 27.

[88] Robert Cleaver, *A Godly Forme of Household Government* (London, 1598), pp. 93–4.

think her self to be, as if it were the overseer of the laws within our house: that she should . . . oversee the stuff, vessel[s] and implements of our house none otherwise than the captain of a garrison overseeth and proveth the soldiers'.[89] Faced with various threats – material and symbolic – to the integrity of their households, it was not, as has sometimes been implied, only exceptional women who were sufficiently resourceful enough to negotiate their legal status under coverture.[90] I have described elsewhere the cultural models of positive feminine force that were resonant with the actions of ordinary women in defending their households. The role of family members, especially mistresses of households, was similarly significant in 'forcible rescues' of goods and livestock – when people used actual or threatened force or violence to recover their property from legal custody such as from the hands of bailiffs or constables or from the local pound in the case of animals.[91] Both the ideology and the practical experience of housewifery – which was often hard, arduous, and absolutely crucial to the household's well-being – invested in married women an authority and responsibility that informed their perspectives and actions.

The higher status of wives in relation to other women is reinforced in a further development in the case of the Brocks, discussed above. Three and a half years after the aforementioned incidents, Margaret Brock, who having recently married was now Margaret Dod, was prosecuted by her brother William and his wife Ann again. This time, the property at issue was not land but moveable goods. In May 1669, Margaret and Mary Catherall (in 1665–6 a servant of Margaret and William's brother, John) entered William and Ann's house while they were absent, marched into the kitchen and, after a struggle with a surprised maidservant, took away a kettle (valued at 1s), a large iron mortar and pestle (valued at 2s), and a pewter dish (worth 6d). When the maidservant asked why on earth she was removing these things while her mistress was out, Margaret 'swore they were her own and [that] she would have them and that she would go through the house and take what was hers'. William and Ann filed an indictment for grand larceny; although the bill was found true, Margaret and Mary were immediately pardoned.[92] It is instructive that it was as

---

[89] *Xenophon's Treatise of Housholde*, trans. Gentian Hervet (London, 1532), fol. 33v. For a recent account of the contradictions inherent in household manuals' advice to women, see Korda, *Shakespeare's Domestic Economies*, ch. 1.

[90] E.g., Nancy E. Wright with Margaret W. Ferguson, 'Introduction' to Wright, Ferguson and Buck, *Women, Property, and the Letters of the Law*, p. 4.

[91] Walker, *Crime, Gender and Social Order*, pp. 86–96, 249–62.

[92] CCLAS: QJB 3/2, fol. 211r; QJF 97/2, fols. 35, 87, 158, 1, 79, 160. The legal record does not contain information about why the pardon was granted.

a married woman that Margaret Dod *née* Brock attempted to regain her property on her own behalf.

Spinsters rarely brought suits to recover or protect their property (unlike widows).[93] Only 6 per cent of forcible entries and disseisins were prosecuted by, or even on behalf of, single women (see Table 4.1). When they did, they tended to prosecute members of their families rather than people with whom they had entered into commercial relationships, such as tenants or landlords. Spinsters were thus grossly under-represented given that at any given time they outnumbered wives and widows together in the general population.[94] Many single women did hold independent interests in property, inherited legacies, and controlled and leased lands on their own behalf. They also frequently exercised a great deal of responsibility within family and household structures. We cannot assume that they were merely passive vessels under their fathers' control. In comparison with their apparent reluctance to sue over land, never-married females constituted one-third of female defendants for forcible detainer and disseisin. Their actual participation was probably greater, however, for they were not always formally prosecuted when they participated as sisters, daughters or maidservants. Mary Parker in 1669 sought to ensure that the house of which her father later took possession was empty by enticing away the maidservant who had been left by her master and mistress 'to keep their house'. Her tactics ranged from simply inviting the girl to go home with her to promising to show her two pied horses in Mr Stanley's stables.[95] Ellen Boote was indicted along with her three brothers and her parents for ejecting, with knives and axes, a man from his messuage in Wilkesley in July 1649.[96] Unmarried sisters Alice and Elizabeth Barber and their yeoman brother Randle were charged in 1645 with the forcible expulsion of a ninety-year-old widow from two closes of land and for further 'violent carriages' towards her thereafter.[97] Bonds between single adult women and their siblings and parents often remained exceptionally strong. Many enjoyed long-term residence with their siblings whether they were married or not.[98] In 1667, the unmarried Elizabeth Minshull had provided a home for her brother, 'a simple man', as well as her

---

[93] Tim Stretton, *Women Waging Law in Elizabethan England* (Cambridge, 1998), pp. 103–8.

[94] Estimates for the period between 1574 and 1821 are 59.2% spinsters, 32.1% married, 8.7% widowed: Peter Laslett, 'Mean household size in England since the sixteenth century', in Peter Laslett and Richard Wall (eds.), *Household and Family in Past Time* (Cambridge, 1972), p. 145, table 4.7.

[95] CCALS: QJF 97/1, fols. 101, 99, 10, 48.   [96] CCLAS: QJF 77/2, fol. 124.

[97] CCLAS: QJF 73/3, fol. 96.

[98] Amy M. Froide, *Never Married: Singlewomen in Early Modern England* (Oxford, 2005), pp. 49–64, 74–9; Ralph A. Houlbrooke, *The English Family 1450–1700* (London, 1984), p. 41.

blind centenarian mother.[99] The participation of single women in forcible
detainers and disseisins lends weight to the view that without the labour,
financial support and other assistance of never-married women, it seems
likely that 'many so-called "nuclear families" would not have survived or
thrived'.[100]

Recognising the active participation of spinsters in crimes committed
by family groupings serves as a corrective to the impression that unmarried women's dealings with the courts were invariably detrimental as a
result of the difficulties inherent in their non-married state and the need
to sustain themselves: petty thievery, prostitution, living out of service,
and bastard bearing, for instance.[101] The significance of the contributions of never-married women to households and household formation is
perhaps the area of recent and current historical research that promises
to revise fundamentally received views about the early modern family.[102]

Conclusion

My focus in this chapter has been upon the family as a unit that engaged in
criminal activities, and that in so doing came into conflict with members
of other households. While I do not wish to deny the reality of violence
perpetrated by family members upon their intimates *within* the early modern household, I have been concerned with somewhat different issues. In
particular, I have shown that household and familial participation in property offences and violent acts did not obey a crude patriarchal model. The
dynamics of collective participation in criminal activities were far more
varied. In a number of ways, we have seen that the theoretical status of
family and household members and the reality of their everyday lives
inform and explain both individual and collective acts for which people
were brought before legal officials.

We considered the bearing of that most central of familial relationships,
that between husbands and wives, on participation in crime. The legal
position of married women was not simply determined by a doctrine of
coverture that denied them a legal identity. Stone argued that the status and rights of wives declined in the sixteenth and early seventeenth
centuries: married women lost the protection both of their wider kin
and of parish priests and religious houses, which left them exposed to

---

[99] CCLAS: QJF 95/1, fol. 152.
[100] Froide, *Never Married*, p. 44.   [101] E.g., ibid., pp. 31, 38.
[102] The history of unmarried or never-married men is even more difficult to reconstruct as
court records do not include men's marital status. However, the proportion of unmarried men in the general population was similar to that of unmarried women, and they
may also have maintained strong bonds with their adult siblings and parents.

exploitation by their husbands. These trends were compounded, he thought, by the 'new emphasis placed by the state and the law on the subordination of the wife to the head of the household as the main guarantee of law and order', and by the Protestant ideals of marriage which strengthened the husband's authority over his wife and the likelihood of women's submission to their husbands.[103] However, as subsequent historians of the family and of women and gender demonstrated, the emphasis on the household as the primary conduit of law and order also *raised* the status and practical authority of wives. As mistresses of households, women gained an authoritative identity that informed active defences of and sometimes offensives on behalf of their households. Some of these acts resulted in legal action being taken against them. In cases where wives had acted alongside their husbands, however, only he might appear in the formal record of the courts.

Moreover, we saw too that there is good reason to believe that unmarried as well as married women's involvement in criminal activity is underestimated in the sources because of their position as subordinate household members. The same, however, is true of male dependants. One practical consequence of the patriarchal theory that demanded submission to fathers and masters meant that indictments and bindings over of household heads might obscure the active participation of other family members in the events for which the former found themselves brought before legal officials. It was unnecessarily expensive to bind to the peace or good behaviour a number of individuals when seeking a recognisance against only the household head might be sufficient to warn adversaries that one meant business. In such cases, husbands, fathers and masters were understood to represent their entire households.

The participation of other family members in crime will hopefully be illuminated further in future research, yet it remains extremely difficult to quantify. Familial ties, whether by blood, marriage or co-habitation, are not systematically recorded in legal records. Married women were, of course, identified in legal records as the wife of so-and-so, and unmarried women who lived at home were identified as the daughters of parents with whom they were prosecuted. But the law did not require that legal documents such as indictments or recognisances stated the relationships of married, unmarried or widowed women nor indeed men of varying marital status to their brothers, sisters, aunts, uncles, mothers, step-parents or cousins, or other members of their households with whom they had participated in an unlawful activity. John Smith senior and John Smith junior, for instance, husbandmen prosecuted together for a riotous

---

[103] Stone, *Family, Sex and Marriage*, p. 202.

assembly, might have been father and son; alternatively, they were perhaps uncle and nephew, grandfather and grandson, cousins, or no relation
at all.[104] Nor was men and women's status as servants or apprentices
routinely entered in the legal record when they acted alongside their
masters, mistresses or employers, or other people with whom they lived.
Although we cannot assume that co-defendants with shared surnames
were inevitably related by blood or marriage, supporting evidence suggests that many were. As many co-habitants did not share surnames even
in basically nuclear households – including household and farm servants,
apprentices, step-parents and step-children, in-laws, and half-siblings –
it is probable that figures such as those I have presented in this chapter
are underestimates.

The practical demands to preserve, defend and further their household's interests were made on *all* family members – not just masters and
mistresses of households. In a society where the household rather than the
individual was widely understood to be the social, economic and political unit that mattered, the male household head's legal claim to ownership of property that was under threat was often neither here nor there.
Early modern people understood property to be held in common by and
for households. If the household suffered, so did all its inhabitants. The
prosperity of households, and sometimes their very social and economic
survival, made it incumbent upon women and men who lived together
to commit unlawful acts both individually and collectively. Crucially for
our argument here, where civil law invested ownership in husbands and
fathers, criminal law sanctioned the use of physical force to protect one's
household and co-habitants. Just as parents could legitimately use violence to protect their children, sons and daughters could do the same
in defence of their parents, and male and female servants in defence
of their masters and mistresses. Historians of the family, including (but
certainly not limited to) Stone, and historians of crime and social order
have privileged the political and symbolic importance of the household
at the expense of its day-to-day significance. They have also paid too
great attention to laws regarding property ownership and not enough
to those regarding the obligations of family members towards each
other.

All of these points have been explored in my case study of the criminal misdemeanours of forcible entry, detainer and disseisin, offences
that have received comparatively little attention from historians of crime,
and which *pace* Stone were engaged in by households of almost all
classes, by individuals of almost all status, and in all regions. Analysis

[104] CCALS: QJF 95/2, fol. 8; QJB 3/1, fol. 271r.

of these offences demonstrated the extent to which legal battles sometimes involved complex competition between competing households of people who were themselves related in some way. The law was one of several weapons used in such disputes, which often had no clear victims or perpetrators. Lawrence Stone's generalisations about the *meaning* of family violence and criminal families that are deduced from assumptions that we can identify in his work about the transition to modernity ultimately tell us little.[105] Evidence of family members collectively defending or acquiring resources through lawful or unlawful means suggests that the early modern family was intrinsically neither united nor divided. Only historical investigation can reveal to us what happened in particular contexts. Stone's trajectory of the history of the family has raised important questions but the history of crime, at least, has also raised equally taxing ones of his own argument.

[105] Walker, 'Modernisation', pp. 39–40, 31–2.

5 Faces in the crowd: Gender and age in the early modern English crowd

John Walter

In early modern England, men did it, women and youths did it, even little children on occasion did it – they all participated in protest. But within the historiography of the crowd that developed in the 1950s and 1960s, the participation of all these groups, to the extent that their separate inclusion in protest was even noted, was largely subsumed within the grand narratives of the emergence of class and the struggle for citizenship. Causation in terms of the grievances of the 'rioters', itself located in underlying narratives of the impact of modernisation, capitalist agriculture, industrialisation, and the growth of the state, was held to explain participation in protest. Thus, when historians began to identify faces in the crowd the faces were those of men, and for the pioneer of this approach in Britain – George Rudé – predominantly those men whose modest property and marginal political participation rescued them from contemporary identifications of protesters as 'the mob'.[1]

Issues of status in terms of gender or age had little or no place in these narratives. The emergence of a feminist/women's history, to which pioneering work on pre-industrial protest made its own contribution, was the first explicitly to challenge the neglect of gender in explaining issues of participation.[2] Much of the inspiration for this work was also shaped by reference to grand narratives, not least those of subordination/resistance and oppression/emancipation. When Lawrence Stone produced *Family, Sex and Marriage*, he was able to draw on this work. 'The evidence suggests', he wrote,

I am grateful to Keith Wrightson, my colleagues Amanda Flather and Clodagh Tait, Alex Shepard, and the editors for their helpful comments.

[1] See the essays collected in G. Rudé, *Paris and London in the Eighteenth Century* (London, 1970).

[2] M. I. Thomis and J. Grimmett, *Women in Protest 1800–1850* (London, 1982). The important work here is, of course, E. P. Thompson, 'The moral economy of the English crowd in the eighteenth century', *Past and Present* 50 (1971). He returned to the issue of women's participation in protests over food in his *Customs in Common* (London, 1991), pp. 305–36.

that married and unmarried women were as submissive and dependent as the conduct books suggested that they ought to be . . . The only two areas where they showed a spirit of independence was in leading food riots and in adhering to dissident religious opinions . . . but in both cases . . . they were relying on the higher moralities of the just price and the true faith to spur them to defy the law.[3]

Stone's brief discussion registered both the then strengths and weaknesses of this body of work. For Stone, women were capable of engaging in protest that concerned their immediate interests in domestic consumption, and they might participate in confessional strife. But they were little involved, if at all, in the politics of class and state. 'Men took direct action against the law when they felt aggrieved, women only in accordance with a higher moral code'.[4]

More recent work has recognised that women were often to the fore in early modern protest, has offered some discussion of the reasons for this, and has more recently begun to extend women's political participation into the politics of the state from which Stone wrongly excluded them.[5] By comparison, there has been more limited recognition of the participation of young males (with the partial exception of the London apprentices). More surprisingly, given the assumption that protest was carried out predominantly by men, there has been little explicit discussion of participation in protest as an expression of, *and* claim to, masculinity.

This chapter seeks to begin an exploration of how contemporary constructions of the social roles of the gendered groups from whom protesters were recruited helps to enrich the explanations for their participation and presence in protest. It points to the family strategies and priorities that often lay behind membership of the crowd. It pays particular attention to how representations of identities defined by age and gender might be manipulated by protesters, and the families and communities whose interests they sought to represent, in an attempt to license a political agency by groups traditionally thought of as dependent and subordinate

---

[3] L. Stone, *The Family, Sex and Marriage in England 1500–1800* (London, 1977), p. 201.

[4] Ibid.

[5] S. H. Mendelson and P. Crawford, *Women in Early Modern England* (Oxford, 1998), ch. 7; R. A. Houlbrooke, 'Women's social life and common action in England from the fifteenth century to the eve of the civil war', *Continuity and Change* 1 (1986), 171–89; P. Crawford, '"The poorest she": Women and citizenship in early modern England', in M. Mendle (ed.), *The Putney Debates: The Army, the Levellers and the English State* (Cambridge, 2001), pp. 197–218; D. P. Ludlow, 'Shaking patriarchy's foundations: Sectarian women in England 1641–1700', in R. L. Greaves (ed.), *Triumph over Silence: Women in Protestant History* (Westport, Conn., 1985), pp. 93–123; A. Hughes, 'Gender and politics in Leveller literature', in S. Dwyer Amussen and M. A. Kishlansky (eds.), *Political Culture and Cultural Politics in Early Modern England: Essays presented to David Underdown* (Manchester, 1995), pp. 162–88.

in early modern society. It explores whether participation by these groups offered a degree of (temporary) empowerment for those otherwise thought to have no political role and, if so, what implications this might have had for gendered identities in early modern England. At the same time, it examines how different aspects of the contested representations of gendered identities were drawn on both by those engaged in, and those prosecuting, protest, respectively to justify and to condemn participation. Since protest and its prosecution offer a contested site where we can see competing representations of age and gender roles in play, it is suggested that greater attention to the gendering of protest might help to meet the call for an explicitly gendered history of change in early modern England.[6]

I

The assumption that most early modern protest was protest by males has meant that grievance, not gender, continues to be held as sufficient explanation of their actions. An attention to gender, however, can deepen our understanding of the reasons for, and the range of meanings involved in, men's membership of the early modern crowd. Recent work on early modern masculinity has suggested that, while the superiority of the patriarchal male may have been a given in prescriptive literature, where it was seen to be grounded in a display of rationality and order guaranteed by contemporary medical/humoral theory, its achievement was in practice harder to secure and to maintain.[7] Moreover, the control of self and others that patriarchal manhood assumed for its exercise was also grounded in part in an independent and self-sufficient mastery that presumed economic independence.[8] Economic change in the period was to make economic autonomy, always problematic for those at the bottom of the social hierarchy, more difficult for growing numbers of adult males to achieve or to maintain. Grievance *and* gender were therefore inextricably linked in explaining male participation in protest.

Seen thus, there is an obvious and direct relationship here with protest within a politics of subsistence where access to land, food and the proper rewards for skilled employment dominated early modern crowd actions. If

---

[6] A. Shepard, 'From anxious patriarchs to refined gentlemen? Manhood in Britain, circa 1500–1700', *Journal of British Studies* 44 (2005), 281–95.

[7] A. Shepard, *Meanings of Manhood in Early Modern England* (Oxford, 2003); 'Manhood, credit and patriarchy in early modern England c. 1580–1640', *Past and Present* 167 (2000), 75–106; E. A. Foyster, *Manhood in Early Modern England: Honour, Sex and Marriage* (Harlow, 1999), and, of course, A. Fletcher, *Gender, Sex and Subordination in England 1500–1800* (New Haven and London, 1995).

[8] Shepard, *Meanings of Manhood*, pp. 16, 37.

the link between economic sufficiency and masculinity was rarely, if ever, explicitly articulated in protest and its judicial aftermath, recognition of this aspect of manhood nevertheless helps to deepen our understanding of the male role in protest. Men's participation might be explained in the familiar terms of a 'breadwinner' politics. But there is also scope for thinking beyond largely economic explanations. Male participation in protest may also have been informed by an 'anxious masculinity',[9] by otherwise unexpressed fears about the threats posed to the full attainment of patriarchal manhood. For an increasing number of men in this period, protest might also have reflected the psychic costs of gaining and maintaining patriarchal manhood. If this was the case, then it is also worth pondering the psychic *gains* to be found in the experience of participation in crowd action. The claims to power that crowds represented, even if only temporarily, offered an opportunity for the deployment of competing constructions of masculinity. Crowds might provide a space for performances that brought compensatory confirmation of manhood for males being increasingly marginalised by social and economic change.

Poverty and the threat to their own and their family's subsistence was a central plank in the justifications offered by male protesters. Underlying these was an appeal to the prescribed sexual division of labour which positioned adult male household heads as providers for their families. Those who described themselves as poor day labourers, involved in a dispute at Childersditch in Essex in 1607, grumbled that if they lost their common rights to wood they would be left with little or no means of livelihood and their wives and children would be utterly undone.[10] This was a common grievance in protests over access to both land and grain. Clothworkers in Gloucestershire, who had attacked barges transporting grain down the River Severn in the dearth of 1586, complained that 'they were dryven to feede their Children with Catts, doggs and rootes of nettles'. Craftsmen in the Wiltshire broadcloth industry grumbled that, because of middlemen in the grain trade, 'they were not able to provide foode for themselves and their families'; Essex weavers, petitioning against abuses in their trade, complained of the unemployment these caused, 'by reason whereof wee are brought into great extreamitye & want and [are] not able to maynteyne our poore wives and Children'; while the humble petition from Somerset of 'many well-affected and poor distressed people' in

---

[9] I have borrowed this phrase from M. Breitenberg, *Anxious Masculinity in Early Modern England* (Cambridge, 1996).

[10] The National Archives [hereafter TNA]: Public Record Office [hereafter PRO], STAC 8/247/8.

the dearth of 1648/9 made direct reference to the male role as providers, asking the magistrates 'effectually to help us, that our poore families be not remed[i]lessely cast away'.[11]

These appeals sought then to legitimise male participation in protest by reference to a consensus about what was the male role within the family. Thus, Wiltshire weavers, examined about their role in assaulting and taking grain from a dealer in grain in 1614, drew on their role as household heads to explain their actions. John Ford told his examiners, 'he would not denye it for he had as leafe [i.e., rather] lo[o]sse his life as to see his wife and Children stearve', words echoed by a fellow weaver, who said 'he [was] verie loth to see his wife and Children to stearve for he had rather dye himselfe'.[12]

If defence of family made honour a central component of early modern aristocratic culture, then similar ideas may also have informed plebeian protest.[13] If less clearly articulated than in elite culture, the resort to violence in protest brought these ideas of honour in the use of male strength to defend essential rights closer to the surface. Protesters who had destroyed enclosures in Feckenham Forest in Worcestershire presented themselves before the county's sheriff, 'w[i]th warlike weapons (vizt. Pikes, fforest Bills, pitchforks, swordes & the like)' and 'did not only slight o[u]r power, but assaulted o[u]r p[er]sons, & p[ro]tested they would fight itt out to the last man before they would y[i]eld'. Opponents who pulled down an emparkment by the lord of the manor at Ryther in Yorkshire in the early seventeenth century were reported to have said 'they would dye in the same place or loose their best blood but they would have it'.[14]

Violence was an ever-present corollary of the association of masculinity with strength and of the emphasis on the requirement, if necessary, physically to defend male integrity and honour. It drew on perhaps more contested constructions of masculinity. *The Homily of the State of Matrimony* might complain that '*the common sort of men* doth judge that . . . moderation should not become a man: for they say that it is a token of womanish cowardness; and therefore they think that it is a man's part to fume in anger, to fight with fist and staff'.[15] But the frequency with

---

[11] TNA: PRO, SP 12/188/47; *Acts of the Privy Council [hereafter APC] 1613–1614*, pp. 457–8; Somerset Record Office [hereafter RO], Q/S Petitions, QS Wells, 24 Charles I; QSOB 1627–38, fol. 140v; Essex RO, Q/SR 266/121.

[12] Wiltshire RO, Q/S Gt. Roll, Trin. 1614, nos. 112–14.

[13] M. James, *English Politics and the Concept of Honour* (*Past & Present*, supplement 3, 1978).

[14] TNA: PRO, SP 16/214/46; STAC 8/250/30.

[15] *The Two Books of Homilies Appointed To be Read in Churches*, ed. J. Griffiths (Oxford, 1859), p. 503 (my emphasis).

which violence was a characteristic of protest (especially against enclosure), and was deployed therein by all social groups from the gentry
down, suggests that it might be premature for the period at least up to
the mid-seventeenth century to see this as an expression of 'oppositional'
masculinity.[16] Whatever the conduct books might advocate, violence in
defence of vital interests was a corollary of the emphasis on strength as
an essential aspect of masculinity and of the need for males to be willing
to use this to defend their 'honour'. A willingness to join in protest might
then prove a test of manhood. Those who failed to join the crowd faced
being labelled cowards, as was the case in protests in the Forest of Dean
in 1612.[17]

The physical destruction that protest against enclosure necessarily
entailed ensured that violence – usually, but not exclusively, against property rather than persons – was a frequent aspect of collective protest. But,
not unsurprisingly, protests involving large crowds of men were marked
by violence – or at least by its threat. The rhetoric and use of violence
seems to have been particularly marked among commoners in forest, fen
and moorland communities who faced large-scale aristocratic or royal-
sponsored enclosures that threatened radically to transform the nature of
their local economies and to supplant their independent subsistence with
new forms of labour discipline. Enclosers and drainers were threatened
with burial in their own dikes or mines, while the erection of gallows
and digging of graves over the disputed land gave symbolic expression to
these threats.[18] In the enclosure disputes prosecuted in Star Chamber, the
pulling down of hedges was often described as the work of large crowds
of men, well armed with an array of agricultural implements and, less frequently, weapons, sometimes marching in military order with their cap-
tains, lieutenants and colours, and usually accompanying their destruction with threats of violence and the issuing of challenges and dares to the
encloser, his servants and workmen.[19] Protesters in Yorkshire announced
'that never a fellow in England should keepe upp the . . . hedges but it
should be pulled downe in dispite', while protesters in Essex, having
thrown down an enclosure, told the encloser's servants, 'wee would see
yo[u]r Maister . . . come himself with his workmen & spade, and take

---

[16] Shepard, *Meanings of Manhood*, p. 105.   [17] TNA: PRO, SP 14/70/49; /160/18.
[18] TNA: PRO, STAC 8/227/35.
[19] For examples, see TNA: PRO, STAC 7/1/7; 8/4/3; /5/21; /7/3; /226/19; /256/17; /265/7;
TNA: PRO, SP 16/188/20; /223/31; /230/50; /242/62; /484/8; SP 18/37/11; *Journal of the
House of Commons*, vol. II , p. 254; House of Lords [hereafter HL] RO, MP HL 14 June
1641, 25 Aug. 1641, 8 Sept. 1641, 15–18 May 1643, 21 March 1645–6; S. R. Gardiner
(ed.), *Reports of Cases in the Courts of Star Chamber and High Commission* (Camden Soc.,
ns. xxxix, 1886), p. 62; J. Rushworth, *Historical Collections of Private Passages of State . . .*
(1659–1701), vol. III, app.

a spitt of earth if he dare'.[20] Violence might be symbolically displaced onto livestock or effigies of the enclosers. But enclosers, their servants, workmen and tenants were all threatened with being buried alive, having their eyes put out, their throats ripped out, or being burnt alive on a bonfire made of the hedges pulled down.[21] Such colourful descriptions owed not a little to the formal requirements needed to bring an action in Star Chamber, but such charges needed to be culturally plausible and can be confirmed from other sources.[22] They underline the combative and testosterone-laden nature of such protest.

This emphasis on violence might be reinforced by a strategic deployment of a rhetoric of *threatened* violence that was intended to coerce opponents and cajole the authorities into taking action. At Kirby Malzeard, opponents of enclosure by Sir Stephen Proctor threatened that they would 'gyve him Hallyfax lawe and thruste him upp', evidently a reference to a local variant of popular 'justice'.[23] The rhetoric of violence deployed by men in protest might take on much of the *braggadocio* and dark humour associated with the competitive male sociability of the alehouse. Told that 'they would be brought into Starr Chamber', a group of Bedfordshire protesters were said to have replied 'that it was their desire to see London for that they wanted one some thing and some an other'. At Riddlesden in Yorkshire, the encloser was warned 'that they would sett upon his skirts & cutt his tether shorte'. Similar threats of emasculation were alleged to have accompanied a dispute over enclosure at Ladbroke in Warwickshire where threats to cut bristles short carried the same message.[24]

Care needs to be exercised here. Victims' emphasis on the violence of male protesters, more lurid than any recoverable reality of violence in such disputes, was intended to secure the protection of courts and authorities. Playing up the violence crowds were said to use was also intended to discredit the validity of protest. Authority and the crowd's victims drew on the other central defining aspect of patriarchal masculinity – reason and control – precisely to suggest that protest was illegitimate. Charges of disorder carried with them not only obvious associations with the threat to social order, but also the accusation that rioters were personally disordered and that therefore no credence need be given to their protest. 'Dissolute', 'disordered', 'ill-disposed' and 'lewd' were frequently used

---

[20] TNA: PRO, STAC 8/144/20; 8/142/8.

[21] For examples of these threats, see TNA: PRO, STAC 8/7/3; /5/21; /194/4; /105/8; /61/35; /12/7; /129/13; /184/2; /121/20; /227/14; /165/18; /220/23; /275/7; /204/30; /197/18; Essex RO, Q/SR 190/40–5; HLRO, MP HL 14 June 1641, 26 June 1643.

[22] T. G. Barnes, 'Star Chamber mythology', *American Journal of Legal History* 5 (1961), 1–11.

[23] TNA: PRO, STAC 8/227/35.   [24] TNA: PRO STAC 8/253/35; /10/18.

adjectives to stigmatise those labelled 'rioters'.[25] Thus, crowds seizing grain in Wiltshire were said to be 'loose and disordered persons'. Rioters in 1603 were said to have 'behaved themselves as persons enraged and stark mad'. Protesters in Essex were accused of being 'all men of like violent & unpeacable disposition'; those at Rippingale in Lincolnshire as 'p[er]sons of very Lewde and dissolute condic[i]on and wilde behavioure'.[26] If, then, disputes on the ground provided an arena for the display of violence as an expression of masculinity, courts provided a site for its stigmatisation. But the frequent descriptions of the combative nature of crowds and of the competitive exchanges protest involved suggest how membership of the crowd might allow men, anxious to defend the social and economic bases of their masculinity, to claim a compensatory masculinity.

II

In the recorded exchanges around incidents of protest, the values of masculinity were more often invoked implicitly, rather than explicitly voiced. What we might term the taciturnity of males has perhaps much to tell us of the extent to which all men in early modern England felt less need openly to articulate masculinity and its values. But when age was combined with masculinity then there was more need and more opportunity for an explicit appeal to contemporary constructions of masculinity. Not unsurprisingly, elderly males were less often to be found in the crowd, though their importance as the community's memory banks meant that they still had a vital role to play, especially in disputes over customary rights.[27] But the participation of males whose youth meant that they had yet to achieve manhood makes it more possible to see how claims to masculinity directly informed men's participation in protest.

In early modern England, as in later societies, the crowd was often a youthful crowd. Contemporary constructions of the intersection between age and gender in early modern England offered considerable licence for the participation of young males in acts of collective protest.[28] Youth was

---

[25] TNA: PRO, SP 14/129/79; *APC 1621–3*, pp. 355–6; *APC 1629–30*, pp. 4–5, 24–5; *APC 1595–6*, pp. 43–4.

[26] TNA: PRO, STAC 8/259/21; /144/20; /274/3.

[27] K. Thomas, *Age and Authority in Early Modern England*, Raleigh Lecture on History 1976, 62 (British Academy, 1976), p. 32.

[28] On youth and masculinity, see P. Griffiths, *Youth and Authority: Formative Experiences in England 1560–1640* (Oxford, 1996); I. Krausman Ben-Amos, *Adolescence and Youth in Early Modern England* (London and New Haven, 1994); Thomas, 'Age and authority'; K. Thomas, 'Children in early modern England', in G. Avery and J. Briggs (eds.), *Children and Their Books: A Celebration of the Work of Iona and Peter Opie* (Oxford, 1989),

held to be 'a slippery age, full of pashion, rashness, wilfulness'.[29] Humoral theory suggested that young male bodies lacked balance, being vulnerable to an excess of heat and moisture. As such, young males were not thought to be able to control either their minds or bodies. Consequently, young men were represented as being too easily given to anger, violence and disorder with, therefore, an innate tendency towards insubordination and disobedience. Such ideas of course informed discourses of order and the need for subordination and control, but they could also be used to license youthful participation in protest. Those ambiguous qualities of manhood associated with the physical strength to which young men were thought to be especially vulnerable – among them fighting, aggression, vandalism – might be drawn on to excuse their involvement in the crowd.

Young people, and the communities from which they came, exploited contemporary constructions of youth as lacking reason and naturally given to disorder both to fashion protest and to explain it away. John Stow's account of the participation of young men in the large-scale destruction of enclosures in London in 1516 provides a telling example of this. On examination by the King's Council, the mayor had reported 'the injury and annoying done to the citizens and to their liberties, which though they would not seek disorderly to redress yet the commonalty and young persons could not be stayed thus to remedy'. The Council's response was to order the young home, 'the mayor departed without more harm', and – Stow records – the land remained unenclosed.[30] Similar tactics were employed elsewhere. When, in the aftermath of the Midlands Rising, the recently erected gibbet was pulled down, the urban authorities reported to an irate earl of Hastings, the lord lieutenant, that it was done by 'Children'. A sceptical Hastings sarcastically replied, 'were not Leicester a place of gov[ern]m[e]nt and to be governed by men of ripp[e] Age and not by the unruly stroke of youthe, happily it might be soe, but I rather thincke yt some of greater poware then Children have done it'. But though he dismissed their excuse itself as 'Childishe', Hastings was left asking to be told the names of 'those children or whatsoev[er] they weare'.[31] Similarly, when an anti-popish panic at Colchester in 1640 led a large crowd of the town's young men to assemble with the idea of searching the nearby houses of Catholic gentry families, the town authorities

pp. 45–77; K. Thomas, *Rule and Misrule in the School of Early Modern England* (Stenton Lecture, University of Reading, 1976); A. Shepard, 'Manhood, credit and patriarchy in early modern England, 1580–1640', *Past and Present* 167 (2000), 75–106; Shepard, *Meanings of Manhood*; Foyster, *Manhood*.

[29] Thomas, *Age and Authority*, p. 16.
[30] J. Stow, *The Survey of London* (1603), ed. H. B. Wheatley (London, 1956), p. 381.
[31] Leicestershire RO, Leicester Hall Papers BR II/18/19/no. 116.

were said 'to make butt a jest of it', reporting, 'it was butt a boyes Drum, and none butt few children and boyes followed it'.[32]

According to contemporary wisdom, 'until a man grow unto the age of twenty-four years' he was 'wild, without judgement and not of sufficient experience to govern himself'.[33] Contemporary thinking of youth as a period of diminished responsibility, when combined with legal ambiguity over the age at which children became legally responsible, meant that youthful participation might be used to excuse protest. This is a tactic for whose effectiveness there is further evidence in the usually more lenient pattern of criminal prosecution of children and adolescents.[34] Young 'rioters' might, like the youthful petitioners cited by Paul Griffiths, 'mould pliable images of youth to present themselves as weak, stupid, ignorant and naturally naive'.[35] For example, apprentices and servants, dismissed as 'boys' in witness statements, who pulled down enclosures on Hounslow Heath made direct reference to these ideas when they informed the House of Lords that '(they being ignorant of the law) did simply doe [it] w[i]thout any appointing consent or direcceon of their Masters'. They went on to say, somewhat disingenuously it might be thought, that had they known the law they would not have pulled down the pales.[36]

Other aspects of the contemporary construction of youthful masculinity could also extend the licence afforded young men and, where they acted with or on behalf of their families, households, craft and communities, might even be taken to grant them some degree of legitimacy for their participation in protest. In early modern, as in later, societies, youth was seen as a period of difficult transition, in which the young were expected to learn and to absorb the values of the adult world. But, as part of that process, it was recognised that they might also challenge and criticise those norms.[37] There was a tradition of communities seeking to employ the associations of youth with those qualities of courage and rashness celebrated in ballad and popular culture to mobilise young men as inheritors, arbiters and defenders of the boundaries and values of the moral community. Accordingly, to try to manage this *rite de passage* young

---

[32] TNA: PRO, SP 16/458/12–13.   [33] Thomas, *Age and Authority*, p. 16.

[34] See the discussions in M. Hale, *Historia Placitorum Coronae*, ed. S. Emlyn, 2 vols. (1736), vol. I, pp. 16–29, 44; W. Hudson, 'A treatise of the court of Star Chamber', in F. Hargrave, *Collectanea Juridicia: Consisting of tracts relative to the law and constitution of England*, 2 vols. (1792), vol. II, p. 141; M. Dalton, *The Countrey Justice, Containing the Practise of the Justices of the Peace out of their Sessions* . . . (1622 edn), p. 201; G. Walker, *Crime, Gender and Social Order in Early Modern England* (Cambridge, 2003), p. 185.

[35] Griffiths, *Youth and Authority*, pp. 53–4.   [36] HLRO, MP HL 2 June 1641.

[37] E. H. Erikson (ed.), *Youth: Change and Challenge* (New York and London, 1963); M. Mitterauer, *A History of Youth* (Oxford, 1992).

males were encouraged to act as the community's enforcers of its values and, paradoxically, instructed in at least some of those values by being permitted to transgress them, at least temporarily, within the confines of the ritualised time of festive culture.

Rogationtide provides an apt example of the former strategy. With its annual procession of the 'ancienter and younger sort', it was intended to mark and memorise the community's physical boundaries. It was deliberately designed to offer its younger participants a corporate manifestation of the moral community as well as of its physical boundaries. As defendants to the charge of pulling down an enclosure at Colby in Lincolnshire during their procession there insisted, they did so 'to the end the Auncient bounds of the said p[ar]ishe should not be blemished nor obscured butt be kept and p[re]served in memorye, and soe lefte in memory to the younger sorte of people of the said Parishe'.[38] A procession that began with a sermon and ritual cursing of any who encroached on their neighbours' land, the Rogation procession provided a perfect script for crowd action against enclosure and licensed action in particular by the young men of the community.

Festive culture offered considerable scope for the latter strategy of socialisation through the ritualised breaking of rules and norms. It too offered an opportunity for young males to express their aspirations for manhood in a form that readily lent itself as a vehicle for protest. In the temporary respite afforded them and other subordinate groups in an otherwise hierarchical society by special days of holiday licence, young men were allowed to invert and challenge social norms. At the same time, festivities on special calendar days provided for forms of competitive sport and homosocial play that deliberately ended in fighting which sought to foster those qualities of adventurousness and aggression for which young men were feted in ballad and print.[39] All this meant that the temporary licence of what Keith Thomas has described as 'acceptable times of youthful pranks', with their disregard for property and 'addiction to mischief', could as easily be used to assemble a crowd and articulate protest.[40] Thus, at Hingham in Norfolk in 1641, young men, variously described as 'young ruffians' or 'zealots', exploited the licensed horseplay allowed them on Plough Monday to pull down the hated altar rails there. Apprentices intent on similar godly reformation at Norwich cathedral chose to time their efforts at iconoclasm on Shrove Tuesday, a day

[38] TNA: PRO, STAC 8/163/30.
[39] C. Pythian-Adams, *Local History and Folklore: A New Framework* (London, 1975); J. R. Gillis, *Youth and History: Tradition and Change in European Age Relations 1770–present* (New York and London, 1974), pp. 1–28.
[40] Thomas, 'Children', pp. 55, 56–7.

with complex religious associations of purification and one which was also associated within the popular calendar as a day of youthful disorder and popular licence.[41]

If, outside of the realms of fiction,[42] early modern England lacked the formal groupings that were said to be characteristic of continental European youth culture, there is nevertheless plenty of evidence to suggest that in England, as in early modern France, young men could act as the 'uproarious voice of the community's conscience'.[43] This was a tradition that stretched back to at least the English Reformation, but which became more pronounced in the English Revolution and confessional politics thereafter.[44] The young men who met in an Essex village to ring the church bells on New Year's Day, 1641 and then went on to pull down the Laudian altar rails saw themselves as acting in precisely this manner. As one of their number said, 'the reason of his so pulling downe the railes was, because theye gave offence to his conscience, and that the placeing of them was against Gods lawes, and the King's'.[45]

Apprentices represented a more persistent and more organised form of youthful participation in protest. (In London and elsewhere the term 'apprentice' was so synonymous for contemporaries with disorder that it was frequently used as a blanket term for others in the crowd.) As such, apprentices are the one group of young males whose participation in protest has attracted serious study.[46] Patterns of work and associated sociability, reinforced by commonalties in dress, culture and address, underwrote apprentices' ability to act as a group, something in turn celebrated in a cheap print (ballads, popular histories, moral tracts, etc.) intended to flatter the heroic self-image of its apprenticeship audience. But their future, if sometimes shaky, expectations of mastership, guild

---

[41] J. Walter, '"Abolishing superstition with sedition"? The politics of popular iconoclasm in England 1640–1642', *Past and Present* 183 (2004), 93–4.

[42] B. Capp, 'English youth groups and the *Pinder of Wakefield*', *Past and Present* 76 (1977), 127–33.

[43] N. Z. Davis, 'The reasons of misrule: Youth groups and charivaris in sixteenth-century France', *Past and Present* 50 (1971), 41–75; N. Z. Davis, 'Some tasks and themes in the study of popular religion', in C. Trinkaus and H. A. Oberman (eds.), *The Pursuit of Holiness in Late Medieval and Renaissance Religion* (Studies in Medieval and Renaissance Thought, x, Leiden, 1974), p. 323; B. Scribner, 'Reformation, carnival and the world turned upside down', *Social History* 3 (1978), 317.

[44] S. Brigden, 'Youth and the English Reformation', *Past and Present* 95 (1982), 37–67; P. Collinson, *The Birthpangs of Protestant England: Religious and Cultural Change in the Sixteenth and Seventeenth Centuries* (London, 1988), p. 106.

[45] Walter, '"Abolishing superstition"', 112–13.

[46] Steven R. Smith, 'The apprentices of London, 1640–1660: A study of revolutionary youth subculture' (PhD thesis, Vanderbilt University, 1971); Steven R. Smith, 'The London apprentices as seventeenth-century adolescents', *Past and Present* 61 (1973), 149–61.

membership (where guilds existed), and citizenship could give apprentice protests greater political clout. As one contemporary noted, a 'prentice is a City-kernell, his master the shell'.[47]

Apprentices participated in a wide range of protests. Like their rural counterparts, they too might join in protests intended to defend the rights of community or craft. Their participation in protest related to the politics of trade and subsistence reflected shared anxieties about their ability to achieve the economic autonomy that permitted the full achievement of patriarchal male adulthood. Apprentices were responsible for one of the few crowd actions over food to have taken place in London. Sent to Billingsgate to buy fish and finding it all forestalled by the fishwives, a group of sixty to eighty apprentices, again described as 'boyes', enacted a form of *taxation populaire* in the dearth of 1595, selling the fish at a popularly determined 'fair price'.[48] The socialisation of young men into the moral values of the community which was a corollary of their apprenticeship, together with contemporary constructions of their liminal status, meant that apprentices both at London and elsewhere were also active in regulative action, famously in the Shrove Tuesday 'riots' in London attacking the brothels.[49] When xenophobia and anti-popery combined with appeals to young men as defenders of the community, apprentices were also to the fore in policing the confessional boundaries of their communities, attacking both Catholic and Puritan nonconformists throughout the period and being central to many of the iconoclastic episodes of the early stages of the English Revolution.[50] What, then, has been seen as 'the ritual appropriation of modes of violent correction' by young males within a 'censure tradition' could also provide a ready-made text and form for protest.[51]

Since marriage defined the achievement of social adulthood in early modern England, and for many marriage might not come until at least their mid-twenties, young males could encompass a very wide age range, from children through to physically mature, but still single, men like Bartholomew Steer and his compatriots in the mooted 'Oxfordshire Rising'. The degree of independence participation brought doubtless varied by age. Young children accompanied their mothers to protest,

---

[47] 'The wandering Jew telling fortunes to Englishmen', repr. in J. O. Halliwell-Phillips, *Books of Characters, illustrating the habits and manners of Englishmen, from the Reign of James I. to the Restoration* (1857), p. 33.

[48] City of London Repertory, Remembrancia II/97.

[49] K. Lindley, 'Riot prevention and control in early Stuart London', *Trans. of the Royal Historical Society*, 5th ser., 33 (1983), 109–26.

[50] Smith, 'Apprentices'; T. Harris, *London Crowds in the Reign of Charles II: Propaganda and politics from the Restoration until the exclusion crisis* (Cambridge, 1987).

[51] Shepard, *Meanings of Manhood*, p. 105; Mitterauer, *History of Youth*, p. 167.

but early employment in agricultural and other forms of labour gave them plenty of opportunity to learn for themselves of the grievances at issue. The dependent status of sons and servants meant that they too might find themselves commanded by masters or mistresses to pull down enclosures.[52] (Nor were daughters and female servants immune from these pressures. Litigation in a dispute in Cheshire records this revealing exchange between a yeoman and his servant, obviously anxious to know whether he would support her if caught: to the question, 'Katherine, cannot thou and Peter Saint's daughter goe and pull down yonder fence?', came the answer 'Maister, will you bear mee out?'[53]) But, as was the case in a dispute over enclosure at Dulwich where the crowd was made up entirely of sons and servants, young people were as likely themselves to join in action to defend the community's common rights on which their family's and their own future subsistence and chances of independence depended.[54] Thus, in a dispute in Windsor Forest in which a group of young girls and boys broke up stones marking out an intended enclosure, one young girl explained, that being

at playe with diverse other yong maidens & children . . . some speeches were then & there used by some of the young people that . . . [the encloser] had threatened very insolently that he would forthwith build a house upon the comon there & would keepe inclosed a greate p[ar]t of ye said wood to his own use in dispight of all men, & that he would debarr all the inhabitants therabouts from their accustomed and Lawfull common therein, upon which speeches and others . . . [she] and div[er]se others there p[re]sent conceiving that by the said course, the inhabitants thereabouts, being eyther parents or masters to the said company & *consequently* themselves should be much hindred & impoverished . . . [the] young maidens and children & this defendant for companyes sake went of their owne heads without any commandment or request . . . and with three or fower axes at the uttermost, without any other engines or weapons, did breake some of the greatest stones & scatter others.[55]

Similarly, in the abortive Oxfordshire Rising of 1596, it was their identification of enclosure as the obstacle to their acquiring the land necessary for marriage and thus full adult male status that prompted a group of servants – 'angry, but ageing young men' – to plan a general campaign against enclosure.[56]

[52] For examples of this, see Somerset RO, Q/SR 3.1/11; TNA: PRO, STAC 8/299/21; /284/31.
[53] M. Campbell, *The English Yeoman in the Tudor and Stuart Age* (London, 1960), p. 86.
[54] TNA: PRO, STAC 8/282/17.   [55] TNA: PRO, STAC 8/20/22 (my emphasis).
[56] J. Walter, '"A Rising of the People"? The Oxfordshire Rising of 1596', *Past and Present* 107 (1985), 90–143.

For physically mature males in particular, participation in protests might offer a welcome opportunity to claim the status of manhood. The qualities participation in crowd protests demanded – aggression, physical bravery and combat – advertised their possession of essential male attributes while the status it bestowed on young males as defenders of 'community' gave them a claim to a political identity and authority otherwise restricted to married male adult householders. As we have seen, a willingness to engage in protest could be seen as a test of the manliness manhood presumed. Was he not of 'faint heart?' asked apprentices in the cloth trade at Norwich, attempting to recruit support for a protest against 'creepers' (unapprenticed labour), when one of their number said they should first tell the mayor.[57] Seeking to recruit support for the rising in Oxfordshire and meeting with a refusal, Bartholomew Steer declared, 'if all men weare of . . . [his] mind, they might live like slaves as he did, but for himself he said happ what would, for he coulde die but once and that he would not allwaies live like a slave'. For Steer, there were what he termed approvingly 'lusty fellowes abroade'; those who showed themselves willing to join in the rising were praised as sound or good fellows.[58] In thinking of young men's participation in agrarian and other forms of protest we might then borrow, from another context, Alex Shepard's telling phrase, 'that the territory being claimed was that of manhood itself'.[59]

III

Women's presence in the early modern crowd has received more explicit attention. Some protests might involve no more than a handful of women, but others could see crowds of wives, widows, daughters and servants (as in protests in the eastern fens) numbered in their hundreds.[60] The frequency with which women participated in protest reflected in part the fact that familiar prescriptions of public (male) and private (female) worlds did not capture the reality of gendered space in which work and worship saw women necessarily operate within a public sphere and develop networks and knowledge on which they could draw to articulate collective action.[61] But a sexual division of labour which assigned women primarily

---

[57] TNA: PRO, SP 14/54/62 i–viii.   [58] TNA: PRO, SP 12/261/10.

[59] A. Shephard, 'Meanings of manhood in early modern England, with special reference to Cambridge' (PhD, University of Cambridge, 1998), p. 156.

[60] TNA: PRO, KB 9/789/1/5–6.

[61] A. Flather, 'The gendering of space in early modern Essex, c.1580–1720' (PhD, University of Essex, 2002); L. Gowing, *Common Bodies: Women, Touch and Power in Seventeenth-Century England* (New Haven and London, 2003); B. Capp, *When Gossips Meet: Women,*

to the demands of their families and household economy may perhaps help to explain the hitherto unremarked absence – if that is what it was – of women from the major rebellions of the period.[62] Women were undoubtedly present in large-scale protests which remained locally based, like those in the eastern fens and western forests or in the Midlands Rising of 1607, where it was reported that the women 'destroyed more than the men' and 'tasted of the smart' as well as they.[63] But understandably women do not appear to have been an active presence in those rebellions that ultimately took the form of mobile armed forces marching over considerable distances, even though they may have shared the sense of mobilising grievance.[64]

Women too drew on contemporary constructions of their gendered identity both to justify their presence in protest and to attempt to escape the punishment that their open challenge to authority might otherwise bring. Petitions to the authorities reflected women's belief that the sexual division of labour gave them special licence, as provisioners of their families, to notify authority of its failings to police illegal enclosure or the grain market. This paralleled the 'maternal or matronly' language women used to justify their petitioning in the English Revolution.[65] If men could justify their protest by reference to their role as 'breadwinner', then so too could women refer to their role as provider within the household and family economy. Involved in protests over food, access to land and taxation,[66] they made frequent use of this gendered identity.

Women were present in almost every protest over food in the period and some crowd actions were exclusively feminine affairs. As the group most involved in the round of face-to-face marketing, they were especially sensitive to price movements and abuses in the market-place.[67] As

---

Family, and Neighbourhood in Early Modern England (Oxford, 2003); D. Willen, 'Women in the public sphere in early modern England: The case of the working poor', *Sixteenth Century Journal* 19 (1988), 559–75.

[62] But see S. Federico, 'The imaginary society: Women in 1381', *Journal of British Studies* 40 (2001), 159–83.

[63] J. Wake (ed.), *The Montagu Musters Book, A.D. 1602–1623* (Northamptonshire Record Society, 7, 1935), p. xlix.

[64] For example, in the year of the Pilgrimage of Grace women armed with shovels and pikes sought to defend St Nicholas's Priory at Exeter against dissolution: P. Crawford (ed.), *Exploring Woman's Past* (London, 1983), p. 57.

[65] S. Achinstein, 'Women on top in the pamphlet literature of the English Revolution', *Women's Studies* 24 (1994), 138; A. M. McEntee, 'The [un]civill-sisterhood of oranges and lemons: Female petitioners and demonstrators, 1642–53', *Women's Studies* 24 (1994), pp. 131–64; Hughes, 'Gender and politics'.

[66] Capp, *When Gossips Meet*, pp. 315–16.

[67] M. Roberts, '"Words they are women, and deeds they are men": Images of work and gender in early modern England', in L. Charles and L. Duffin (eds.), *Women and Work in Pre-Industrial England* (London, 1985), p. 153.

the social group most intimately connected with the everyday life of the community, they were able to gauge popular feelings and to voice these in effective collective action that drew on women's networks. In protests over food, women drew on their gendered responsibility for the subsistence of their family to justify their participation. 'Being in pou[er]tie and wanting victual for her Children' was the succinct justification offered by Elizabeth Sturgeon, for her participation in the first crowd action over food at Maldon in 1629, in which women, accompanied by their children, forced Flemish sailors to fill their caps and aprons with some of the grain about to be exported.[68]

A similar concern with the threat to their family's subsistence and to their ability to fulfil their role prompted women's frequent participation in protests over enclosure and customary rights. In a protest in Norfolk against the lord of the manor's over-commoning his sheep, women sought to mobilise other women by telling them, 'this would take away their comon from them and force them and theire children to begg, leaving them void of all succour'. Similarly, women who threw down enclosures at Gnossal in Staffordshire claimed that they had done so in a peaceable manner since enclosure would ruin their husbands and children. One of those involved in a long-running dispute over enclosure at Grewelthorpe Moor in Yorkshire described herself as a very poor woman great with child who had but one cow; if it were no longer allowed to go on the moor she was 'beggared' since she had no money for feed. In 1608 a large crowd of women assembled at the site of the enclosure on the moor, 'and fallinge down upon their knees, and some of them weepinge for the losse of their Com[m]on, desired . . . [the encloser, Sir Stephen Proctor] to be good unto them'.[69] The subsequent violent turn of events in this episode suggests that this display of female weakness was merely tactical.

It was not uncommon for women, as in the first protest against the export of grain at Maldon, to be accompanied by their younger children. Their presence doubtless lent symbolic force to the women's appeals. But in one particular enclosure dispute motherhood offered a more direct 'excuse' for their participation. Charged with throwing down the enclosures and depasturing the disputed land 'by way of insurrection and rebellion', the women offered an alternative description of the episode. They countered that, sending their children and servants to pasture their cattle,

---

[68] J. Walter, 'Grain riot and popular attitudes to the law: Maldon and the crisis of 1629', in J. Brewer and J. Styles (eds.), *An Ungovernable People: The English and their Law in the Seventeenth and Eighteenth Centuries* (London, 1980), p. 54.

[69] TNA: PRO, STAC 8/17/11; /12/7; /227/3.

there 'was an outcrie in the Towne that the children w[hi]ch kept the . . .
beasts were staid in the Cow pasture & laid hold on to be whipped . . .
thereon the women . . . that had Children there . . . being affrighted
therew[i]th did goe to the Cow pasture to save their . . . Children from
whipping'.[70] Women might also hope to use motherhood to escape punishment. When mercy was sought for a group of women who had pulled
down enclosures at Enfield Chase in 1589, it was said of some of them
that they were 'greate with child and expecting every hour to travaile',
a plea with echoes of the 'benefit of belly' by which women accused of
criminal acts sought to escape punishment.[71]

Women's participation in protest might also reflect a knowing exploitation of the licence afforded them by their ambivalent legal status at the
margins of the law's competence. The assumption in manorial courts that
fathers and husbands were legally responsible for offences committed by
wives and daughters compounded legal uncertainty over women's culpability.[72] Despite the attempts of courts like Star Chamber to clarify the law
and to prevent women from 'hiding behind their sex', the legal position
of women in crowds remained very unclear in early modern England.[73]
As William Lambarde, author of the standard textbook of early modern
magistracy, informed his readers: 'if a number of women (or children
under the age of discretion) do flocke together for their own cause, this is
none assembly punishable by these statutes, unless a man of discretion
moved them to assemble for the doing of some unlawfull act'.[74]

Women demonstrated an awareness of the uncertainties of the law in
agrarian protests, telling each other and taunting their victims that women
were not answerable at law. As a victim of the destruction of enclosure by
a crowd of women complained, they acted 'upon the[i]re phantasticall
ymaginac[i]ons conceaved amongst themselves, that women were law-
lesse, and not subiect to the lawes of the realme as men are but might
in such cases offend without drede or punishment of law'.[75] Such ideas

[70] TNA: PRO, STAC 8/308/13.
[71] W. Page (ed.), *Victoria County History of Middlesex* (1911), vol. II, p. 91; P. Lawson,
    'Patriarchy, crime and the courts: The criminality of women in late Tudor and early
    Stuart England', in G. T. Smith, A. N. May and S. Devereux (eds.), *Criminal Justice in
    the Old World and New World: Essays in Honour of John Beattie* (Toronto, 1998), p. 40.
[72] C. S. Orwin and C. S. Orwin, *The Open Fields* (Oxford, 1967), pp. 141–2.
[73] N. Z. Davis, 'Women on top', in her *Society and Culture in Early Modern France*
    (Oxford, 1978), p. 146 (quotation); J. Hawarde, *Les Reportes del Cases in Camera Stellata.
    1593–1609*, ed. W. P. Baildon (1894), pp. 103–4, 247; Hudson, 'Treatise', pp. 140–1;
    T[homas] E[dgar], (ed.) *The Lawes Resolutions of Womens Rights: Or, The Lawes provision
    for Woemen* . . . (London, 1632), section xiii.
[74] W. Lambarde, *Eirenarcha, or The Office of the Justice of Peace, in foure Bookes* (1619 edn),
    p. 180.
[75] TNA: PRO, STAC 8/223/7.

seem to have circulated widely and were widely drawn on. At Osmington in Dorset, a 'Company of disordered unruly and willfull woeman and Children' were mobilised, it was said, with tales 'of div[er]s & sundry hedges & ditches that had beene cast downe w[i]thin . . . [the] County of Dorset by weomen & boyes . . . [and they] that did destroy them had escaped without any punishm[en]t or question for the same'. Similarly, the women at Grewelthorpe Moor were said to have boasted how 'the wyves of Thorpe had long before that tyme done the like against the Earle of Derbyes Anncestors and were nev[er] punished for the same'.[76]

The perception that women might protest and yet escape punishment was reinforced by women's sometimes playful exploitation of their gendered identity. Women's strategic self-presentation of womanly weakness in court pleadings and of their 'frail condition' in petitioning[77] could also be used to claim a licence in protest. Contemporary constructions of women associated womanhood with a weakness both mental and physical. Women were thought to suffer from a lack of reason and a vulnerability to disorder, with the imbalances attributed to them by medical/humoral theory reinforced by notions, still current, of their vulnerability to hysteria brought on by the phenomenon of a wandering womb. These naturalised 'deficiencies' were drawn on to justify their subordination under a system of patriarchy. But, as Natalie Zemon Davies has shown, women could also exploit the image of the unruly woman, in thrall to lower passions and not accountable for what they did.[78] 'Disorderly women', celebrated in both ballad and proverb, could therefore invert commonly accepted ideas of women's frailty to claim for themselves a licence to protest.[79]

As with young men, the particular licence granted women within festive culture as temporary compensation for their subordination might also be drawn on to facilitate protest. Women who pulled down enclosures in Lancashire, on the understanding that 'woeman [*sic*] were lawles[s] and that they mighte boldly [do so] without anie ffeare of punishment', sought double immunity for their actions by carrying out their destruction on Shrove Tuesday. In a similarly timed protest against enclosure in

[76] TNA: PRO, STAC 8/293/12; /227/3.
[77] L. Gowing, 'Gender and the language of insult in early modern London', *History Workshop Journal* 35 (1993); Walker, *Crime, Gender and Social Order*, p. 271; T. Stretton, 'Women and litigation in the Elizabethan Court of Requests' (PhD, University of Cambridge, 1993), p. 210; Achinstein, 'Women on top', p. 138.
[78] Davis, 'Women on top', esp. pp. 146–7.
[79] J. Wiltenburg, *Disorderly Women and Female Power in the Street Literature of Early Modern England and Germany* (Charlottesville and London, 1992); M. Ingram, 'Ridings, rough music and the "Reform of Popular Culture" in early modern England', *Past and Present* 105 (1984), 98.

Oxfordshire, a crowd of women managed both to refer to their household duties and to make a more playful reference to the liminality of Shrove Tuesday by claiming that 'they would cut downe all the . . . pales and make pancake wood thereof'. Another group of women at Childerditch in Essex in 1607 staged their protest after 'meeting together to make merrie' on 'the twelthtide', while women in the same county who chose Candlemas Day for pulling down and burning the Laudian altar rails in their parish church demonstrated the sophistication such crowds could deploy when they took advantage of that day's explicitly gendered association in both the liturgical and popular calendar with purification of the church by women.[80]

Contemporary constructions of women as weak might also lead to an expectation on the part of women that this might make it difficult for their victims or those charged with maintaining order to repress or punish their protest. As one of the hundred or so women involved in the destruction of enclosures at Kingswinford in Staffordshire later said under examination, they did it because they believed that more violence would have been offered to their husbands if they had attempted it.[81] Protests by women might be thought to pose a less serious threat than that by male householders. In protesting, women were able to turn their marginal relationship to the structure of power (of which their legal dependence was only one aspect) to their temporary advantage, since their intervention, if short-lived, might be thought less likely to threaten the underlying relationship between subordinates and their governors. Opponents of enclosure in 1608 were said to have believed that its destruction would give greater offence and be more grievously punished if done by men.[82]

Whatever the debated merits of the 'chivalry thesis' in modern criminology in explaining the attitudes of criminal courts to women, the experience of early modern 'rioters' suggests something of its potential force.[83] Punishing women at a time of tension might exacerbate an already difficult situation. If women did not follow the protocols of protest and, in accordance with the construction of them as weak and simple, acknowledge their fault, then, as was the case for many women once indicted in ordinary criminal business,[84] they might experience the full penalty of the law. But the episode of protest against the export of food at Maldon for which Ann Carter of Maldon was executed was exceptional, a response

---

[80] TNA: PRO, STAC 8/153/2; /279/11; /247/8; British Library [hereafter BL], Harleian MS 454, fol. 38v. For discussion of the symbolic significance of the choice of Candlemas Day, see Walter, '"Abolishing superstition"', 94–5.

[81] TNA: PRO, STAC 8/259/21.   [82] TNA: PRO, STAC 8/42/11.

[83] Lawson, 'Patriarchy', pp. 37–9.

[84] Ibid., pp. 38–42; Walker, *Crime, Gender and Social Order*, pp. 135–6, 178.

to her leading not one, but two 'riots' within as many months, the second as captain to a crowd of several hundred men, and at a time of political as well as economic crisis. In cases of riot, it seems that if women played up to their contemporary representation as 'soon stirred to wrath' and as '*the weaker vessel*'[85] then they might hope to escape or to mitigate punishment. This was clearly the strategy of a group of Yorkshire women brought to court for pulling down an enclosure at Slaidburn, who claimed that being 'poor and ignorant' women they had thought it was lawful for them to do it in defence of their husbands' common right. The women arrested and ordered to be fined for their part in the attack on the bishop of Lincoln's enclosures at Buckden demonstrated the possible reward of this strategy. Although the attacks there had involved some hundreds of women, they had petitioned for their release 'in tender Considerac[i]on of woemen's weakness'. In response, the House of Lords had ordered that 'the women are to be spared'.[86]

Women too might employ a rhetoric of violence, giving full reign to the 'weapon' with which they were most commonly and misogynistically associated – their tongues. In the politics of protest, as in the politics of the street, women claimed the linguistic power insult was said to give them.[87] The threat to their ability to meet their family's subsistence needs prompted furious outbursts. The widow Anne Samwayes who, in an angry exchange with the sellers of grain in Dorchester market in the dearth of 1630, threatened 'to cut holes in their baggs for that they sold all to the millers', was said by a witness to have later accused the local minister 'that he did starve the Cuntry' 'and [used] many other unseemly words for a quarter of an howre spare'.[88] After a crowd had seized sacks of grain being moved out of the port of Colchester in early 1674, the victim of their actions reported that one woman 'came up to him in furious maner & s[ai]d if theie would be ruled by her the next yt came by with Corne theie would be theire Butchers', while in 1709 in the same county, 'a multitude of above 100 women armed with clubbs' were reported to 'have threat[e]ned to fire diverse houses & shoot several persons, by reason they have been dealers in corn to London, on pr[e]tence they make ye same dear'.[89]

---

[85] *Two Books of Homilies*, p. 503.
[86] TNA: PRO, STAC 8/285/5; HLRO, MP HL 8 July 1641; *Journal of the House of Lords*, vol. II, pp. 281, 289.
[87] L. Gowing, 'Language, power, and the law: Women's slander litigation in early modern London', in J. Kermode and G. Walker (eds.), *Women, Crime and the Courts in Early Modern England* (London, 1994), p. 36.
[88] Dorset RO, DC/DOB 8/1, fols. 46r, 54.
[89] Essex RO (Colchester), D/B5/Sb2/9, fol. 221; BL, Additional MS 61608, fol. 159.

Despite their presumed weakness, and allowing again for the exaggerations of their opponents, participation in crowds often allowed women also to claim a power through violence. Requests to women in the May Day crowd at Kirkby Overblow to stop pulling down the enclosure were met with the threat that they had brought ropes to bind, and mastiffs to bite, any who opposed them, while women protesting against enclosure in Cheshire were reported to have said that they would kill or be killed but they would keep the land common. At Buckden, a large crowd of women and children, having thrown down the bishop of Lincoln's enclosures, kept their ground and, armed with pitchforks and staves, announced that 'they were there ready to fight w[i]th anie that shold come to remoove them'.[90] Reflecting the everyday violence that individual women were capable of showing when called on to defend the integrity of the household,[91] crowds of women backed their threats with force. When their tearful and humble entreaties failed to stop the enclosure on Grewelthorpe Moor, a crowd of wives and widows, led by one Dorothy Dawson, '(termed and com[m]onlie called for her bould and auddacious attempts Captaine Dorothie)', proceeded to pull down the enclosures and, taking it in turns by pairs, assaulted the encloser's workmen. In so doing, they did

most gr[i]evouslie pull . . . [them] by the haires of their heads and did strike them on their faces with their fists and on their shynnes w[i]th their feete, having shoes of purpose tacked with Iron nayles. And did likewise furiouslie teare in peeces and spoyle divers of the said workmen's clothes and apparell and did often throw dirt in their faces and provoke them to strike and hurte the said women. And to terrifie the said workmen more . . . did sweare by many horrible and blaspemous Oathes and threates that they had whetted and sharpened their said knyves ['great Cole knyves'] all the waye as they came to cutt the throates of the said workemen, and that they would cutt them . . . and bury them alive in the said dytches.

Violent attacks could also accompany protests over food. From Northampton in 1693 it was reported that 'great numbers of women came into the market with knives stuck in their girdles to force corn at their own rates'. In Hertfordshire in 1595, a group of women assaulted a man at Bishops Stortford, tore open a bag of grain and helped themselves to wheat. After being refused the loan of a bushel of wheat by the collector of the poor because it had all been bought up in the market, a Hertfordshire widow in the same year encouraged a group

---

[90] TNA:, STAC 8/311/34; /247/18; HLRO, MP HL 21 June 1641.
[91] Walker, *Crime, Gender and Social Order*, pp. 76–7, 89, 261.

of women, including her daughter, to attack a grain dealer in the market.[92]

Violence and the rhetoric of violence were by no means, then, restricted to those protests involving men. As members of a crowd, women might feel emboldened to assault men, though their frequent use of stoning as a form of protest might suggest a desire to avoid close physical combat. Stoning seems to have been a form of violence particularly associated with women. For example, women stoned middlemen in Oxford market in 1693, and both the crowd of some two hundred women at Slaidburn, and those protesting against enclosure in the eastern fens, stoned those trying to measure and divide up their commons.[93]

Women protesters might also display a black humour. A group at Maldon in Essex, having thrown down hedges and not finding the encloser, said 'he was then squat somewhere in the bushes & . . . they wold bast him & set the dogg mastive they here hadd upon him'. The women at Childerditch, finding labourers ditching, demanded 'yf they wanted any workfolkes, . . . [and] sett themselves a worke, and wished the ditchers to goe on with theire worke and they would throw yt downe as fast'. Those at Gnossal in Staffordshire, 'boastinge they had done that w[hi]ch they came for & that there was no law againste women', were said to have offered the JP who called on them to stop their destruction of the enclosures 'a dozen of ales for his labour or paynes, & used menacing words to him'. Women's humour in protest seems to have been particularly associated with their delight at being able as members of a crowd to triumph over men. It is doubtful, however, whether their victims found any amusement in the gendered inflection of the common threat – a playful reference to women's domestic duties within the family – to cut their opponents 'as small as herbs to the pot'.[94]

Women might hope to use contemporary constructions of their weakness to explain and excuse their participation in protest. The common misogynistic strand in early modern thought offered authority an opportunity to pardon women's involvement. For example, the *Homily of the State of Matrimony* required the minister to tell his parishioners annually 'that the woman is a weak creature . . . therefore they be the sooner disquieted, and they be the more prone to all weak affections . . . and lighter they be and more vain in their fantasies and opinions'.[95] As one

[92] Hertfordshire RO, HAT/SR 10/52, 78; M. Beloff, *Public Order and Popular Disturbances 1660–1714* (Oxford, 1938), p. 64.

[93] E. P. Thompson, *Customs in Common* (London, 1991), p. 323; TNA: PRO, STAC 8/216/29; SP 16/113/38.i.

[94] TNA: PRO, STAC 8/12/7; Essex RO, D/B3/3/423/14; PRO, STAC 8/247/8.

[95] *Two Books of Homilies*, p. 503.

contemporary ballad had it: 'Dust is lighter than a feather, / And the wind more lighter than either, / But a woman's fickle minde/ More light than feather, dust or wind.'[96] But this was a double-edged sword, since it also allowed their victims to draw on the same set of constructions both to dismiss protests involving women and to discredit the legitimacy of their grievances. Opposition to royal enclosure at Theobalds by 'a showre of Shrews' led Sir Fulke Greville to note, 'you may see, how easilie this light sea of busie people is raysed up with every wynde'.[97]

In seeking to discredit women protesters, victims could also refer to the dominant prescriptive construction of women's duty to be both obedient and submissive. Given women's very participation in protest, let alone their actions as a crowd, this was a powerful set of ideas to mobilise against them. Women in a dispute in the Forest of Waltham were accused of acting in a 'Rude, barbarous and Savage Man[n]er . . . bragging on that which they had done', while those at Osmington were labelled 'a Company of disorderly, unruly and wilful woemen and Children'.[98] It was an easy and frequently used tactic to emphasise how such protests fundamentally transgressed norms that prescribed modesty and restraint and, in theory at least, restricted women to the private sphere of family and household. Thus, women who pulled down enclosures in Shropshire were described as behaving 'in sight and viewe of diverse of yo[u]r highnes' subiects in most uncivill, undecent and unwomanlike sort', while those at Gnosal were reported as 'setting a p[ar]te ye modestye becomeinge theire sexe'. The latter's threat to the pregnant wife of the encloser 'to burie her quicke' was offered as further confirmation of their abandonment of even those tenderer qualities conventionally associated with women. Elsewhere, wives who had 'pitilessly injured some ewes' during an enclosure dispute found themselves simply labelled: 'not women'.[99] It was all too easy therefore to represent women's actions in protest as being not only unlawful, but also unnatural.[100]

IV

Women or young men were clearly capable of acting alone and in pursuit of their own interests. But, as in the case of older men, they usually

---

[96] J. O. Halliwell and T. Wright (eds.), *A Collection of Seventy-Nine Black Letter Ballads . . . 1559–1597* (London, 1867), p. 193.

[97] TNA: PRO, SP 14/91/50. It should be noted however that Greville ended by advising that 'a tender proceeding with them can be no preuidice'.

[98] TNA: PRO, STAC 8/12516; /293/12.

[99] M. Ingram, '"Scolding women cucked or washed": A crisis in gender relations in early modern England?', in Kermode and Walker, *Women, Crime and the Courts*, p. 67.

[100] TNA: PRO, STAC 8/12/7; PRO, STAC 8/207/15.

operated on behalf of, and drew support from, the wider community for whom the crowd acted. If much of the politics of subsistence was grounded in defence of the interests of the family and community, then it should not surprise us that crowds were more often mixed in terms of both age and gender. Claims before Star Chamber that when women pulled down enclosures armed groups of men stood some way off, countered in turn by women's insistence that their husbands had not known of their actions, were to be explained in part by litigation strategies. Plaintiffs sought to undercut their opponents' strategy of attributing protest to women whose 'weaknesse' or 'lawlessness' might allow communities to evade punishment. But the reality was that many crowds were made up of men and women, husbands and wives, servants and children. This reflected the family strategies that lay at the heart of the politics of subsistence.

Further exploration of gender roles in protest would need, then, to examine the complex interplay between gender and other sources of power and status within 'the grids of power' of early modern society that formed the infrastructure of early modern crowds.[101] The frequent claim by the crowd's victims that those of superior wealth and status were behind the protest, and, therefore, that subordinate groups necessarily acted at the command of their 'betters', needs to be treated with caution. In making such claims, gentlemen victims sought to take advantage of the 'fact' of riot to disadvantage their rivals within landed society. Nevertheless, it is clear that the hierarchies operating within age and gender groups were also to be found in the early modern crowd. Age and status as house-holding males gave some married men and masters greater authority in the crowd and, as in the everyday politics of the parish, wealth and social standing could reinforce their authority over other men, as well as women, in protest. Wives and widows exercised similar authority in female crowds, with claims, for example, that poorer women were threatened with loss of alms if they did not join the crowd pointing to similar hierarchies at work. But, as we have seen, protest could at the same time create its own, if temporary, hierarchies, offering status and authority to groups otherwise subordinated within the early modern matrix of gender, age and social standing. As Ann Carter at Maldon experienced, and Bartholomew Steer in Oxfordshire hoped, crowds could empower those otherwise subordinated by age and gender.

---

[101] For a discussion of the notion of 'grids of power', see M. J. Braddick and J. Walter, 'Grids of power: Order, hierarchy and subordination in early modern society', in their *Negotiating Power in Early Modern Society: Order, Hierarchy and Subordination in Britain and Ireland* (Cambridge, 2001), pp. 1–42.

Further work would also need to pay more attention to the consequences of the dynamics of the *inter-gendered* nature of some protests.
Although the evidence is slighter for the early modern period than for
later ones, gender differences could divide as well as unite. Women's
increasing exclusion from production and from the public defence of
custom, it has been argued, helped to define the masculinity of skilled
male groups like the Derbyshire lead miners.[102] By contrast, protest
as members of a crowd also allowed women temporarily to dominate
over those unfortunate males who were their victims. Since one important aim of crowd actions was to stigmatise and shame those who
failed to observe the norms of the moral community, we need to think
more about how within the dynamics of protest actions by women
might bring a heightened sense of shame and humiliation to their male
victims.

Crowds always operated at a disadvantage in a society that privileged
wealth and social status and that criminalised protest as riot. However,
in a society where constructions of status by gender and age were multi-
faceted and therefore neither consistent nor stable, there remained plenty
of scope for early modern crowds to exploit these to their advantage. This
perhaps helps to explain the tendency of those in authority and the targets
of protest to privilege the interaction of social status with age and gender in
identifying faces in the crowd. Thus, women who pulled down enclosures
at Brigstock Park, claiming that there was no law for them, became a
'troop of lewd women', and the case against them detailed their moral and
social failings: one was 'suspected among her neighbours for wytcherie
& light fingered besid[e]s'; another, a widow, was 'a Comon Charwoman
and releived weekelie by the Almes of the towne'; while a third was 'an
ill liver [who] had a bastard two yeares before she was married & [was]
great with child againe at the tyme of her marriage'. That their failings
were a product of their marginality was made clear in the dismissive reply
of another witness, that the women 'are thought to be of bad behaviour &
verie poore'.[103] Similarly, the women in the protest at Slaidburn were said
to be 'divers & sundry turbulent p[er]sons being people of the basest and
meanest sort . . . having no meanes or estates whereby to be punished'.[104]
Such accusations were commonplace. Their use against men as well as
women serve as a reminder of how disabling the intersection of gender

---

[102] A. Wood, *Politics of Social Conflict: The Peak Country 1520–1770* (Cambridge, 1999),
pp. 5–6, 172–4, 254–6.
[103] TNA: PRO, STAC 8/122/3; P. A. J. Pettit, *The Royal Forests of Northamptonshire: A
Study in Their Economy 1558–1714* (Northamptonshire Record Society, xxiii, 1968),
p. 172.
[104] TNA: PRO, STAC 8/216/29.

and class might be for those whose social marginality merely confirmed their failure to live up to the dominant gendered expectations. Thus, protesters in the Forest of Leighfield were said to be 'such as were of small credit and reputac[i]on that had little to loose'; those in the Forest of Dean were said to be 'very beggerly and naughty people and such as he never saw or took notice of'; those at Manchester in 1603, 'many most ydle, vagrant, and yll disposed people'; while male enclosure 'rioters' in Leicestershire were of the 'base, carelesse & meaner sorte'. One plaintiff's accusation succinctly summarised this strategy – the rioters were 'men of no value'.[105]

Against the ambiguity of the categories of age and gender, a discourse of the crowd as 'the many-headed monster' offered a more certain means of discrediting protesters (though this representation too would continue to be contested through competing discourses, including increasingly those of entitlement and rights among the honest and respectable poor). As the examples quoted above suggest, self-serving notions of civility already lay behind some of the earlier criticisms of 'riotous' behaviour; witness the frequency with which the adjective 'lewd', rich in its many meanings, was used to describe 'rioters'.

It is unfortunate that the abolition of Star Chamber means that it is not possible after the mid-seventeenth century to trace through its rich records the growing impact of discourses of civility and the increasing condemnation of violence on the gendering of protest. This is not the place to attempt that project, but it is perhaps possible to suggest something of its trajectory. The tighter integration of wealth and social status that was a product of the incorporation of the middling sort of capitalist farmers, merchants and traders carried prescriptive discourses of gendered behaviour deeper into local society, discrediting other forms of male behaviour and denying increasing numbers of plebeian men the political voice of a patriarchal manhood. At the same time, these changes sharpened distinctions between the public and private in ways that increasingly challenged in particular poorer women's ability to claim a public voice. These, and the economic changes that brought growing landlessness and dependence on waged labour in both agriculture and handicraft industry, left those threatened by change without necessary leadership and vulnerable to more certain victimisation since the state was now able to rely on the local deployment of social power on its behalf by local elites who were the beneficiaries of these same developments.

Change was, of course, never as complete or as regionally or socially uniform as this sketch implies. Within the politics of the trade, as in

---

[105] TNA: PRO, STAC 8/32/10; /195/5; /216/12; /270/23.

the politics of subsistence, crowds of journeymen and artisans became more common after the middle of the seventeenth century. For the latter, reference to the duties placed on them by a normative patriarchal masculinity became, if anything, more urgent, while the politics of the former might also veer between what has been termed *subordinate* and *anti-patriarchal* masculinities.[106] Protests over access to food became more common than those over land and common rights later in the seventeenth century, and with this the continuing involvement of women in protest, for whom the licence and legitimation afforded them by contemporary constructions of their gendered identity with its familial responsibilities also became even more important as an increasingly classed reading of civility offered growing condemnation of their immodest and uncivil behaviour.[107]

Over much of the countryside, the growing imposition of enclosure and the growth of landlessness saw, with a few but significant regional exceptions, a collapse in collective protest that became more marked after the middle of the seventeenth century.[108] If the participation of marginalised groups in protest had always been driven in part by fear and desperation, then the temporary access to power and authority that protest as a crowd allowed these otherwise subordinated groups continued to be reflected in the sheer enjoyment and carnivalesque quality their actions often took, with their accompaniments of music, feasting and drinking. For men in general, and young men and plebeians in particular, the attack on other men allowed them to assert their claims to a masculinity that we might be tempted to label 'oppositional' were it not for the fact that its key characteristics, especially those that emphasised the physical attributes of manhood, remained an uneasy component of the dominant discourse of patriarchal manhood. For women too, protest as a crowd allowed them a feeling of power and authority that they could not claim in their normal lives. This had led one group of women 'rioters' at Twickenham in the early seventeenth century to meet in the alehouse a year to the day after their protest, where they were said to have boasted of a 'valiant' deed worthy to be remembered 'in the Chronicles' and to promise among themselves to hold a feast every year for 'remembrance' sake.[109] But the

---

[106] For these categories, see Shepard, 'From anxious patriarchs', 290–1.

[107] On the latter, see S. Mendelson, 'The civility of women in seventeenth century England', in P. Burke, B. Harrison and P. Slack (eds.), *Civil Histories: Essays presented to Sir Keith Thomas* (Oxford, 2000), pp. 111–25.

[108] J. Walter, 'Changement agraire et disparition de la paysannerie en Angleterre 1500–1800', in H. Frechet (ed.), *La terre et les paysans en France et en Grande-Bretagne de 1600 à 1800* (Paris, 1998), pp. 137–67.

[109] TNA: PRO, STAC 8/235/2.

disempowerment and subordination later changes brought many labouring males might suggest that we see in the aggressively heightened violence of the anonymous threatening letter or in the minor skirmishes of poaching claims to a compensatory masculinity that the increasing need for a public display of deference and humility otherwise denied them.

V

In a culture of obedience that sought to naturalise subordination in terms of age and gender hierarchies, the intersections of gender and age could, then, be drawn on both to explain *and* excuse protest, as well as to condemn it. Married men's role as householders and the political identity this brought them may have given protest by male crowds extra clout, but as such it made retaliation perhaps more certain. By contrast, the gendered and subordinate identities of women and young men gave these groups greater licence and the hope, not always realised, that they might escape punishment. Women and youths might exploit cultural constructions of their irresponsibility and play up to negative representations.

But the multivalent meanings of gender in early modern England meant that while gendering the crowd might allow the authorities scope to acknowledge and negotiate grievances, gendering the crowd could also be a strategy by which to challenge the legitimacy of protest and to question the reality of grievances. By emphasising the role played by groups whose lack of reason denied them a public political voice, the crowd's victims could seek to rubbish the validity of their complaints. By emphasising the subordinate status of those from whom obedience was to be expected, the crowd's victims could emphasise the threat to order their disorderly and disobedient actions posed. By either showing how the behaviour of those who made up early modern crowds challenged the norms by which they were meant to fulfil their social role (men abandoning reason for violence, women throwing off modesty and young men restraint) or, paradoxically, by showing how their behaviour confirmed fears of the gendered defects readily attributed to women and youth, the crowd's victims sought to emphasise the larger threat to society represented by such inversionary disorder.

This may offer a further explanation for the discipline and avoidance of violent disorder that so often characterised early modern crowds. Both in the discipline their ritualised display and symbolic displacement of violence exhibited, and in their subsequent rebuttals of the charge of riot and restatement of rights, protesters sought to emphasise more positive constructions of their identity – the control their behaviour demonstrated, the rationality that lay behind their just grievances, and the proper fulfilment of social roles that their defence displayed. Men acted with restraint under provocation, young men with courage, maids with their mistresses' blessing, and women 'according to their small strengths',[110] all to defend their rights.

[110] TNA: PRO, STAC 8/247/8.

'Without the cry of any neighbours':
       A Cumbrian family and the poor
       law authorities, *c.* 1690–1730

Steve Hindle

'Poverty', argued Lawrence Stone in 1977, 'is an acid that erodes both physical beauty and affective relations.'[1] Stone's depiction of family life among the labouring poor of seventeenth- and eighteenth-century England was, accordingly, bleak in the extreme. Poor men spent much of their time in the alehouse, their drunkenness inducing temporary forgetfulness of a working life spent in dreary and degrading jobs.[2] Poor women began life in servitude in the parental home, moved in early adolescence to servitude in their employer's home, and ended in servitude to their husbands in the marital home. Amid the drudgery of domestic purification, 'the whitened doorstep was the only symbol of self-esteem' to which they could aspire.[3] In the one- or two-roomed cottages, hovels or tenements in which the poor huddled, privacy was neither a practical possibility nor even a theoretical aspiration. The absence of sexual privacy merely compounded problems created by the lack of cleanliness. The indigent were dirty, exhausted and suffered from reduced libido. Relentless hardship of this kind meant that it was 'simply not conceivable' that affective individualism, the modernising force that Stone placed at the centre of his account of the emergence of the modern family, had any purchase among the poor.[4]

Notoriously, Stone argued that poverty was corrosive of affective relations not only between adults, but also between parents and children, which were dictated above all by economic circumstances. Offspring, he was convinced, were 'greedy little competitors for an inadequate food supply' and were 'bound to be treated with at best neglect and at worst deliberate hostility'.[5] The 'indifferent, cruel, erratic and unpredictable' behaviour of the poor towards their children, he suggested,

This essay has benefited very significantly from close readings offered by Bernard Capp, Susannah Ottaway and Keith Wrightson, and especially by the editors, to all of whom thanks are due.
[1] Lawrence Stone, *The Family, Sex and Marriage in England 1500–1800* (London, 1977), p. 201.
[2] Ibid., p. 393.   [3] Ibid., p. 374.   [4] Ibid., pp. 255–6, 487–8.   [5] Ibid., p. 477.

might either have been cultural (a product of deprivation and displacement), or economic (because sustained emotional concern was a luxury).[6] Either way, parent-child relations among the very poor were 'brutal' and 'exploitative', characterised by illegitimacy, infanticide, child abandonment, aggressive begging and sexual abuse.[7] In turn, he argued, older children were increasingly shedding responsibility for the support of the elderly and transferring it to the community at large, and the rise of parish relief might therefore be read as an index of the declining responsibilities of kin (even, perhaps especially, immediate kin) among the poorer classes.[8]

Stone's views on the family lives of the poor provoked dismay and embarrassment among his critics and apologists alike, and ultimately even in Stone himself. Edward Thompson noted that Stone's hypotheses about the labouring poor 'reproduce, with comical accuracy, the ideology and sensibility of eighteenth-century upper-class paternalists'.[9] In reflecting, perhaps even inadvertently echoing, the condescension towards the poor that characterised the age, Stone was arguably guilty of one of those 'failures of sympathy' of which Peter Laslett had first warned in 1965 and about which he was still concerned in 1983.[10] By the time the abridged version of The Family, Sex and Marriage was published in 1979, Stone had recognised the fragility of his generalisations about the lower classes, and had not only the good sense to excise them almost entirely from the text, but also the good grace to retract some of them in the preface.[11] He might therefore plausibly be excused some of his wilder assumptions, not least because his experiment in family history was so precocious, being conceived long in advance of the effective conceptualisation of the issues in the field.[12] It is hardly surprising that, as the historiography of the family has developed, Stone's assumptions that the poor lived lives devoid of emotion and were moved merely by the scramble for livelihood has been challenged, perhaps most effectively in those analyses of consistory court depositions in which attitudes towards courtship,

---

[6] Ibid., p. 470.   [7] Ibid., pp. 451, 470–8.   [8] Ibid., pp. 148–9, 403.

[9] Edward Thompson. 'Happy families [Review of Stone, The Family, Sex and Marriage]', New Society 41 (8 Sept. 1977), reprinted in Thompson, Persons and Polemics: Historical Essays (London, 1994), p. 308.

[10] Peter Laslett, The World We Have Lost (London, 1965), p. 239; and Peter Laslett, The World We Have Lost Further Explored (London, 1983), p. 285.

[11] Lawrence Stone, The Family, Sex and Marriage in England 1500–1800 (abridged edn, London, 1979), pp. 17, 294–9.

[12] For a critical review of the development of the historiography of the family, see Keith Wrightson, 'The family in early modern England: Continuity and change', in Stephen Taylor, Richard Connors and Clyve Jones (eds.), Hanoverian Britain and Empire: Essays in Memory of Philip Lawson (Woodbridge, Suffolk, 1998), pp. 1–22.

marriage and parenthood among subordinate groups are vividly disclosed.[13] Stone was, moreover, writing before the historiography of social welfare had developed to the point where the potential of the archive of parish relief for reconstructing the history of the family had been recognised.[14] Even so, his generalisations about family life among the poor have not unreasonably occasioned widespread criticism, sometimes even outrage. In a coruscating critique, Alan Macfarlane provided a devastating list of Stone's unintentionally hilarious assertions about plebeian sentiments and behaviour (some of them quoted above), concluding that 'since no evidence is given in support of these views, there is clearly no need to take them seriously'.[15]

While Macfarlane emphasised Stone's distortion or ignorance of appropriate evidence, Thompson was more concerned with his more profound conceptual failure. Stone had, he insisted, isolated 'the family' as an institution, thus artificially displacing it from its embedded context in the neighbourhood and the community. This failure of imagination was particularly pernicious with respect to the households of the poor, among and between whom, Thompson suggested, 'feeling may be *more*, rather than less, tender or intense *because* relations are "economic" and critical to mutual survival'.[16] To study the families of the labouring poor, Thompson argued, 'and to detect the signs and gestures which disclose their interior emotional life, we must attend very closely indeed to "economics" – or to that daily occupation (farming, fishing, weaving, begging) which gives us their way of living: a way of living which was not merely a way of surviving but also a way of relating and of valuing'.[17] Just as Macfarlane and Thompson were fulminating against Stone's casual indictment of the indifference of the poor toward their own children, moreover, a younger generation of scholars, especially those early modernists working at the intersection of social and demographic history at (or under the influence of) the Cambridge Group for the History of Population and Social Structure, were beginning to explore the implications of the fact that the family, or more properly the household, was not merely a unit of reproduction but also one of production. Taking his lead from

---

[13] For plebeian attitudes towards sexuality and courtship, see Laura Gowing, *Domestic Dangers: Women, Words and Sex in Early Modern London* (Oxford, 1996); Diana O'Hara, *Courtship and Constraint: Rethinking the Making of Marriage in Tudor England* (Manchester, 2000); and Bernard Capp, *When Gossips Meet: Women, Family, and Neighbourhood in Early Modern England* (Oxford, 2003).

[14] Paul Fideler, 'Introduction: Impressions of a century of historiography [Symposium: The study of the early modern poor and poverty relief]', *Albion* 32 (2000), 381–407.

[15] Alan Macfarlane, '[Review of] *The Family, Sex and Marriage in England 1500–1800*', *History and Theory* 18 (1979), 109–10.

[16] Thompson, 'Happy families', 307, 309.   [17] Ibid., 309.

European scholars of cottage industry, David Levine offered a vision of the industrialising villages of seventeenth- and eighteenth-century Leicestershire in which family formation was influenced by a desire to secure child labour within the households of stocking-knitters.[18] In turn, collaborating with Keith Wrightson, Levine reconstructed the demographic structures of Terling (Essex), an agricultural village that was experiencing rapid social polarisation. In analysing its 'local social system', Wrightson and Levine paid very close attention not only to the network of kinship and to the degree of kin recognition within village society in general, but also to relations within the nuclear family in particular, including those of inheritance, at every social level.[19]

Although hampered by archival attrition, especially the disappearance of the seventeenth-century poor law records for the parish of Terling, Wrightson and Levine also made a preliminary attempt at reconstructing the impact of social welfare provision, and especially of the institutions through which it was administered, on the households of the poor.[20] Where the archive did include extant overseers' accounts, however, historians were able to locate the family life of the poor in the context not only of the labour and market relations of the local economy, but also of the power structures of the civil parish. In two celebrated essays, published together in 1984, Tim Wales and William Newman-Brown offered the first attempts to correlate the demographic record of baptisms, marriages and burials with the lists of disbursements itemised by parish officers.[21] Between them, they demonstrated that the poor law intersected with the experience of poverty at certain specific stages of the life-cycle, not only (as might be expected) in old age, but also in the years immediately after marriage when parents were overburdened with young children.[22] Whereas the elderly (especially widows) were almost invariably regarded as deserving objects of charity and dominated the lengthening relief rolls

---

[18] David Levine, *Family Formation in an Age of Nascent Capitalism* (New York, 1977), p. 80. Cf. Hans Medick, 'The proto-industrial family economy: The structural function of household and family during the transition from peasant society to industrial capitalism', *Social History* 3 (1976), 291–316. For the subsequent development of Levine's views on the 'proto-industrial family', see David Levine, *Reproducing Families: The Political Economy of English Population History* (Cambridge, 1987).

[19] Keith Wrightson and David Levine, *Poverty and Piety in an English Village: Terling 1525–1700* ([1979] 2nd edn, Oxford, 1995), pp. 73–109.

[20] Ibid., pp. 103–9, 110–41.

[21] Tim Wales, 'Poverty, poor relief and the life-cycle: Some evidence from seventeenth-century Norfolk', and William Newman-Brown, 'The receipt of poor relief and family situation: Aldenham, Hertfordshire 1630–90', both in R. M. Smith (ed.), *Land, Kinship and Life-Cycle* (Cambridge, 1984), pp. 351–404, 405–22.

[22] Wales, 'Poverty, poor relief', pp. 364–7; Newman-Brown, 'The receipt of poor relief', pp. 412–14.

of the later seventeenth century, the plight of the children of the labouring poor was much more problematic. The presence of children in fragile household economies raised awkward questions both about the nature and value of their labour and about the desirability of removing them to parish apprenticeships where those ethics of industry and thrift so obviously wanting at home could be inculcated.[23] Analysis of the overseers' accounts of Aldenham (Hertfordshire) and Hedenham (Norfolk) in turn demonstrated that parish officers were fine-tuning the nature and scale of relief in accordance with the capacity of both widows and poor households to support themselves through their labour.[24]

While the next generation of scholars working in the field recognised the value of this quasi-demographic approach to the reconstruction of family life among the poorer sort, they generally shied away from actually undertaking it, not least because it was felt likely to prove impossibly time-consuming to practise within the framework of a doctoral thesis.[25] On balance, they preferred to reconstruct the *experience* of poverty through studying the words and lives of the poor themselves, a historiographical development that bore fruit in the significant collection of essays edited by Hitchcock *et al.*, under the title *Chronicling Poverty* (1997).[26] Through the analysis of pauper letters, settlement examinations and parish inventories, the contributors to *Chronicling Poverty* were able to penetrate the popular mentalities of subordination, and in turn the experience of coping not only with poverty itself but also with the poor law authorities whose obligation it was to alleviate its burden. One key set of sources was, however, neglected in *Chronicling Poverty*.

Petitions to the county bench to compel the parish officers to fulfil their obligations to relieve the poor under the terms of the Elizabethan statutes were a prominent feature of poor law administration from as early as 1594, and their numbers rose significantly across the seventeenth and eighteenth centuries.[27] They are particularly valuable for the analysis of affective relations within and beyond poor households because they

---

[23] Wales, 'Poverty, poor relief', pp. 375–6; Newman-Brown, 'The receipt of poor relief', pp. 417–19.

[24] Wales, 'Poverty, poor relief', pp. 360–7; Newman-Brown, 'The receipt of poor relief', pp. 412–15.

[25] For an important exception, see Lynn Botelho, 'Provisions for the elderly in two early modern Suffolk communities' (PhD, University of Cambridge, 1996), now published as *Old Age and the English Poor Law, 1500–1700* (Woodbridge, Suffolk, 2004).

[26] Tim Hitchcock, Peter King and Pamela Sharpe (eds.), *Chronicling Poverty: The Voices and Strategies of the English Poor 1640–1840* (Basingstoke, 1997).

[27] The potential of this source was first recognised in Anthony Fletcher, *Reform in the Provinces: The Government of Stuart England* (New Haven, 1986), p. 188; and is fully exploited in Steve Hindle, *On the Parish? The Micro-Politics of Poor Relief in Rural England c.1550–1750* (Oxford, 2004), ch. 6.4.

confirm the suspicion, raised by the relatively low value of the pensions accounted for by parish officers, that not only before but also indeed long after overseers were required to make provision for an indigent family, informal networks of support remained crucial to plebeian survival strategies. Petitions of this kind nonetheless present considerable problems of interpretation, and especially of 'authorship'. Literate householders like Roger Lowe of Ashton-in-Makerfield (Lancashire) or Thomas Turner of East Hoathly (Sussex) often wrote petitions, letters or wills on behalf of their poorer neighbours, and it may well be that in many a village men like them were called upon to draw up, perhaps even to compose, applications for poor relief. It is equally possible that petitioners themselves deliberately chose advocates who embodied particular social or moral authority – the parish clergyman, for instance, a leading ratepayer, perhaps, or even a retired parish officer. Office-holders and vestrymen were certainly favoured by applicants who sought collective subscription to testimonials of their deservingness from 'the parish'.

Either way, petitioners pleaded their case in a wide variety of ways, and there is little or nothing formulaic about their pitifully sad stories. There are, of course, very great dangers involved in taking these narratives at face value. They (like the paupers' letters of the later eighteenth and early nineteenth centuries) were, after all, designed to make a case.[28] Even though they deployed a subtle blend of deference, exaggeration and distortion, the effectiveness of the petitions depended on the credibility of claims that might more easily have been verified by magistrates at the time than by historians at a distance of over three hundred years.[29] Indeed, only the most painstaking record linkage of parish registers and overseers' accounts would now corroborate the applicants' references to their age or infirmity, to the burden of bringing up their children, or to their previous independence of support.

These caveats notwithstanding, this chapter analyses one particularly rich series of petitions for relief in order to reconstruct the nature and quality of social relations both within and between poor households. Instead of deploying either the selective reading of the correspondence of the gentry or the aggregate macro-historical techniques favoured by

[28] Cf. *Essex Pauper Letters, 1731–1837*, ed. Thomas Sokoll (British Academy, Records of Social and Economic History, new ser., 30, Oxford, 2001). Sokoll very subtly explains the problems of interpretation associated with these remarkable sources at pp. 44–70.

[29] For useful discussions of the interpretative problems surrounding petitions of this kind, see James Stephen Taylor, 'Voices in the crowd: The Kirkby Lonsdale township letters, 1809–36', in Hitchcock *et al.*, *Chronicling Poverty*, pp. 112–14; Donna Andrew, 'To the charitable and humane: Appeals for assistance in the eighteenth-century London press', in Hugh Cunningham and Joanna Innes (eds.), *Charity, Philanthropy and Reform* (London and New York, 1998), pp. 91–3.

the demographers, this experiment in the history of the family adopts a micro-historical perspective, with all the strengths and limitations that the technique of 'observing trifles' implies.[30] Like most micro-histories, the case study offered here reduces the scale of observation to a single community, even to a single household; emphasises the role of the particular (though not, it should be emphasised, at the expense of wider social and economic context); focuses on narrative and its reception; and, above all, complicates what might at first sight seem to be a simple account.[31] It cannot, however, speak to issues of long-term change, and neither does it pretend to typicality, Rather, it presents what Edoardo Grendi has described as the 'exceptional normal', a realistic but simultaneously less mechanistic representation of historical experience.[32]

What follows is not, however, a community study of the kind made possible by the fortuitous and coincident survival of a reliable parish register, an exhaustive set of overseers' accounts and a detailed vestry book.[33] On the contrary, it is the study of the experience of a single family within a community for which the overseers' accounts themselves have conspicuously failed to survive. By using poor relief petitions and orders to reconstruct the triangular series of encounters between the Bowman family, the parish officers of Kirkoswald and the county magistrates of Cumberland over the course of some two decades at the end of the seventeenth and the beginning of the eighteenth centuries, it illuminates the extent to which the administration of poor relief not only permeated social and economic relations in the local community but also intersected with the survival strategies of individual paupers and their families. In both of these respects, therefore, the paper speaks to issues that have been central to the work of Anthony Fletcher over the last three decades: the practice of magisterial authority; the administration of social policy; the exercise of social power; and the experience of gender, sex and subordination. In sum, the story of the Bowman family and the parish officers of Kirkoswald demonstrates the extraordinary potential of the poor law archive to

---

[30] Edward Muir, 'Introduction: Observing trifles', in Edward Muir and Guido Ruggiero (eds), *Microhistory and the Lost Peoples of Europe: Selections from Quaderni Storici* (Baltimore, 1991), pp. vii–xxviii. Cf. Carlo Ginzburg, 'Micro-history: Two or three things that I know about it', *Critical Inquiry* 20 (Autumn 1993), 10–35.

[31] For these characteristics of the genre, see Giovanni Levi, 'On microhistory', in Peter Burke (ed.), *New Perspectives on Historical Writing* (Cambridge, 1991), p. 110.

[32] Grendi, quoted in Levi, 'On microhistory', p. 109.

[33] See, for example, Lynn Botelho, 'Aged and impotent: Parish relief of the aged poor in early modern Suffolk', in Martin Daunton (ed.), *Charity, Self-Interest and Welfare in the English Past* (London, 1996), pp. 91–112; Steve Hindle, 'Power, poor relief and social relations in Holland Fen, *c.*1600–1800', *Historical Journal* 41 (1998), 67–96; Steven King, 'Locating and characterising poor households in late seventeenth century Bolton: Sources and interpretations', *Local Population Studies* 68 (2000), 42–62.

facilitate the writing of what Tim Hitchcock has recently christened a 'new history from below'.[34]

I. Ann Bowman

In July 1710, widow Ann Bowman of Kirkoswald (Cumberland) pleaded with the county magistrates to compel the overseers of the poor to house her adequately and to provide her with a regular pension:

> I being old feeble and infirm desire I may not be confined to an old ruinous house which is without the cry of any neighbours of which the officers in [the parish] were speaking: for that unmerciful and savage behaviour would have pined me to death with hunger . . . [they] would confine me to a dismal corner where none might relieve or help me in my hunger bitten condition. I humbly beg of this honourable court that my pension be ascertained & the days or the weeks when to be payd nominated . . . that in my feeble old age I perish not with hunger for a piece of bread when God has blessed the land with plenty.[35]

This is the fourth of seven extant petitions, amounting in total to over twelve hundred words, sent by Ann Bowman to the Cumberland bench in the period 1694 to 1711. Several of its features are of interest to the historian seeking to analyse the relationships between the households of the poor, the neighbourhoods in which they lived and the institutions of the civil parish in early modern England. It discloses the desperation of an elderly widow seeking to cobble together a living both from parish relief and from neighbourly charity; the bitterness of her dispute with the overseers of the poor; and the pitiful rhetoric that might be deployed to mobilise the paternalism of the magistracy. Taken together with the full sequence of her numerous appeals to the county bench and the relief orders which they provoked, Ann Bowman's account offers a narrative not only of the affective relationships within and beyond one particularly poor household but also of the perceptions of the family lives of the labouring poor among the vestrymen who repeatedly attempted to withdraw her pension and among the magistrates who patiently sought to arbitrate the case. On the one hand, this is a narrative of distress: of disease, bereavement, physical incapacity, mental illness, debt, eviction, destitution and, above all, of hunger. On the other, it conveys a vision of affective relations in motion: the spontaneous kindnesses of both neighbour and stranger, the casual alms of the charitable, the reciprocal obligations felt between a mother and her children. To be sure, few claimants for poor relief were as tenacious, and fewer still as vigorous or candid,

---

[34] Tim Hitchcock, 'A new history from below', *History Workshop Journal* 57 (2004), 294–8.
[35] Cumbria Record Office, Carlisle [hereafter CRO] Q/11/1/96/25 (Midsummer 1710).

as Bowman.[36] But the sheer vividness of her accounts of making shift in this remote Cumbrian parish renders her petitions particularly useful for the reconstruction of familial and neighbourly relations at this, the most humble of all social levels. In what follows, Bowman's narrative is successively placed in numerous contexts: first, the economy of Kirkoswald; second, the nature and scale of provision for the poor in the parish; third, what little is known of Bowman's own family circumstances; and fourth, her career as pensioner. Finally, analysis of the content of her petitions explores their relevance for the historical understanding of affective relations both beyond and within poor households.

II.   The economy of Kirkoswald

Kirkoswald was a small Cumberland town in the Eden Valley some eight miles north of Penrith and thirteen miles south of Carlisle. The parish of which it formed part stretched over almost 13,000 acres of mountainous common.[37] It contained two townships: the larger settlement of Kirkoswald was itself an ancient market town; neighbouring Staffield was but a small hamlet. Although the parish experienced mortality crises in 1587, 1623 and 1649, its population seems to have grown from approximately 300 in 1563 to around 560 in 1642.[38] When Thomas Denton passed through in the late 1680s, he estimated that the parish had perhaps 620 inhabitants, a total that Frederick Morton Eden thought had swollen by the 1790s to 937, some two-thirds of whom lived in Kirkoswald itself.

[36] Serial petitioners for continued or improved pensions were relatively rare, but see, for example, the cases of widow Margaret Doughty in dispute with the overseers of Salford (Warwicks.) between 1619 and 1652; and Mary Franklin in dispute with the overseers of Great Horwood (Bucks.) between 1693 and 1710 in *Warwick County Records*, ed. S. C. Radcliff, H. C. Johnson and N. J. Williams (9 vols., Warwick, 1935–64), vol. I, pp. 19, 25, 60, 162, 172; vol. II, pp. 139, 141, 199, 251; vol. III, p. 106; and *County of Buckingham: Calendar to the Sessions Records*, ed. W. Le Hardy and G. L. Reckitt (4 vols., Aylesbury, 1934–51), vol. I, pp. 461, 472; vol. II, pp. 29, 259, 278; vol. III, pp. 59, 62, 136, 214–15.

[37] Except where noted the following account is based on F. M. Eden, *The State of the Poor: or, An History of the Labouring Classes in England* (3 vols., London, 1797), vol. II, pp. 83–7; Angus J. L. Winchester (ed.), *Thomas Denton: A Perambulation of Cumberland, 1687–88, including Descriptions of Westmorland, the Isle of Man and Ireland* (Surtees Society, 207, Woodbridge, Suffolk, 2003), pp. 326–9; T. Fetherstonhaugh, *Our Cumberland Village* (Carlisle, 1925).

[38] Susan Scott and Christopher Duncan, *Human Demography and Disease* (Cambridge, 1998), p. 52. *The Diocesan Population Returns for 1563 and 1603*, ed. Alan Dyer and David M. Palliser (British Academy, Records of Social and Economic History, new ser., 31, Oxford, 2005), p. 69 lists 60 households in Kirkoswald in 1563. For subsequent population estimates (450 in the Compton census of 1676 and 527 in 1688), see Peter Clark and Jean Hosking, *Population Estimates of English Small Towns, 1550–1851* (rev. edn, Leicester, 1993), pp. 25–6.

Staffield seems to have been the wealthier of the two townships, having almost twice as many rateable households in the 1664 hearth tax as its neighbour, where the number of exempt was almost certainly proportionately higher.[39] This was a mixed farming area. The land was relatively fertile: fallowing, liming and dunging ensured that while cereal crops might be grown on the clay, the lighter soils might successfully be sown with turnips, clover and grass. By the end of the eighteenth century, the men of the twenty-two agricultural labouring families might earn between twelve and fourteen pence plus victuals if they could secure a day's work during harvest. These men's time was largely, however, spent in rearing the ubiquitous sheep, of which Eden thought there were some six thousand. Kirkoswald's status as a decayed market town was nonetheless reflected in its diversified occupational structure, the parish teeming with tailors, weavers, blacksmiths, masons and joiners. Mining and papermaking were also practised here. The women, as might be expected, were overwhelmingly employed in spinning lint or flax, and were desperately poorly paid. Their wages were 'inconsiderable', a woman having to 'labour hard at her wheel, 10 or 11 hours in the day' to earn fourpence. Eden therefore concluded that in Kirkoswald, as in those other parts of northern England 'where spinning is much attended to, many more women than men are necessitated to solicit parochial assistance'.[40] That solicitation, as we shall see, was not invariably successful.

III. Provision for the poor in Kirkoswald

Although Kirkoswald was almost certainly running a rate-funded parish relief scheme by the end of the seventeenth century, the absence of overseers' accounts before the 1780s renders impossible any estimate of the social distribution of liability for, or the scale of expenditure on, the poor during Ann Bowman's lifetime. It is clear, however, that the parish was endowed with relatively generous seasonal doles.[41] From the 1680s onwards, the churchwardens' accounts refer to a stock of almost

---

[39] CRO DX/129/14 (Kirkoswald Hearth Tax, 1664) lists 68 rateable households, only 25 (36.8%) of them in Kirkoswald township. Although exemption certificates for the hearth tax do not, regrettably, survive, the pattern of exemption from the late eighteenth century window tax is suggestive. While only 32.8% of the households in Staffield township were exempt, the corresponding rate in Kirkoswald was 58.2%. Eden, *The State of the Poor*, vol. II, p. 84.

[40] Eden, *The State of the Poor*, vol. II, p. 84.

[41] Except where noted, the following account is based on an analysis of CRO PR9/5 (Kirkoswald Parish Churchwardens' Account Book, 1641–1786), unfol. A general survey of the content of what is effectively a 'vestry book' is provided in Fetherstonhaugh, *Our Cumberland Village*, pp. 153–61 ('Local government').

£22 that was lent out at interest (of some 6.6 per cent), the yield of which was then disbursed to the poor.[42] In the 1720s, these doles, ranging in value from sixpence to two-and-sixpence, were distributed to as many as twenty-one poor parishioners, twelve of them women. In 1821, the charity commissioners noted that the doles, which were distributed 'on Christmas eve yearly to the poor of the parish who do not receive relief', generally benefited fourteen or fifteen persons. They nonetheless could not discover by whom or when this money had been left.[43] By the 1750s, the churchwardens were finally beginning to record the names of those who received regular pensions. Typically, there were no more than four paupers on the relief rolls at any one time in that decade, at a time when the realities of life-cycle poverty in a parish of perhaps eight hundred souls could expect a significant degree of indigence among its elderly inhabitants. While doles financed by the parish stock might provide seasonal relief for as many as two dozen inhabitants, the parish pension was evidently far more circumscribed in its impact. The calculus of eligibility for relief was, apparently, applied rigorously by the parish officers.

This suspicion is confirmed by analysis of the half-dozen relief petitions from other Kirkoswald inhabitants that survive in the Cumberland sessions papers. These suggest that Ann Bowman was not the only widow in Kirkoswald who was frustrated in her demand for poor relief in the late seventeenth and early eighteenth centuries. Katherine Coulthard pleaded with the bench to coerce the overseers when her pension fell into arrears in October 1710. Although she was 'almost a hundred yeares old and not able to guide herself', she claimed to have received nothing 'but one farthing since lammas day', some three months previously. Perhaps she had made the strategic error of referring to the fact that she was cared for by her daughter, an admission that gave the magistrates a welcome opportunity to enforce the little-used kin obligation clause of the Elizabethan statutes, for they tersely subscribed her petition, 'nil'.[44] The parish officers, indeed, consistently kept one eye upon the possibility that applicants for relief in Kirkoswald, as elsewhere, might secure support from their immediate kinfolk, especially their children, rather than from the ratepayers. In 1730, they successfully persuaded the bench that although

---

[42] Cf. the arrangements that prevailed in the Durham parishes discussed by Peter Rushton, 'The poor law, the parish and the community in north-east England, 1600–1800', *Northern History* 25 (1989), 138–9.

[43] 'Report from commissioners: Charities in England and Wales', *Parliamentary Papers* (1821), vol. XII, p. 153.

[44] CRO Q/11/1/97/10 (Michaelmas 1710). For the kin obligation clause, see Hindle, *On the Parish?*, pp. 49–50.

George Ameson and his wife had become chargeable, they had a son resident in the parish who was able to maintain them. Ameson's pension was, accordingly, to be kept down to ninepence a week, with his son paying some forty shillings a year towards his maintenance.[45] Yet another single woman, this one abandoned rather than widowed, also struggled to constrain the parish officers. Jane Harrison's husband had been impressed as a soldier, leaving her 'very poor and destitute of reliefe being now sickly and not able to work wherewithal to maintain her and her [three] poor children'. Although she 'humbly' desired 'a pension towards her maintenance', the magistrates were unsympathetic and applied the usual laconic, negative notation to her petition.[46] Like Bowman, however, Harrison fought back, alleging that she had been 'falsely and slanderously' denied relief by the overseers, although her appeal appears to have been fruitless.[47]

Only one of the Kirkoswald petitioners can, indeed, be shown to have met with anything like success in dealings with the county magistrates in this period. This victory was all the more unusual in that the successful petitioner was the only widower of Kirkoswald who can be shown to have petitioned the Cumberland bench for arrears in these years.[48] Thomas Smith rehearsed a time-honoured formula when describing himself in 1711 to the justices as 'reduced to poverty by reason of great age and infirmity', though he was at pains to emphasise that he had both been long resident and was legally settled in the parish. Whichever of these assertions secured the sympathy of the bench is unclear, but he was awarded a relief order for a shilling a week, and seems to have died 'on the parish' some eight years later.[49]

Perhaps the parish officers were controlling the purse strings so tightly because the parish had as recently as 1703–4 contested and lost a settlement case, incurring not only the immediate costs of litigation but also long-term liability for Mary Percival, whom they had sought to have removed to Addingham, her place of birth some three miles distant, when she had become 'distracted'. The justices nonetheless ruled that a year's domestic service during her long residence in Kirkoswald had secured her

---

[45] CRO Q6/2, unfol. (Carlisle sessions, 15 July 1730).
[46] CRO Q/11/1/97/21 (Michaelmas 1710).
[47] CRO Q/11/1/101/17 (Michaelmas 1711).
[48] Wales, 'Poverty, poor relief', p. 360 emphasises the preponderance of women, especially widows, on relief in late seventeenth-century Norfolk. Cf. the emphasis on the increasing number of males receiving pensions in eighteenth-century parishes in Richard M. Smith, 'Ageing and well-being in early modern England: Pension trends and gender preferences under the English old poor law, *c.*1650–1800', in Paul Johnson and Pat Thane (eds.), *Old Age from Antiquity to Post-Modernity* (London, 1998), p. 76.
[49] CRO Q/11/1/99/17 (Easter 1711); PR9/2, unfol. (2 Feb. 1719).

settlement there and ordered Percival back to the parish.[50] Even before
this disaster befell them, however, the Kirkoswald parish officers had
been concerned about the heavy costs incurred in housing the poor. 'The
parishioners' had complained in 1699 that 'there are several families lately
come into the parish and not yet legally settled and that there are several others that yet reside and are maintained in Kirkoswald township in
cottages for which the parishioners pay 20s a piece'. They could, they
suggested, 'take better houses in other parts of the parish for 2 shillings
a house'.[51] The differentials across the various parts of the parish both
in rental costs and in the burden of liability for the poor were ultimately
to come to a head in 1730. The ratepayers of Staffield township complained that they had always had their own officers and maintained their
own poor until 'of late years' they were drawn in to help Kirkoswald's
relief, agreeing to do so partly because the poor were 'very few and small
at first' and partly to prevent controversy. The population of Kirkoswald
had, however, lately grown and 'divers new dwelling houses had been
builded upon new foundacions', 'divers ancient dwelling houses have
been divided' and 'divers out-houses had been converted into dwelling
houses'. This proliferation of rental accommodation had attracted many
poor migrants – 'inmates and poor people who are not able to maintain
themselves' – to settle there, and 'more dayly indeavour to settle there to
beg in the town and to trespass in the ancient commons and woods to
get fuel'. All this, they insisted, was the product of the negligence of
the overseers of Kirkoswald township, from whose slack relief regime
they sought a prompt secession. These claims were sufficiently controversial to polarise magisterial opinion, with the justices voting only by a
majority of five to four in favour of dividing the two townships.[52] The
policing of the thresholds of belonging in the parish had, moreover, been
practised since 1703 when, for the first time, the annual meeting of the
parishioners resulted not only in the election of the traditional parish officers – overseers, churchwardens, constables – but also men who would
'take particular care that noe inmates come within the said parish and
give notice to those that are inmates already to remove forthwith'.[53] As

---

[50] CRO Q/11/1/70/8 (Epiphany 1703–4); Q6/1, fol. 336 (Cockermouth sessions, 2 Jan.
1704).

[51] CRO Q/11/1/46/44 (Easter 1698); Q6/1, fol. 91 (Carlisle sessions, 19 April 1699).

[52] CRO Q11/1/158/3 (Midsummer 1730). The idea of dividing responsibility for the poor
so that each of the townships looked after their own had been in the air since at least
1708, when the bench was anticipating an imminent order 'for devideing the parish'.
CRO Q/11/1/88/9 (Midsummer 1708); Q6/1, fols. 517, 519 (Carlisle sessions, 13 July
1708).

[53] CRO PR9/5, unfol. (meeting of 25 Jan. 1703).

we shall see, Ann Bowman was herself to fall foul of officers on the hunt for inmates in 1710.

The lack of overseers' accounts makes it impossible to calculate whether the burden of poverty was more pressing, or the scale of relief more generous, than in other communities of this kind. It is nonetheless instructive that by the 1790s, when there were approximately 195 households in Kirkoswald, Eden could count only fifteen adult paupers (eleven of them widows, a twelfth a deserted wife) in the whole parish. Another six or seven families in Staffield, he estimated, were housed at parish expense, while an unspecified number in Kirkoswald township received casual relief.[54] It would be a mistake, however, to assume that the elderly entirely dominated the relief rolls in this or indeed in any other Cumberland parish. In the twelve Cumberland parishes investigated by Eden and analysed by Susannah Ottaway, Kirkoswald's proportion (40 per cent) of those on relief who were aged sixty or more was characteristic of the sample as a whole (43.6 per cent). If anything, those elderly pensioners who were relieved were treated slightly more generously in Kirkoswald, where they received almost twenty-three pence per week on average, than in neighbouring parishes, where they had to make do with less than thirteen pence a week.[55] Whether there were similar differentials in generosity towards the illegitimate children who had fallen on the parish, of whom there were nine in Kirkoswald, is unclear. On balance, it seems, the parish officers had enjoyed long-term success in preventing what they considered to be the unnecessary inflation of welfare costs, an achievement that bore fruit for that relatively small number of paupers to whom relatively generous pensions were paid.

IV.   The Bowman family

As might be expected in the case of such a humble individual, and particularly one of her gender, virtually nothing is known of Ann Bowman or her family aside from what is revealed in her encounters with the poor law authorities. Even the parish registers, extant from 1577, furnish only the terminal one of the very many significant demographic facts about her with which the social historian of family life in poor households might work. All that can be said with any confidence is that Ann Bowman was

---

[54] Eden, *The State of the Poor*, vol. II, pp. 85–6.

[55] These figures are derived from an analysis of the twelve Cumberland parishes whose provision for the elderly is reported in Susannah R. Ottaway, *The Decline of Life: Old Age in Eighteenth-Century England* (Cambridge, 2004), p. 187 (table 5.2).

buried in Kirkoswald on 18 January 1714.[56] She was almost certainly baptised and married elsewhere, though the surprising lack of reference to the baptisms of her own children in the parish is probably due to the deficiencies in the register in the years before 1684. The rest of her life-history can be reconstructed only from incidental references in her numerous petitions to the Cumberland magistracy, an invaluable source to which we shall return. The vicar and churchwardens claimed on her behalf in 1708 that she was then aged seventy-six, which implies that she was born in 1632 and lived into her eighty-third year.[57] As we shall see, however, there is evidence elsewhere in the petitioning archive that her last child was born around 1689 (when Ann would have been at the putative age of fifty-seven!), which would suggest some special pleading on the part of her patrons, for Bowman was almost certainly younger than seventy-six in 1708. It is possible, of course, that no-one, herself included, really knew her age and that she simply appeared 'old'. Perhaps, conversely, she deliberately exaggerated her age to solicit sympathy. In the absence of the relevant parish register entries, these contradictions are unlikely ever to be resolved.[58]

Ann was married to Robert Bowman, who described himself in 1693 as 'of Buskarrig' in the parish of Kirkoswald, though when and where the wedding took place is uncertain.[59] In the late 1680s, she appears to have been working as a servant to Humphrey Bell, a gentleman resident in neighbouring Lazonby, who complained in 1687 that she was still in possession of eleven shillingsworth of his property. She protested in turn that he owed her ten shillings in wages. By this time, she described herself as resident in Fieldgate in Staffield and she and Robert were regular participants in manorial court disputes over non-payment for goods and services rendered: for three shillingsworth of ale; for fourteen shillingsworth of hay; and for five shillingsworth of dung.[60] Debt litigation of this kind suggests that the Bowmans were deeply enmeshed in local networks of credit, eking out a living from a variety of sources including ale-selling,

---

[56] CRO PR9/2 (Kirkoswald Parish Register, 1659–1809), unfol. The notes concerning baptisms recorded on the first two pages of this register between 1659 and 1684 are clearly incomplete and are probably copied from an earlier register which does not now survive. The preceding register, CRO PR9/1 (1577–1659), is also, apparently, seriously deficient.

[57] CRO Q/11/1/88/9 (Midsummer 1708).

[58] For the ambiguities surrounding knowledge of, and claims about, the precise ages of non-elite individuals, see Ottaway, *The Decline of Life*, pp. 45–7, 51, 53, 59–63.

[59] CRO Q/11/1/26/31 (Midsummer 1693).

[60] CRO D/Mus/1/7/1/1 (Court Book of Kirkoswald-cum-membris, 1682–96), unfol. (meetings of Michaelmas 1682, Michaelmas 1687, Michaelmas 1689).

hay-making and muck-raking.[61] Robert died well before Ann, possibly as early as 1694, more likely in 1698, at which time he described himself as a (chimney-)sweep.[62] Like very many women in early modern England, therefore, Ann Bowman spent a long time, perhaps as many as twenty years, as a widow. That status, it should be emphasised, should not be taken to imply that she had no ongoing responsibility for her offspring. As was the case with thousands of other widows, Bowman was bereaved with several children, two of them (in her case at least) infants.

Only one of the twelve extant petitions to the Cumberland sessions concerning Bowman's poor relief yields information of any value about the majority of her offspring. Unfortunately, however, this is the only undated document in the collection.[63] If, as seems likely, it originates in 1704, it would suggest that Ann had by then borne five children, the eldest of whom (a boy named Abraham) was already dead. Although the ratepayers did not bother even to mention the names of the remaining children, all four, they alleged, had either already left home or were already old enough to be put to apprenticeship or service. The eldest, a daughter, was allegedly 'very well settled by marriage'. The second, a son, was a labourer at 'the Greves', presumably a farm or estate in or near the parish. The two youngest 'were able to earn their living', the younger of them 'being a boy of fifteen or sixteen yeares of age', who had therefore been born in 1689.[64] The younger daughter, who was then aged at least twenty-one, was still living with (and, as we shall see, helping to support) her mother in 1710.[65]

Only for Abraham Bowman, the eldest of Ann's children, is there any further detail. Abraham appears to have suffered from mental illness. The parishioners of Kirkoswald variously described him as 'melancolly' in 1694 and as 'lunatic' in 1697, reporting that they had already incurred

---

[61] For the importance of credit, and especially of debts forgiven, in poor households, see Craig Muldrew, *The Economy of Obligation: The Culture of Credit and Social Relations in Early Modern England* (Basingstoke, 1998), pp. 303–12.

[62] CRO PR9/2, unfol., records the burial of one Robert Bowman 'sweeper' on 14 Nov. 1698, though this could only be Ann's husband if the petition in which the parishioners of Kirkoswald refer to his recent death has been erroneously filed with the petitions of 1694 in the sessions papers.

[63] CRO Q/11/1/136/11 (stray and mutilated petition filed with those of 1719). Only the middle portion of this petition survives, but its content correlates with an order issued at the Epiphany sessions at Cockermouth in 1704, CRO Q6/1, fol. 341 (Cockermouth sessions, 2 Jan. 1704). The only alternative, that it provoked the order at Carlisle sessions on 14 April 1697, can be discounted on the grounds that such a dating would place the birth-date of the Bowman's youngest child in 1682, with the consequence that the boy would surely have been too old to be described by his father as 'small' in 1693.

[64] CRO Q/11/1/26/31 (Midsummer 1693).

[65] CRO Q/11/1/96/25 (Midsummer 1710).

a great deal of expenditure on his behalf and that he was likely to remain a significant liability for a long time to come.[66] Ann's own description of him was naturally much more sympathetic, though it makes no less distressing reading for all that. She reported that, 'being distracted', Abraham had been 'bound in chains and [had] a keeper set over him by the parish'.[67] The parish officers, 'perceiving him to have some lucid intervals knokt off his fetters and sett him at liberty upon which he distractedly ran into the woods where he lay a fortnight'. He had, she went on, wandered into Westmorland where, 'not being capable of giving any account of himself', he was committed to the county gaol at Appleby, where he was forced to lie 'among the felons in great misery and want'.[68] Abraham nonetheless seems to have made some sort of recovery. By 1697, the inhabitants alleged that he was 'sound of body and mind and in service and has £3 per annum paid him for his wages'. How long Abraham enjoyed his sanity is far from clear, however, and by 1704 he was dead.[69]

By the time she lost her eldest son in the first decade of the eighteenth century, Ann Bowman had already been widowed ten years. The minister, churchwardens and overseers nonetheless thought she was fit enough to contribute to her own maintenance, and pleaded with the bench to withdraw altogether, or at least reduce, her weekly pension.[70] She nonetheless survived another ten years, most of them, as we shall see, engaged in attritional conflict with the parish officers over the nature and scale of her relief. It is to her experience of relief that we must now turn.

V.   The Bowman family on the parish

The longevity of some parish pensioners' careers has not gone unnoticed by historians. Five of those admitted to pensions in Gnosall (Staffordshire) in the 1670s and 1680s, for example, remained on the parish

---

[66] CRO Q/11/1/31/2 (Midsummer 1694). Provision for the mentally ill in northern parishes under the terms of the Elizabethan poor laws is described in Alfred Fessler, 'The management of lunacy in seventeenth-century England: An investigation of quarter sessions records', *Proceedings of the Royal Society of Medicine (History Section)* 49 (1956), 901–7; Peter Rushton, 'Lunatics and idiots: Mental disorder, the community and the poor law in north-east England, 1600–1800', *Medical History* 32 (1988), 34–50.

[67] For other instances where poor law authorities placed a premium on securing the mentally ill with locks and chains, see Fessler, 'The management of lunacy', 903; Rushton, 'Lunatics and idiots', 44.

[68] CRO Q/11/1/31/28 (Midsummer 1694).

[69] CRO Q6/1, fol. 24 (Carlisle sessions, 14 April 1697); Q/11/1/136/11 (?1704). In 1700 an agricultural labourer might usually expect to earn £9 a year if he could secure regular employment.

[70] CRO Q/11/1/136/11 (?1704).

for between eleven and sixteen years. Ann Foster's career in receipt of
a pension in Whitchurch (Oxfordshire) lasted some twenty-one years.
Three widows of Hedenham (Norfolk) who were on the relief rolls in
1662 continued to receive collection for thirty years. In cases of chronic
illness or mental incapacity, the period of dependency could be even
longer. Goodwife Wells spent thirty-six years on the parish at Cowden (Kent), while Cicely Badger was forty-eight years on the parish of
Gnosall.[71]

Robert and Ann Bowman are typical of this profile. Ann herself seems
to have been on the parish from the early 1690s, and Robert was first
licensed to beg and subsequently admitted to a pension in July 1693.[72]
Ann herself was still receiving collection in April 1711, almost eighteen
years later. Her experience of parish relief was, however, anything but
consistent. Nor does it sit easily alongside the results of Tim Wales's
painstaking analysis of the pattern of disbursements to the pensioners of
Hedenham (Norfolk) in the years 1662 to 1707, where payments were
fine-tuned to meet the increasing needs of individual paupers and their
families. Wales demonstrated that pensions were ratcheted up incremen-
tally as age and illness remorselessly undermined the capacity of the
poor to contribute to their own maintenance through their labour.[73]
Were it rendered possible by the survival of overseers' accounts, analysis of the careers of the comparatively small number of collection-
ers on the parish of Kirkoswald may well have revealed a similar
pattern. But Bowman's experience would stand out in any context,
for the rhythm of disbursement faltered as Bowman and the overseers
of the poor engaged in a protracted and bitter tug of war over parish
resources. The history of the Bowmans' pension arrangements can be
summarised as follows.

As was so often the case, Ann Bowman was receiving a pension even
before she was widowed. In the early 1690s, she was granted a pension of a shilling a week to support her two small children. In July
1693, Robert Bowman himself was granted a pension of tenpence a
week, and the sum was increased to eighteen pence a week the following

---

[71] Edward Turner, 'Ancient parochial account book of Cowden', *Sussex Archaeological Collections* 20 (1882), 114; Smith, 'Ageing and well-being', pp. 80–1; Wales, 'Poverty, poor
relief', p. 364; S. A. Cutlack, 'The Gnosall records, 1679 to 1837: Poor law administration', *Collections for a History of Staffordshire, Part I* (1936), 38.
[72] The separate treatment of Robert and Ann by the Kirkoswald overseers was by the
standards of the rest of England relatively unusual. The parish seems to have authorised
a begging licence for Robert, while at the same time paying Ann a pension. When
Robert was no longer able to beg, a single pension was paid to the household, which
Ann 'inherited' on his death.
[73] Wales, 'Poverty, poor relief', pp. 362–4 (figure 11.1).

October.[74] After Robert's death (possibly as early as the following year), the parish sought to have the pension (which Ann was apparently still drawing) cancelled on the grounds that she could support herself through her labour. She protested that she needed a shilling a week for herself, and a further shilling to take care of her son Abraham (then afflicted with mental illness), but succeeded only in securing sixpence a week on his behalf.[75] When he recovered his sanity, the bench stopped his relief but insisted that Ann should continue to receive a shilling a week. By January 1704, the parish was claiming that her children were no longer a burden and that her pension should be cancelled altogether. The bench was not entirely unpersuaded and reduced it to sixpence.[76] In autumn 1704 and again in autumn 1706 she unsuccessfully appealed to have the full shilling restored. By July 1708, getting the overseers to pay her even sixpence a week was beyond her and she protested that one of them, Thomas Jameson, 'very positively saieth that he will never pay her anything'.[77] By April 1710, despite threats to the parish officers of coercion from the bench, Bowman's pension was very seriously in arrears and the overseers were refusing point blank to pay, which led her into debt and, in July 1710, into eviction and destitution.[78] By autumn 1710, when she was owed over thirty-five shillings back-pay by the parish, the bench was altogether running out of patience with both parties. They insisted that the arrears be paid up, and that Bowman be housed with a continuing pension of sixpence a week, but stipulated that she wear the parish badge in recognition of her dependency.[79] By Easter 1711, she was once more destitute, having been 'by the overseers means driven out of [her] house' the preceding January. Once again, she complained of the recalcitrance of the parish officers and sought the arrears on her pension, this time on a relief order for a full shilling a week.[80]

Over the two decades through which the dispute had dragged on, the bench had delegated at least half-a-dozen magistrates, either singly or in pairs, to investigate the case, and some of them must have become

[74] CRO Q/11/1/26/31 (Midsummer 1693), 27/3 (Michaelmas 1693).
[75] CRO Q/11/1/32/1, 28 (Midsummer, 1694).
[76] CRO Q6/1, fols. 24 (Carlisle sessions, 14 April 1697), 341 (Cockermouth sessions, 2 Jan. 1704).
[77] CRO Q/11/1/73/27 (Michaelmas 1704); 81/12 (Michaelmas 1706); 88/9 (Midsummer 1708).
[78] CRO Q6/1, fols. 517, 519 (Carlisle, 13 July 1708), 524 (Penrith, 6 Oct. 1708); Q6/2, fol. 41 (Carlisle, 19 April 1710).
[79] CRO Q/11/1/97/7 (Michaelmas 1710). Cf. Steve Hindle, 'Dependency, shame and belonging: Badging the deserving poor, c.1550–1750', *Cultural and Social History* 1 (2004), 6–35.
[80] CRO Q/11/1/99/28 (Easter 1711).

familiar with the family's circumstances.[81] As a last resort, however, it took the relatively unusual step of referring the matter to the most senior clerical JP on what has been described as a 'quasi-theocratic' county bench: Bishop Nicolson of Carlisle.[82] Both Bowman and the parish officers were required to appear before the bishop, and the clerk of the peace was empowered to indict the overseers for contempt if the matter was not resolved to his satisfaction.[83] Although Bishop Nicolson's diary is extant for the year 1711, he unfortunately did not see fit to record for posterity his encounter with Ann Bowman and the parish officers.[84] With the bishop's visit to Kirkoswald pending, Ann Bowman disappears from the archive, resurfacing only when the parish clerk tersely recorded her burial in January 1714. Whether she died 'on the parish', with the overseers paying her funeral expenses, cannot be ascertained.[85] The parish clerk conspicuously failed to make reference to her poverty at burial, at a time when he was happy to do so in other cases, for the register records the funeral of Mary Dowson 'pauper' in 1697; Ann Nicolson widow 'pauper' in 1711; Thomas Smith 'pauper' in 1719; Joseph Brown 'a poor householder' in 1729; Margaret Latton 'pentioner' in 1729; and Barbary Bowman (possibly one of Ann Bowman's daughters) 'a poor householder' in 1730.[86] Perhaps then, Bowman's career as a pensioner finally ended some time between her last petition in 1711 and her death almost three years later. Whether she, like widow Martha Thompson of Little Crosby (Lancashire), took the highly unusual step of voluntarily refusing to accept her weekly allowance (and the badge that symbolised it) is equally uncertain.[87] It is more likely that, as had happened so often

---

[81] The orders variously require the intervention and/or mediation of Justices Aglionby, Blencow (twice), Hetherstone, Hutton and Musgrave (twice).

[82] CRO Q6/2, fol. 75 (Carlisle sessions, 11 April 1711). For Nicolson's career, see F. G. James, *North Country Bishop: A Biography of William Nicolson* (New Haven, 1956), esp. pp. 147–9 for his role as a magistrate (and quoting p. 149 on county government as a theocracy).

[83] The clumsy process of indictment was generally regarded as a matter of last resort, initiated (as in this case) only after threats of binding over to good behaviour had proved ineffective. For Nicolson's brief diary references to his dealings with the destitute, see, e.g., 'Bishop Nicolson's Diaries, part IV', *Transactions of the Cumberland and Westmorland Antiquarian and Archaeological Society*, new ser., IV (1904), 8 (removing a vagabond woman from Dalston, 27 August 1707), 42 ('hardly' dismissing a 'graceless and silly' beggar woman with a crown in cash, 3 November 1707).

[84] Nicolson did, however, dine with the Aglionbys at Nunnery in Kirkoswald on 9 July 1711, noting the 'perfection of the cookery and good husbandry' there, so perhaps this was the occasion of his visit to settle the poor law dispute. 'Bishop Nicolson's Diaries, part IV', 53.

[85] For pauper funerals, see Hindle, *On the Parish?*, pp. 279–82.

[86] CRO PR9/2, unfol. (11 Feb. 1697, 7 Jan. 1711, 9 Sept 1719, 4 April 1729, [undated] 1729, 14 Feb. 1730).

[87] Cf. Hindle, *On the Parish?*, p. 450.

during her lengthy career as a pensioner, Ann Bowman had fallen foul of the parish officers and had her collection suspended, or perhaps even withdrawn altogether.

VI.   The Bowman family petitions

The Kirkoswald poor law dispute was fought out in at least fifteen petitions to the Cumberland bench over a period of almost twenty years. Of these petitions, twelve are extant, and the existence of a further three, which have failed to survive but which would almost certainly plug substantial gaps in the narrative, is implied by surviving quarter sessions orders. Of the nine surviving petitions from the Bowman family, two were drawn up by, or on behalf of, Robert, and seven by, or on behalf of, Ann after his death. The remaining three petitions claimed to represent the views of 'the parish' of Kirkoswald, and it is to these that our discussion will turn first.

The first of these documents speaks of the petitioners only as those who have 'formerly been charged with the payment' for the poor, a formulation that implies not only the parish officers but also the ratepayers in general, a group whose principal interest lay in the reduction of relief expenditure. This petition was the first of several to refer to the ratepayers' desire to reduce Ann Bowman's pension. The motivation for this request seems to have been purely economic. If the parish officers had other grounds for hostility against Bowman – perhaps because she was alienated from the parish in some way, either as a nonconformist or as a resident who was delinquent or negligent in her parish obligations – they did not choose to disclose them to the bench. Their priority was apparently to ensure that pensions were not granted to those who could contribute (or who had offspring who might contribute) towards their maintenance. In this respect, the ambiguity over Bowman's age might well have been decisive, since any attempt on her part to exaggerate her inability to support herself would be construed as malingering.

The second and third petitions are, however, much more revealing in that they suggest that both Bowman herself and the overseers of the poor were at various times able to convince the most substantial parishioners of the justice of their claims. As early as 1704, 'the minister churchwardens and overseers' of the parish were pleading on behalf of the ratepayers that Bowman's family circumstances were such that she no longer needed a pension.[88] By 1708, Bowman had retaliated by securing a certificate from

[88] CRO Q/11/1/136/11 (?1704).

'the minister and churchwardens' that the overseer of the poor, Thomas Jameson, was unjustly withholding her pension.[89] Both protagonists evidently understood the importance of mobilising respectable opinion in support of their cause. Although the turnover in the tenure of the principal parish office probably explains the change of allegiance of the churchwardens, the fact that the minister, John Rumney, was prepared to speak on behalf of both parties within the space of a few short years perfectly captures the ambiguous position of the clergyman in the politics of the parish.[90]

The Bowmans' own petitions are altogether more idiosyncratic. Although all are superficially humble and deferential in tone, their content is truculent and embittered. None of them is written in a consistent hand and all are unsigned and unmarked, probably written on either Robert or Ann's behalf by a local scrivener, perhaps one of their neighbours. Like hundreds of other applicants for parish relief, therefore, the Bowmans relied upon 'epistolatory advocates'.[91]

VII.   Poor households in the neighbourhood

The petitions are nonetheless extremely revealing about the relationship between this particular poor family and the community in which they lived. Both Robert and Ann were consistently at pains to explain just how dependent they were on the goodwill of their neighbours. Indeed, so rich was the tradition of neighbourly hospitality in this part of Cumberland that it was by no means unusual, even in the 1690s, for the county justices to license the poor to beg rather than to require the overseers to raise money for them by taxation. Thus the Penrith sessions of May 1693 ordered that Robert Bowman 'should be relieved by the parish of Kirkoswald with meate and drinke weekly at the several houses belonging to the said parish'. Bowman himself seems to have been content with traipsing round Kirkoswald in search of off-cuts and scraps from the tables of his neighbours, who, he argued, afforded him 'some smale relief'.[92] When his legs failed him, however, he was no longer able to beg and the bench fell back on the expedient of a ten-pence weekly pension

---

[89] CRO Q/11/1/88/9 (Midsummer 1708).

[90] Cf. Steve Hindle, 'Introduction: The clergy and the politics of poor relief in a Hertfordshire parish', in Heather Falvey and Steve Hindle (eds.), *'This Little Commonwealth': Layston Parish Memorandum Book, 1607–c.1650 & 1704–c.1747* (Hertfordshire Record Publications, 19, Hertford, 2003), pp. xi–xlvii.

[91] Thomas Sokoll, 'Old age in poverty: The record of Essex pauper letters, 1780–1834', in Hitchcock *et al.*, *Chronicling Poverty*, p. 135. Cf. Hindle, *On the Parish?*, ch. 6.4(a).

[92] CRO Q/11/1/26/31 (Midsummer 1693).

together with a promise to house the family at parish expense. It was here, however, that the first of the numerous tensions between the Bowmans and the ratepayers became evident. Although the overseers did house them, they placed them some three miles away from the town centre, so 'remote from any house' that the whole family were 'rendered destitute of all charity and assistance' except the pension.[93] The clear implication was that unless they were housed sufficiently close to town that Ann and her young children could beg from their neighbours' kitchen doors at meal-times, collection itself would not support them. Some seventeen years later, Ann Bowman herself was (as we have seen) singing from the same hymn-sheet. Being 'feeble and infirm', she pleaded that she should 'not be confined to an old ruinous house which is without the cry of any neighbours'. The overseers, she feared, would 'confine me to a dismal corner where none might relieve or help me in my hunger bitten condition'.[94] This allusive remark, which might at first be taken as a lament for the prospective absence of any near dwellers at all, is in fact highly suggestive about conflicted contemporary understandings of the term 'neighbours'. After all, Bowman implied a distinction between *ratepayers* (whom modern historians tend to identify as neighbours in the formal sense of being fellow residents of the parish) and *neighbours* (a group defined by Bowman in the rather more restricted sense of those individuals, probably other poor residents, who lived in sufficiently close proximity to her to provide her with practical aid). In Bowman's view, good neighbourliness seems to have been less a matter of fulfilling one's impersonal legal duty to pay the parish rate, than of offering spontaneous succour and support on the doorstep and in the street. Poor householders arguably preferred to identify themselves with the ancient tradition of indiscriminate mutual aid out of which neighbourhoods were constructed than with the growing machinery of discretionary social welfare created by the Elizabethan poor laws.

The Bowmans and the overseers evidently had wildly differing views about the nature and extent of the neighbourly support that Ann might be afforded even in her widowhood. By the summer of 1710, Ann was living alone with her youngest daughter who was earning just enough to provide a room for them. When the overseer Thomas Tetherston discovered that Ann was effectively lodging with her daughter, he was apparently so enraged that he threatened the landlady, Catherine Cowper, with prosecution under the 1589 inmates' statute: after all, it was one of the fundamental principles of the Elizabethan poor laws that relief was only to be granted if children were unable to support their aged

---

[93] CRO Q/11/1/27/3 (Michaelmas 1693).   [94] CRO Q/11/1/96/25 (Midsummer 1710).

parents.[95] Cowper was so terrified that she threw all Bowman's goods out into the street, 'where they lay for four and twenty hours so that [her] lodging in that house [was] very precarious and not to be depended upon'. Effectively destitute, Bowman no longer had the means to lubricate the machinery of credit on which she had evidently long depended. Without the cash flow implied by a relief order, let alone a pension on whose payment she could actually count, she had no hope of discharging her credit or releasing those goods she had already lodged with the town's pawnbrokers, and would be forced to give pledges of what little was left of her property simply to buy bread. Tetherston, she alleged, nonetheless threatened to starve her and 'abused people with ill words that either trusted [her] or gave [her] anything' in her 'piteous lamentable necessity'. Bowman was emphatic in her demands for her arrears and continuing pension, insisting that 'my pension be ascertained & the days or the weeks when to be payd nominated'.[96]

This request was not, it should be emphasised, a matter of ensuring an income on which she could actually live, but simply a means of keeping the revolving doors of credit in motion.[97] The payment of arrears would in itself only allow her, she argued, to 'get my pawns loosed against approaching winter to happ [i.e., clothe] me'. These fears, expressed in July 1710, about the freezing up of the stream of credit had become more acute by the following October, by which time she was claiming that 'those who ventured to lend me anything upon the credit of [the bench's] order are discouraged from helping me anymore'. The overseers were whipping up feeling against her and 'such persons as either trust or sell me anything are thretned for it'. 'My goods that I have layd to pawn for bread', she pleaded, 'will not be restored to me against winter unless I have money to loose them with in this poor desolate starving condition'.[98] Her final petition, of Easter 1711, was especially erudite in its depiction of the dilemma of the destitute. To get money to feed herself, her only assets were the clothes that she might pledge with the pawnbroker: Bowman claimed that she was effectively 'starved with cold to prevent being famished to death'. Again she insisted on a determination of exactly 'at

---

[95] 31 Elizabeth I, c. 7 (1589). This threat was entirely characteristic of the Kirkoswald overseers' attitude towards inmates, for whom regular searches were made. See above, pp. 138–9; and cf. Hindle, *On the Parish?*, ch. 5 ('Exclusion').

[96] CRO Q/11/1/97/7 (Michaelmas 1710). For the importance of pawnbrokers to the poor, see Alannah Tomkins, 'Pawnbroking and the survival strategies of the urban poor in 1770s York', in Steve King and Alannah Tomkins (eds.), *The Poor in England, 1700–1850: An Economy of Makeshifts* (Manchester, 2003), pp. 166–98; and Hindle, *On the Parish?*, pp. 78–81.

[97] Cf. Muldrew, *The Economy of Obligation*, pp. 303–12.

[98] CRO Q/11/1/97/7 (Michaelmas 1710).

what tyme I should be paid' and requested arrears that 'I might repay what I have borrowed'.[99]

In the light of her concern about the flow of credit, it is evident that Bowman did not regard the pension as a living in itself. As Lynn Botelho has recently shown, previous estimates about the increasing generosity of the parish pension during the course of the seventeenth century have proved to be unreasonably optimistic. Botelho's brilliant reconstruction of the declining purchasing power of the parish pension over time effectively undermines the notion that pensioners were by 1700 able to live comfortably without supplementing their incomes from other sources. There is, as Botelho wisely points out, 'no exact formula for a successful economy of makeshifts', but her exhaustive calculations make it abundantly clear that 'shift' would have had to contribute nearly half of the aged poor's annual budget even at the end of the seventeenth century.[100] To this extent, the pension, even the promise of a pension implied by a relief order, was simply another means of keeping the pawnbrokers happy.

The Bowman family's petitions therefore disclose the myriad ways in which an impoverished family might shift for itself in late seventeenth- and eighteenth-century England: the kindness of neighbours and the circulation of credit perforce had to be fitted in and around the provision of collection and habitation by the parish officers. The chink of the small change of neighbourliness – the shopkeepers who cared sufficiently to sell her food on trust or gave her outright gifts, even in defiance of the overseers; the boatman who clandestinely ferried her across the River Eden without accepting a fee; the servant of the Aglionbys, to whom she referred as 'the worthy family of Nunnery', who brought 'voluntary alms' after she had been evicted[101] – is faintly audible above the hiss of invective Bowman spat at the overseers. Her recollections testify not only to the resilience of the tradition of mutual aid from which local communities were constructed but also to the immersion of even the poorest of households within that tradition.

VIII.   The family and the poor law authorities

The petitions in the Kirkoswald poor law dispute are highly revealing of the tensions that existed between the poor and the poor law authorities over various aspects of family life. Four sets of inter-related issues – the

---

[99] CRO Q/11/1/99/28 (Easter 1711).
[100] Botelho, *Old Age and the English Poor Law*, p. 151; cf. Wales, 'Poverty, Poor Relief', p. 356.
[101] CRO Q/11/1/96/25 (Midsummer 1710 (the overseer's harassment of the charitable)); 97/7 (Michaelmas 1710 (Kirkoswald boatman)); 99/28 (Easter 1711 (Aglionby's servant)).

attenuated role of extended kin; the significance of immediate kin; the contribution of children to the household economy; and the putative causes of idleness – deserve detailed consideration here, on each of which Stone's *Family, Sex and Marriage* jumped to conclusions without bothering to exploit the plentiful records that might have disclosed a more complex reality.

A principal theme of Stone's book was the significance of extended kin in structuring the affective relationships of family life. He argued that over the course of the early modern period, the role of kin, by which he meant the extended family (uncles, aunts, cousins, etc.), declined and that the family was transformed from a structure and series of relationships that were permeable to the influence of more extensive kinship networks, to one that was nuclear in form and in which relationships were focused upon a much smaller, and usually co-resident, group. His work was, of course, focused on the elite, among whom notions of lineage were paramount, and it is accordingly no surprise that issues of cousinage and affinity should be so central to his argument. Analysis of poor law petitions suggests, however, that wider kin were almost irrelevant to the survival strategies of pauper households. It was Ann Bowman's husband and children, rather than her more distant relatives, who played a central part in her relief. Her settlement had, after all, almost certainly been secured by service, and her lateral kin may accordingly have been very remote. Even had they been living as neighbours, however, it is unlikely that Ann would have mentioned them. There was, of course, no need to draw attention to the likely charitable contributions of lateral kin, since neither magistrates nor parish officers would have factored them into their calculations of her situation. It is nonetheless striking that none of the Kirkoswald residents who petitioned for relief in this period made any reference to kin other than their spouses or offspring in outlining their case for relief. The evidence presented here suggests, in fact, that neighbours rather than extended kin were the primary providers of charity to poor households.

The second issue is the importance of the nuclear, or at least the lineal, family in providing support for poor households. Stone regarded the institutionalisation of the poor laws as an index of the declining responsibilities of immediate kin for the poor. 'Parish relief', he insisted, effectively relieved the conjugal family of their previous 'sense of obligation to provide relief to the sick and the indigent to save them from starvation'. Children, he believed, 'were increasingly shedding responsibility' for the support of their aged parents, 'and transferring it to the community at large' in the guise of the ratepayers.[102] More attention to the fine

[102] Stone, *The Family, Sex and Marriage*, pp. 148–9, 403.

detail of the Elizabethan statutes themselves in fact suggests that the poor laws were in some respects designed to bolster rather than to obviate the responsibility of children to maintain their elderly parents. Although the kin obligation clause was not very widely enforced, it is revealing that so many petitioners for parish relief were at pains to explain that they had no 'friends' (i.e., immediate kin) to maintain them. Bowman's own career in collection suggests in fact that even in her widowhood she relied on a combination of a weekly pension and her daughter's earnings to keep a roof over her head. That two of her contemporaries were also denied relief on the grounds that their children were able to support them suggests that the parish officers of Kirkoswald were all too aware of just how valuable the kin obligation clause might be in helping them drive down relief expenditure.

This raises in turn the related issue of the perceived economic utility of children. The attitudes of parents on the one hand and overseers on the other towards the role of children in poor households tended to diverge. Both Robert and Ann were at pains to emphasise that their children, especially those who were still 'smale' in the early 1690s, were legitimate objects of 'charity and assistance'. In turn, one of those very young children had some seventeen years later become her mother's only source of support. Bowman pleaded in 1710 that she had 'no other livelihood then what she [her daughter] can earn by her labour for a house for me'.[103] The language used by the overseers was, by contrast, forthright in its emphasis on the high costs of maintaining her offspring and on the desirability of removing her children. They had, they reported, been at 'great charge' with Abraham by 1694, and feared that they were 'like to be at much more', since his disability rendered him vulnerable to an extended, perhaps even a permanent, period during which he could be treated only as a child. They wrote of her surviving children in 1704 that all four were either 'gone from her or serviceable', a formulation that rehearses the agenda of poor law manuals, from the anonymous *Ease for Overseers of the Poor* (1601) to Samuel Carter's *Legal Provisions for the Poor* (1710), that children were a burden rather than a blessing to most poor families; and that both parties would accordingly benefit from their removal.[104] Although Bowman and the parish officers might not have disagreed about the importance or legitimacy of relieving her vulnerable offspring, they had widely differing views about the most appropriate locus of their care.

---

[103] CRO Q/11/1/27/3 (Michaelmas 1693); 96/25 (Midsummer 1710).
[104] CRO Q/11/1/136/11 (?1704); *An Ease for Overseers of the Poor* (Cambridge, 1601), p. 26. S[amuel] C[arter], *Legal Provisions for the Poor* (London, 1710), pp. 48–75.

This leads, finally, to the possibility that the ratepayers regarded dependency as an inherited, perhaps even as a congenital, condition, transmitted lineally in the households of the idle. The overseers were savagely critical of Ann's apparent preference for hand-outs rather than elbow-grease and were determined to make life as a pensioner as uncomfortable as possible for her and her children. They repeatedly insisted (in 1694) that she was 'able to work' and (in 1704) that she was a '*fresh* woman able to *travel* for her own maintenance', though whether their antiquated verb implied that she might work or beg for her living is unclear. The adjective 'fresh' is itself no less interesting, since it implied that Ann was thriving and vigorous, and perhaps even suggested that she was still of childbearing age.[105] Ann's own reading of her situation was diametrically opposed; she described herself in 1704 as 'now very impotent insomuch that she is not able to subsist on 6d a week'; in 1706 as 'very impotent so that she is not able to work or doe anything'; in 1710 as 'old, feeble and infirm'; and later that year as 'almost out of strength' and 'not able to go so often from place [?to place]'. She reported that destitution in the depths of winter 1711 meant that she had 'to lye without a bed upon the cold floor, which has gone very near to kill me and has almost made me a cripple'.[106] Its patience exhausted, the bench decided to call Bowman's bluff by testing her resolve to be on the parish at all, insisting in October 1710 that her pension be conditional on her 'wearing a badge as the law directs'.[107] The 1697 statute on which this order was based required not only the parish pensioner herself, but also the dependent children, to 'take the patch', exempting only those sons and daughters who contributed to the maintenance of their parents. Pensioners who accepted the badge were in turn vulnerable to having their children apprenticed, which perhaps explains why so many of those who refused it were women.[108] From the ratepayers' point of view, therefore, apprenticeship was a way of breaking the cycle of deprivation in which feckless parents like Bowman transmitted habits of idleness to their offspring. Their hopes might even have been fulfilled by 1730 when the parish clerk recorded at her

---

[105] CRO Q/11/1/1/31/2 (Midsummer 1694), 136/11 (?1704) (emphases added). For the end of childbearing, see Lynn Botelho, 'Old age and menopause in rural women of early modern Suffolk', in Lynn Botelho and Pat Thane (eds.), *Women and Ageing in British Society Since 1500* (Harlow, 2001), pp. 43–65.

[106] CRO Q/11/1/73/27 (Michaelmas 1704), 81/12 (Michaelmas 1706), 96/25 (Midsummer 1710), 97/20 (Michaelmas 1710), 99/28 (Easter 1711).

[107] CRO Q6/2, fol. 58 (Penrith sessions, 4 Oct. 1710). This is the only order of the period in which the Cumberland bench *explicitly* ordered a pensioner to wear a badge, although any overseer who paid a pension to a pauper without insisting on the badge was technically liable for a twenty-shilling fine.

[108] Hindle, 'Dependency, shame and belonging', 27, 30.

burial that one of Bowman's daughters had died, almost certainly as she had lived, as 'a poor householder' rather than as a pauper.[109] From the pensioner's perspective, the earning (perhaps even the begging) power of their children was an invaluable supplement to the shifts through which poor families survived, and the removal of a child might irreparably damage the gears of the household economy.[110] In all these respects, then, the Bowmans' petitions suggest that the relationship between the poor law authorities and the households of the poor was far more complex than Stone assumed, and that the institutional structures of the civil parish were a very significant component of those matrices of mutuality and obligation within which plebeian families conducted their emotional lives.

IX.   Forgotten norms, obsolete rituals, hidden gestures

Just about the only observation Stone made about the families of the poor that has withstood the scrutiny of almost thirty years' research is that women without men, such as spinsters, widows and deserted wives, 'bulked large on the relief rolls'.[111] The Bowman case nonetheless suggests that even widows were expected to work, perhaps (at least in some parts of the country) to beg, into extreme old age, and that there was no inevitability about securing the coveted, but ambiguous, status of an 'object of charity'. Her petitions demonstrate that although the poor might have at least some agency in the negotiations that took place over the allocation of relief, and although even a 'poor desolate' widow might seek to shame the overseers into complying with the relief orders of the bench, the parish officers enjoyed very significant powers to dictate the domestic and residential arrangements of those who claimed relief. The households of the poor might be fractured and reconstituted according to the dictates of labour discipline and the demands on parish resources. Children were exported to more prosperous households both to relieve their parents of the burden and to receive some training in husbandry or housewifery. The elderly might be rotated through the parish housing stock, perhaps starting with subsidised rent for a room, continuing with a habitation order for a cottage, maybe even culminating in the gown and stipend associated with a place in an endowed almshouse. If more expedient co-residential arrangements were attempted, especially where parents or children lodged each other as inmates without prior permission, the parish officers were not above removing them either to more

---

[109] CRO PR9/2, unfol. (14 Feb. 1730).   [110] Cf. Hindle, *On the Parish?*, pp. 223–6.
[111] Stone, *The Family, Sex and Marriage*, p. 201.

suitable accommodation or from the parish altogether. Conversely, they might insist on co-residential arrangements if it was felt that they might relieve the burden on the ratepayers. In all these respects, the households of the poor were pieces on the parish chessboard to be moved in accordance with the gambits of the overseers.

But Bowman's petitions (and thousands of others like them) are most valuable for the reconstruction of affective relations within and between plebeian households when they are read against the grain. As we have seen, petitioners like Ann Bowman inadvertently revealed not only the family circumstances that had contributed to their indigence but also the survival strategies through which they had made shift up until the point where they could no longer support themselves. In her case, poverty was a consequence of widowhood, of the mental illness of her son, and of increasing old age and disability; while 'shift' implied co-residence with her daughter, the pledging of goods for pawn, the begging of food from neighbours, the casual charity of the prosperous and countless expressions of the tradition of mutual aid: debts forgiven, goods borrowed, favours proffered. To be sure, this lifestyle can be glimpsed between the lines of Bowman's petitions precisely because she was so articulate and determined in her attempt to expose the callousness of the overseers. Analysis of other petitions of this kind would doubtless reveal different family circumstances and varying household strategies. But all would probably demonstrate the impossibility, to say nothing of the undesirability, of studying affective relations in plebeian households in isolation from the wider structures of kinship, of neighbourhood and of authority.

An enormous amount has, therefore, been learned about the lives of the indigent since *The Family, Sex and Marriage* was published in 1977. If Stone had, however subconsciously, captured the spirit of the age in patronising the poor, it has become clear that condescension was conjoined with suspicion in the minds of the middling sort and the magistracy alike. The poor law authorities, both justices and vestrymen, consistently denied the poor any real autonomy in family life. The penal suspension of relief was used in a variety of circumstances, not least to punish idleness, drunkenness or pilfering.[112] But it was also a very effective strategy for a propertied elite that was determined to regulate the family lives of the poor: pensions were withdrawn where aging parents 'harboured' their daughters living out of service; where the labouring poor refused to surrender children as young as seven to apprenticeship; and where families refused to countenance the loss of independence represented

---

[112] Hindle, *On the Parish?*, pp. 383–6, 386–7, 394.

by moving to the workhouse.[113] Even the right to transmit to the next generation what little property the poor enjoyed was undermined by the vestry's insistence that applicants for relief sign their goods over to the parish before their names were engrossed onto the relief rolls.[114] Strategies such as these might be obviated altogether if the parish officers could prevent the settlement, better still the marriage, of poor couples who were thought likely to breed up a charge on the poor rate.[115] In reconstructing these policies, and the attitudes that underpinned them, two generations of historians of the old poor law have developed very considerable imaginative sympathy towards those whose lives were so fundamentally influenced by its administration. But even so, this is a field in which the scholarship repeatedly bumps up against the limits of what is historically possible. Despite the achievements of the new social history, the doors of the humblest households remain, if not closed altogether, then at least only just ajar.

'The history of the "lower sort of people" between 1500 and 1800', Edward Thompson argued, 'discloses many different familial modes.' 'Some', he wrote, 'may seem to us to be rough, lacking in any foresight, picaresque: others may seem to be cold and bound to elemental needs.' But even petitions as rich and detailed as Ann Bowman's do not enable the historian to fulfil to any great extent the obligations that Thompson identified as the essential objectives of the history of the family: to 'reconstruct the forgotten norms, decode the obsolete rituals and detect the hidden gestures' that disclose the nature and quality of affective relations within and beyond the households, even the poorest households, of seventeenth-century England.[116] On the one hand, then, the misguided nature of Lawrence Stone's revelation of his own prejudices regarding the poor is self-evident. On the other, historians of family life at this social level still find it enormously difficult thirty years later to get beyond the stereotypes, and not merely the stereotypes rehearsed by the likes of the Reverend Alexander Strange or Chief Justice Mathew Hale, but also those purveyed by the poor themselves.[117] After all, in claiming that they had been long resident, that they had always been charitable to their neighbours, that they had consistently taken pains to bring up their children with appropriate habits of industry and deference, claimants for relief were telling the magistrates exactly what they wanted to hear. Even in the case of a family like the Bowmans who have left extensive documentary footprints, it remains extremely difficult to penetrate the world of the poor beyond the most superficial reconstruction of some aspects of the

---

[113] Ibid., pp. 186–90, 390–1, 391–3.   [114] Ibid., pp. 281–2.   [115] Ibid., pp. 337–53.
[116] Thompson, 'Happy families', p. 310.   [117] Hindle, *On the Parish?*, pp. 224–6.

economic problems they faced and the survival strategies they adopted. To explore the further issues of emotion and of affect raised by Stone is, in large measure, impossible. The historian may almost say of Ann Bowman, as did the clergyman Henry Newcome of the poor man whose sickbed he visited in Gawesworth (Cheshire) in 1655, that 'I have dealt as well as I could with [her] . . . [but] how hard it is to get *within* poor persons.'[118]

---

[118] *The Autobiography of Henry Newcome*, ed. R. Parkinson (2 vols., Chetham Society, old ser., 26–7, 1852), vol. I, p. 53 (emphasis added).

7   Childless men in early modern England

Helen Berry and Elizabeth Foyster

On the very first page of that most famous of diaries, Samuel Pepys recorded an intimate detail of his married life from the winter of 1659: 'My wife, after the absence of her terms for seven weeks, gave me hopes of her being with child.' When he wrote this, he and Elizabeth had already been married for five years, but although they were both young, the hoped-for pregnancy had not materialised and the resumption of her cycle at the end of December that year proved yet another disappointment.[1] One year later, having a child was still on their minds: Pepys recorded in his diary that they were referring to their bedroom as 'the Nursery'. By 1662, however, he had begun to countenance 'the possibility there is of my having no child'.[2] Nonetheless, even in the context of his failing marriage, he did not give up his desire to be a father easily. In 1667 he wished a friend's child ('a very pretty little boy' whom he liked 'very well') was his own.[3] He admitted to himself that he was troubled by the idea that he could be left without a brother or a son to continue his family name, a circumstance that did indeed materialise.[4] As with so many other subjects, Pepys's diary provides a rare and detailed account of one man's hopes and fears, in this instance, his attitudes towards fatherhood and his personal sense of loss that he did not have children of his own.

Research for this chapter was made possible in part by an Arts and Humanities Research Fund award from the University of Newcastle upon Tyne. The authors would also like to thank Joanne Bailey, Jeremy Boulton, Malcolm Gaskill, Karen Harvey, Jennie Jordan, Jason Kelly, Wendy Moore, Jim Oeppen and Richard Wall for their helpful comments and references. This chapter is the starting point for a large-scale research project planned by the present authors on the history of infertility in Britain.

[1] In Robert Latham and William Matthews (eds.), *The Diary of Samuel Pepys* (London, 1970), vol. II, p. 1 (1 January 1660).

[2] Ibid., vol. II , p. 127 (28 June 1661); vol. III, p. 16 (23 January 1662).

[3] Ibid., vol. II, p. 442 (19 September 1667).

[4] Tom, Pepys's brother, died a bachelor in 1664. For more details of Pepys's arrangements for his inheritance, see below.

In his pioneering work on family history, Lawrence Stone mined Pepys's diary for evidence of sexual behaviour, but failed to comment on the diarist's inability to start a family. Stone has often been criticised for his lack of insight into the position and treatment of women,[5] but his analysis of Pepys's life-story further reveals some of his preconceptions about early modern men as well as women. Despite Samuel's evident concern that he was missing out on fatherhood, it was Elizabeth Pepys, not her husband, whom Stone described as 'childless and lonely'.[6] Subsequently, historians have continued to impose their own deeply gendered ideas about reproductive problems upon the past, often portraying women as the sole carriers of blame and disappointment, but this seriously misrepresents how couples in the early modern period explained and experienced childlessness.[7] This chapter aims to begin to redress this situation by providing a fuller understanding of the social and cultural importance placed upon reproduction for men as well as women, which hitherto has been an under-explored aspect of family history. In particular, this chapter demonstrates how far the experience of being fathers was a component both of men's gender identity and of their roles as patriarchs within early modern family life.

Thirty years ago, few people had contemplated studying the history of masculinity as a discrete subject. The history of early modern manhood, as a subset of gender history, has received a great deal more attention in the last decade. This innovation has taken the form of debates concerning the importance of honour to ideas of manhood and the history of domestic violence, politeness and masculinity, male youth culture and apprenticeship, 'codes' of masculinity and behaviour among students, and male sexuality.[8] It is now widely accepted that early modern society was broadly patriarchal in theory if not in practice, even if Stone's model for considering the transition from 'despotic' patriarchy to modern companionate marriage has been considerably revised.[9] The work of

---

[5] See Stone's list of ten commandments for historians of women, for example, in 'Only women', *The New York Review of Books* (11 April 1985), 21.

[6] Pepys's relationship with Mary Skinner, which continued for thirty-three years after Elizabeth's death, also remained childless, but neither does this receive comment: see L. Stone, *The Family, Sex and Marriage in England 1500–1800* (London, 1977), pp. 552–9.

[7] Laura Gowing, for example, argues that 'the possibility of male seed failing was rarely considered', and that 'male infertility . . . was seen in terms of physical impotence', in *Common Bodies: Women, Touch and Power in Seventeenth-Century England* (New Haven and London, 2003), pp. 114–15.

[8] See, for example, Alan Bray, *Homosexuality in Renaissance England* (London, 1982); E. A. Foyster, *Manhood in Early Modern England: Honour, Sex and Marriage* (Harlow, 1999); Philip Carter, *Men and the Emergence of Polite Society, Britain 1660–1800* (London, 2001); and Alexandra Shepard, *Meanings of Manhood in Early Modern England* (Oxford, 2003).

[9] Stone, *Family, Sex and Marriage*, Part III.

Anthony Fletcher, for example, has subsequently demonstrated how the legitimation of male authority changed over the course of the early modern period (manifested not in a single, over-arching 'patriarchy' but in 'patriarchies'), with one principle remaining the same: the maintenance of the authority of husbands within the little kingdom of the family (an authority that was mirrored in the super-structures of the kingdom at large), most frequently expressed through the idea of a powerful 'husband and father'.[10] But what happened if men became husbands, but not fathers? That is, what if they married, but did not have children (a circumstance referred to by demographers as 'primary sterility')?[11] If a couple failed to produce children, were they stigmatised in their local community and within their own family? More specifically, to what extent was a man's reputation impaired by childlessness?

'To understand fatherhood historically', argues one historian, 'is to explore a major part of what it means to be a man, to define a key part of masculine identity.'[12] The study of those men who did not conform to this model provides a gauge for judging more precisely the *extent* to which fatherhood was a constituent element of masculinity and patriarchal authority, but currently there has been little research on attitudes towards childless men in early modern society.[13] This chapter focuses upon evidence for early modern medico-legal understanding of male infertility, social attitudes towards childless men, and their experiences, as found in a wide range of primary sources, from religious and devotional literature to popular print culture, medical texts, court records, and personal documents. Evidence presented here suggests that the assumption made by Stone's contemporary, Randolph Trumbach, that childlessness would be seen as 'the result of a woman's barrenness rather than any incapacity of her husband', is long overdue for revision.[14]

---

[10] Anthony Fletcher, *Gender, Sex and Subordination in England 1500–1800* (New Haven and London, 1995) remains one of the most widely cited and authoritative single volumes on the subject. For further discussion of patriarchy and its meaning, see the chapter by Ingrid Tague in this collection.

[11] Cases where a couple had no more than one child were known as 'secondary sterility', which although relevant are beyond the scope of the present chapter. For detailed definition of these commonly accepted terms and their implications, see E. A. Wrigley, R. S. Davies, J. E. Oeppen and R. S. Schofield, *English Population History from Family Reconstitution, 1580–1837* (Cambridge, 1997), pp. 357–61.

[12] See Robert L. Griswold's introduction to a special issue on the history of fatherhood, *Journal of Family History* 24, 3 (1999), 251.

[13] Amy M. Froide, *Never Married: Singlewomen in Early Modern England* (Oxford, 2005), p. 1 observes that more work is needed on single men in this period ('a patriarch was, after all, the married head of a family and a household').

[14] Randolph Trumbach, *The Rise of the Egalitarian Family: Aristocratic Kinship and Domestic Relations in Eighteenth-Century England* (New York, 1978), p. 167; see also Angus

Demographic data provides an important context for considering early modern English attitudes towards childlessness, since it indicates how common, or exceptional, the instances of primary sterility were within the population as a whole. Married couples' anxiety over their inability to conceive, whether temporary or permanent, is well attested in the sources, and was particularly acute at the higher end of the social spectrum, where dynastic pressures meant that a couple's procreative success came under particularly close scrutiny by their kin.[15] Records relating to elite families, who were so concerned with proving ancient lineage and preserving estates in the family name, can produce the clearest evidence of when marriages failed to produce heirs. Hence Stone's argument that there was a 'crisis of the aristocracy' in the early modern period was based partly on his estimates that 19 per cent of all first marriages among the nobility between 1540 and 1660 were childless. Although remarriages after the death of one spouse were frequent among this social group, 48 per cent of these second or subsequent marriages were childless, possibly due to the older age of the couple.[16] It was failure to produce a male heir, rather than children *per se*, that was particularly disruptive for these families in the context of male primogeniture. County studies have suggested the effects of this upon family fortunes: in Nottinghamshire, for example, eighteen knightly families failed in the male line in the fifteenth century, and in Yorkshire between 1558 and 1642 nearly a fifth of resident gentry families died out in the male line.[17]

Lower down the social scale, quantifying the rates of sub-fecundity and actual primary or secondary sterility puts this widely articulated anxiety into perspective, but has proved extremely complex for demographers to measure.[18] Modern and historical studies estimate that primary sterility affects between 5 per cent and 13 per cent of all couples, but both the levels and causes of sterility vary over time.[19] Late age at marriage

McLaren, *Reproductive Rituals: The Perception of Fertility in England from the Sixteenth Century to the Nineteenth Century* (London, 1984), p. 38.

[15] Linda A. Pollock, 'Embarking on a rough passage: The experience of pregnancy in early-modern society', and Patricia Crawford, 'The construction and experience of maternity in seventeenth-century England', both in V. Fildes (ed.), *Women as Mothers in Pre-Industrial England: Essays in Honour of Dorothy McLaren* (London, 1990), pp. 39–42; 19–20.

[16] Lawrence Stone, *The Crisis of the Aristocracy 1558–1641* (Oxford, 1965), p. 168; see also Lawrence Stone and Jeanne C. Fawtier Stone, *An Open Elite? England 1540–1880* (Oxford, 1984), pp. 76–101.

[17] Felicity Heal and Clive Holmes, *The Gentry in England and Wales 1500–1700* (Basingstoke, 1994), p. 24.

[18] For a detailed discussion, see Wrigley *et al.*, *English Population History*, pp. 354–62 and *passim*.

[19] In the early modern period the problem was exacerbated by the high rate of 'incomplete' marriage, with as many as 50% of unions terminated by the early death of one partner.

during the best part of the three centuries in question impacted upon not only the likely number of live births per couple, but also the chances of conceiving per monthly cycle as both partners grew older, with women experiencing a particular downturn in conception after the age of thirty-five.[20] Current and historical data indicate that men in their forties and older also conceive fewer children than younger men, although measuring the overall rates of male sterility is extremely difficult, even in modern populations. The scientific literature on male sterility is still in its infancy, and the concern over possible rising levels of infertility due, for example, to modern environmental factors is a relatively recent phenomenon.[21]

Several other factors adversely affect the fecundity of adult men and women (including disease and malnutrition, as well as somatic problems such as congenital defects in the sex organs which may limit the body's reproductive capacity), all of which were present in pre-modern societies.[22] From the data available in sixteen English parish registers, demographers have estimated that, between 1550 and 1849, just under 5 per cent of women who married between the ages of 20 and 24 did not conceive within the first five years of marriage: over the same duration of marriage this rose to just over 9 per cent of women who married at ages 25 to 29, compared with 24 per cent of those marrying at 35 to 39, and nearly 44 per cent of those who married aged between 40 and 44.[23] These findings are broadly comparable among populations with natural fertility across different cultures.[24] Thus, in addition to those who never

See Stone, *Crisis of the Aristocracy*, pp. 167–8. The Royal Commission on Population of 1944–9 (which was based upon the 1911 census data) estimated that involuntary sterility rendered 5 to 8% of British marriages childless in the early twentieth century, see Simon Szreter, *Fertility, Class and Gender in Britain, 1860–1940* (Cambridge, 1996), p. 555. In twentieth-century America, infertility rates affected around 10 to 13% of all married couples, see M. Marsh and W. Ronner, *The Empty Cradle: Infertility in America from Colonial Times to the Present* (Baltimore, 1996), pp. 1–2.

[20] J. Trussell and C. Wilson, 'Sterility in a population with natural fertility', *Population Studies* 39 (1985), 269–86. For discussion of the age and impact of the female menopause in this period see L. Botelho, 'Old age and menopause in rural women of early modern Suffolk', in L. Botelho and P. Thane (eds.), *Women and Ageing in British Society since 1500* (Harlow, 2001), pp. 43–65.

[21] See for example Ulla Larsen and Jane Menken, 'Individual-level sterility: A new method of estimation with application to sub-Saharan Africa', *Demography* 28, 2 (1991), 229–47.

[22] Joseph A. McFalls and Marguerite Harvey McFalls, *Disease and Fertility* (New York and London, 1984), pp. 59–62.

[23] Trussell and Wilson, 'Sterility', Table 8, p. 281. These statistics are drawn from one of the founders of historical demography, Louis Henry. Data quoted here do not take account of those who conceived in each cohort after five years of marriage, nor of those who never bore children.

[24] H. Hyrenius, 'Fertility and reproduction in a Swedish population group without family limitation', *Population Studies* 12, 2 (1958), 121–30; see also John C. Barrett, 'The estimation of natural sterility', *Genus* 17, 3–4 (1986), 27.

had children, many married couples in early modern England experienced childlessness as a 'life-stage' before the birth of their first child, especially those who married or remarried when the wife was in her mid- to late thirties or older. It is also important to take into consideration the fact that the single greatest factor (apart from late age at marriage) that limited population growth in early modern England was the high rate of non-marriage. This varied according to geographical location and social status, but of all English people born between 1575 and 1700, an estimated 13 to 27 per cent of the population never married.[25] This was especially notable among the gentry and nobility, where at the start of the eighteenth century some 15 to 20 per cent were destined never to marry, although some unmarried men fathered illegitimate children. If the never-married, and couples who had not conceived after at least five years of marriage, are considered together (especially those who married in later years) the experience of being without legitimate children was far from uncommon.

Demographic trends and economic opportunities or pressures undoubtedly frame social attitudes towards reproduction, although positing an exact causal relationship between these factors is problematic.[26] In certain contexts, there are particular pressures upon populations to marry young and produce a large number of children.[27] Factors such as war, subsistence crises, population mobility and settlement undoubtedly affect patterns of nuptial fertility. One such example is the settler society of early colonial America, where married couples were encouraged to produce large numbers of children, New England ministers preached against celibacy, and only 3 to 4 per cent of women never married.[28] By contrast, the English population sustained remarkably steady growth up until the last quarter of the eighteenth century, with only sporadic and localised subsistence crises altering the balance between birth and death rates.

---

[25] Froide, *Never Married*, p. 2.

[26] The complex causal factors at play influencing marriage decisions and birth rates are explored in E. A. Wrigley, 'Fertility strategy for the individual and the group', in C. Tilly (ed.), *Historical Studies of Changing Fertility* (Princeton, 1978), pp. 135–54; see also the series of essays by Wrigley in *People, Cities and Wealth: The Transformation of Traditional Society* (Oxford, 1987), *passim*.

[27] Historically, social attitudes provide an important context not only for the decision whether to marry and to whom, but on the timing of marriage and its likely impact upon family size. See, for example, D. Levine, *Family Formation in an Age of Nascent Capitalism* (New York, 1977), and *Reproducing Families: The Political Economy of English Population History* (Cambridge, 1987); J. R. Gillis, *For Better, For Worse: British Marriages, 1600 to the Present* (Oxford, 1985), pp. 123, 127–8.

[28] Erik R. Seeman, '"It is better to marry than to burn": Anglo-American attitudes towards celibacy, 1600–1800', *Journal of Family History* 24, 4 (1999), 397–419.

Alan Macfarlane contrasts the steady population growth of early modern England with modern developing countries such as India and those in sub-Saharan Africa, where the poor tend to marry young and produce large numbers of children.[29] In societies such as these, fertility is linked to both spiritual and economic success, male virility is celebrated, and infertility is highly stigmatised, indeed regarded as catastrophic.[30] However, Macfarlane argues that early modern England was a society in which barrenness was regarded as a misfortune rather than a disaster, a hypothesis that seems largely plausible in the light of evidence presented here.

Religion has traditionally framed prevailing attitudes towards marriage, sex and reproduction. The three monotheistic world religions have been remarkably consistent in stigmatising women for barrenness. In Judaism, Islam and pre-Reformation Catholicism, there was no difference in that the professed main aim of marriage was the procreation of children. Among Arab-speaking Jews living in the Mediterranean region during the high Middle Ages, for example, bigamy was practised if a marriage proved without issue for ten years, on the assumption of the wife's barrenness.[31] The Islamic law schools of the Umayyad empire permitted polygamy (which lessened the likelihood of childlessness for men capable of fathering children), although unilateral, male-initiated divorce continued to be permitted on the grounds of a wife's barrenness, and there was a strong oral tradition that a woman's duty was to bear her husband children.[32] Among Christians, across pre-Reformation Europe, barren women sought solace and a cure at shrines devoted to the Virgin Mary, St Rita and St Lucy.[33] The Reformation marked a shift in emphasis: celibacy was no longer privileged as the most desirable condition for God's ministers, but at the same time it was recognised that marriage for both clergy and lay people was not just about procreation. Protestant ministers in England still taught that having children was one of the primary ends of marriage, but the *Book of Common Prayer* also gave greater priority to companionship as a reason for marrying, and provided

---

[29] Alan Macfarlane, *Marriage and Love in England: Modes of Reproduction 1300–1840* (Oxford, 1986), pp. 51–5.

[30] Ibid., pp. 58–9.

[31] S. D. Goitein, *A Mediterranean Society: The Jewish Communities of the World as Portrayed in the Documents of the Cairo Geniza.* Vol. II: *The Family* (Berkeley, Los Angeles and London, 1978), p. 205.

[32] Leila Ahmed, *Women and Gender in Islam: Historical Roots of a Modern Debate* (New Haven and London, 1992), pp. 89–92.

[33] Olwen Hufton, 'What is religious history now?' in D. Cannadine (ed.), *What is History Now?* (New York and London, 2002), p. 70; J. Gélis, *History of Childbirth: Fertility, Pregnancy and Birth in Early Modern Europe*, trans. R. Morris (Cambridge, 1991), p. 17; B. J. Harris, *English Aristocratic Women, 1450–1550: Marriage and Family, Property and Careers* (Oxford, 2002), pp. 100–1.

a form of wording for a marriage ceremony where the wife was beyond childbearing age.[34] There is even some evidence that after the Reformation the English started to regard having a large number of children as a suspiciously 'Catholic' and irresponsible practice, especially poor law administrators who took a dim view of paupers marrying without the means of supporting their offspring.[35]

Changing attitudes towards the importance of children in marriage are evident not only among Protestant ministers but also in wider society from the sixteenth century onwards. It was a widely repeated maxim in early modern England that children were a providential blessing from God, an idea that was reinforced through the divine injunction in Genesis to procreate, the biblical precedent for regarding pregnancy as a mark of God's favour (which was apparently possible even in extreme old age), and Christ's blessing upon children, even though he himself was unmarried and childless.[36] In late sixteenth-century Puritan culture, some people may have regarded barrenness as a form of divine punishment, since Puritan providentialism emphasised the 'inexorability of supernatural justice', especially around the 'occult processes of conception and birth'.[37] This idea was encapsulated by one Jacobean author in *A Discourse of the Married and Single Life* (1621). One of the hazards for a man if he married was that his wife could prove to be barren, in which case 'the husband liues then in great discontent, esteeming himselfe to be in hatred with God and nature'. Though the emphasis here was upon a wife's inability to conceive, and the tone is satirical, the author implies that a childless man's reputation could be damaged among his peers, 'Whereby he shameth to accompany with men, as seeming himselfe to be lesse then a man'.[38]

---

[34] 'This prayer next folowyng shal be omitted where the woman is past chide birth', *Book of Common Prayer* (1559); 'This Prayer next following shall be omitted, where the Woman is past child-bearing' (1662 version); see also E. Leites, 'The duty to desire: Love, friendship and sexuality in some Puritan theories of marriage', *Journal of Social History* 15, 3 (1982), 383–408; Anthony Fletcher, 'The Protestant idea of marriage in early modern England', in A. Fletcher and P. Roberts (eds.), *Religion, Culture and Society in Early Modern Britain: Essays in Honour of Patrick Collinson* (Cambridge, 1994), pp. 161–81.

[35] Macfarlane, *Marriage and Love*, p. 57. See also Steve Hindle, 'The problem of pauper marriage in seventeenth-century England', *Transactions of the Royal Historical Society*, 6th ser., 8 (1998), 71–89.

[36] Gen. 2:28; Gen. 17:17 ('Shall *a child* be born unto him [Abraham] that is an hundred years old? And shall Sarah, that is ninety years old, bear?'); Luke 1:18, the birth of John the Baptist foretold ('And Zacharias said unto the angel, Whereby shall I know this? For I am an old man, and my wife well stricken in years'); Mark 10:14.

[37] Alexandra Walsham, *Providence in Early Modern England* (Oxford, 1999), pp. 77, 82, 96–7 and *passim*.

[38] Anon., *A Discourse of the Married and Single Life, Wherein, by Discovering the Misery of the One, is Plainely Declared the Felicity of the Other* (London, 1621), pp. 25–6.

By the eighteenth century, the providential interpretation of infertility had shifted, not least because the meaning of providence had changed. Many Anglicans now used providence as a form of solace, through which they reconciled themselves to misfortunes such as childlessness. '*Why was* Barrenness *counted a* greater Curse *in the* Levitical Law *than in the* present Age?' wrote one anonymous late seventeenth-century correspondent to a well-known London periodical.[39] He or she received the reply that either Jewish women laboured more easily because they lived in more temperate climates than England, or they experienced greater disappointment 'because the *Women* all expected to be the *Mother* of their *promised Messiah*'. For as much as this reference parroted spurious stereotypes about Jews, it also suggests contemporary reflection that general attitudes towards barrenness were not only culturally specific and variable, but relatively mild in their own day. Another popular text from this period, the *Ladies Dictionary* (1694), contains an account of Lycurgus, whose Spartan laws (readers were informed) decreed that those who remained '*unmarried* and *childless*' should be 'debarr'd from all sports, and forced to go naked in the Winter about the Market-place'.[40] Printed discussions of the stigma attached to barrenness in other times and places were thus in part a self-reflexive satire upon the relative tolerance afforded to individuals who contributed to the demonstrably high rate of non-marriage, nuptial postponement and sub-fecundity in the late-Stuart era.

The exception to this trend was among the highest tier of English society. There is no doubt that here the idea of blood kinship was an especially strong motivating force for having children, bringing legitimate continuation of a family name and honour. In families who could name their forbears for more than two preceding generations, a powerful rhetoric surrounded the idea of the continuation of a legitimate bloodline through marriage. As one anonymous author wrote, 'there are sacred Channels cut, in which one stream of blood perpetually runs, from one Generation to another'.[41] This idea was of utmost importance among the great families of England, and among these the notion of sustaining an unbroken royal bloodline was supreme. The problem of producing legitimate heirs had, of course, dogged hereditary monarchs for as long as the institution had existed. In the early modern period, marital childlessness generated dynastic problems for Mary Tudor, Charles II and William and Mary. The issue of succession was of course also critical during the reigns of

---

[39] *Athenian Gazette, or Casuistical Mercury*, 2, 27 (Aug. 1691).
[40] *The Ladies Dictionary. Being a General Entertainment for the Fair Sex* (London, 1694), p. 236.
[41] Anon., *An Account of Marriage, or the Interests of Marriage Considered and Defended against the Unjust Attacques of this Age* (London, 1672), p. 43.

Henry VIII and Queen Anne due to high infant mortality, and that of the never-married Elizabeth I. At the time of his marriage to Katherine of Aragon, Henry VIII believed that his inability to father a male child who survived beyond infancy was a divine judgement upon him for marrying his dead brother's wife (thus breaking Levitical proscription), and considered himself childless even though he had fathered a daughter, Mary, and an illegitimate son.[42] Charles II, who demonstrably *could* father children, but refused to countenance making one of his bastard sons his legitimate heir, was the subject of pamphlets circulated in Restoration England, which debated in particular whether the king could legitimately divorce his barren wife, Catherine of Braganza.[43] Problems with marital fertility could thus have implications for the entire nation, and were enshrined in a rhetoric of potency and impotence that recognised the political character of sexual performance and its reproductive consequences among the ruling elite.[44]

Beyond the ruling household and its court, the economic and political significance of men's dynastic duties was rather different, although evidence from popular culture suggests that men of even modest social status could be subject to ridicule from their friends, neighbours and family if they did not father children in marriage. In ballad literature there is the recurrent theme of the newlywed scolding bride who chastises her husband for his lack of sexual potency. The young bride in one merry book, *The Ten Pleasures of Marriage* (1682), complains to her husband about her barrenness and blames him for her failure to conceive, 'oftentimes calling him a Fumbler, a dry-boots, and a good man Dolittle, &c.'.[45] The refrain of 'The Young Woman's Complaint', a seventeenth-century ballad advising maids to spurn elderly suitors, was '*What shall a young woman do with an Old Man?*' Senile husbands, the ballad warns, will 'scratch and grumble' at night instead of showing a young woman 'Love's blisses' in bed. The wife in this scenario laments, 'with him I must never expect any

---

[42] J. J. Scarisbrick, *Henry VIII* (2nd edn, New Haven and London, 1997); E. Ives, *Anne Boleyn* (Oxford, 1986). Our thanks to Mary Robertson for this point.

[43] See for example William Lawrence, *Two Great Questions Determined by the Principles of Reason and Divinity* (1681).

[44] The study of the connections between family life and high politics remains relatively unexplored. See Elaine Chalus, *Elite Women in English Political Life, c.1754–1790* (Oxford, 2005); Judith S. Lewis, *Sacred to Female Patriotism: Gender, Class, and Politics in Late Georgian Britain* (New York and London, 2003); Rachel Weil, *Political Passions: Gender, the Family and Political Argument in England 1680–1714* (Manchester, 1999); Kathleen Wilson, 'The good, the bad, and the impotent: Imperialism and the politics of identity in Georgian England', in A. Bermingham and J. Brewer (eds.), *The Consumption of Culture, 1600–1800: Image, Object, Text* (London, 1995), pp. 239–62.

[45] A. Marsh, *The Ten Pleasures of Marriage Relating All the Delights and Contentments that are Mask'd Under the Bands of Matrimony* (1682), p. 79.

joy;/ [but] Which vexes me worse, I shall ne'r have a boy'.[46] In a similar scenario, a 'married maid' whose elderly husband gives her sugar plums but no sexual satisfaction, laments, 'I wish'd that [I'd wed] as my neighbours have done;/ to get [joy from] a delicate daughter or son.'[47] There was also the sinister suspicion that, wherever women gathered together, whether at the local market, laundry or childbirthing room, they compared notes about their husbands' performance (or lack of it) in bed.[48] In *The Ten Pleasures of Marriage* the childless wife goes 'a prattling by her Neighbours', Mistress Breedwell and Mistress Wanton, discussing 'most shamlesly . . . what hath passed between her and her husband, twixt the [bed]curtains'.[49] The 'Complaining Maid' feels excluded from the all-female circle of mothers, and laments, 'I long to enjoy the sweet gossiping crew.'[50] Court records that provide incidental references to women's everyday conversations suggest that talk about men's sexual prowess was indeed one among many themes discussed between women, although the frequency with which this was represented in popular culture may have fuelled a disproportionate amount of concern among childless men that their private lives were under female scrutiny.[51]

Overall, beyond the exclusive circles of the royalty and nobility, prevailing social, moral and religious attitudes suggested that having children in early modern England was regarded as desirable in moderation. Certainly, in the popular satirical literature of the time, those who sought to avoid having children by not having sex within marriage or using '*Means physical or diabolical, to prevent Conception*' were regarded as perverse: 'for a Man or Woman to marry, and then say, they desire to have no Children, that is a Piece of preposterous Nonsense, next to Lunacy'.[52] There was considerable stigma directed against *deliberately* avoiding conception, encapsulated in literature that railed against the 'sterile' effects of male masturbation and *coitus interruptus*. Though some couples may have avoided having children through voluntary sexual abstinence, this was strongly opposed by the prevailing idea that procreation was one of the main aims of marriage. Pressure from the customary expectations

---

[46] 'The Young Woman's Complaint; or, A Caveat to all Maids to Have Care How They be Married to Old Men', in J. W. Ebsworth (ed.), *The Roxburghe Ballads* (London, 1883–99), vol. VIII, part III, pp. 679–81.

[47] 'The Complaining Maid', in Ebsworth (ed.), *Roxburghe Ballads*, vol. VIII, part I–II, p. 199.

[48] Bernard Capp, *When Gossips Meet: Women, Family and Neighbourhood in Early Modern England* (Oxford, 2003), pp. 63–4 and *passim*.

[49] Marsh, *Ten Pleasures of Marriage*, pp. 76–7.   [50] 'Complaining Maid', p. 199.

[51] Laura Gowing, *Domestic Dangers: Women, Words and Sex in Early Modern London* (Oxford, 1996), esp. chs. 3 and 4.

[52] Daniel Defoe, *Conjugal Lewdness, or Matrimonial Whoredom* (London, 1727), pp. 123, 130.

of the wider community should not be underestimated, as recorded in ballads such as 'The Discontented Bride', which ridiculed the figure of Will the Baker who 'sow'd himself up in a Blanket every Night going to Bed, for fear of Enlarging his family'.[53] Fatherhood avoided the threat of stigma, and even promised men a form of immortality; as Sir Francis Bacon famously observed, children may 'increase the cares of life, but they mitigate the remembrance of death'.[54] Fewer people believed by the eighteenth century that barrenness was a mark of divine displeasure, although this did not mean that it was not potentially a source of personal disappointment and frustrated hope for both parties in a childless marriage.

One unfortunate side-effect of the modern preoccupation with sexuality and sexual identity has been a tendency to disassociate reproduction from the erotic sensibilities and sexual experiences of early modern men and women.[55] This trend has only recently begun to be revised. As research by Karen Harvey has shown, contrary to a modern focus upon sexual pleasure without reproductive consequences, in the eighteenth century a sexy body was a fertile body, evidenced by erotica that was 'deeply concerned with reproduction'.[56] Indeed, the early modern period saw a proliferation of printed literature that offered advice to couples about how to conceive.[57] Midwives' manuals contained substantial sections detailing how fertility could be enhanced, and childlessness remedied, and it is to these influential sources of advice that we now turn our attention.

Men could be held responsible for infertility in four ways. The first, which could be detected most easily, was impotence. The inability to achieve an erection, or 'absolute impotency', was defined by medical writers as 'a total incapacity of fruition', which was 'manifest of itself'.[58]

---

[53] 'The Discontented Bride', in W. G. Day (ed.), *The Pepys Ballads*, vol. IV (Cambridge, 1987), p. 119.

[54] Patricia Crawford, *Blood, Bodies and Families in Early Modern England* (Harlow, 2004), p. 115; Bacon quoted in Macfarlane, *Marriage and Love*, p. 56.

[55] See for example Thomas A. Foster, 'Deficient husbands: Manhood, sexual incapacity, and male sexuality in seventeenth-century New England', *William and Mary Quarterly* 56, 4 (1999), 723–44.

[56] Karen Harvey, *Reading Sex in the Eighteenth Century: Bodies and Gender in English Erotic Culture* (Cambridge, 2004), p. 97. See also pp. 111–16, 134–5, 139.

[57] The most widely read sex manual of the period, *Aristotle's Masterpiece*, first published in 1684, was primarily concerned with reproduction; see R. Porter, '"The secrets of generation display'd": *Aristotle's Master-piece* in Eighteenth-Century England', in R. P. Maccubin (ed.), *'Tis Nature's Fault: Unauthorised Sexuality during the Enlightenment* (Cambridge, 1987), pp. 1–21.

[58] *A Practical Discourse on Barrenness in Women, and Impotency, Infertility, and Seminal Weakness in Men* (London, 1739), p. 60.

There is no doubt that this was the most commonly understood male cause of infertility. It received the greatest attention in popular literature, and because it could prevent the consumption of a marriage as well as the procreation of children, proof of impotence was a legal ground for the annulment of marriage. The second cause of infertility was related to 'absolute impotence'. This was the belief that a man's penis could be in some way 'deficient', so that penetration could not follow from erection. 'Many diseases are incident to the Yard,' thought Jane Sharp, the author of an influential seventeenth-century guide for midwives, but it was the ravages of venereal disease that could be most damaging to the penis.[59] Unusual size could also lead to deficiency. Sharp believed that 'some men, but chiefly fools, have yards so long that they are useless for generation', but a penis that was 'too diminutive' was also problematic. This would have too little 'proper force to eject the seed', and would lack the 'capacity to fill the pudenda in such manner as it should be'.[60] Fat men were thought more likely to be hampered by small sexual organs, but environment and climate were also believed to play a part. A penis that was longer than seven inches, and thicker than four, was 'unwieldy', explained the Frenchman Nicholas Venette, 'for which reason the inhabitants of the southern countries are not so proper for generation as we'.[61]

It is easy to see why such beliefs would provoke both anxious self-examination and bawdy humour among men, but ideas about how men's bodies could be responsible for childlessness were not limited to these phallocentric causes: the third commonly understood cause of infertility in men was an inability to produce semen, or 'seed,' of sufficient quantity and quality. As Jacob Rueff put it in 1637, 'We say, that sterility or barrenness . . . is not only a disability and unaptness of bringing forth children in women . . . but in men also of ingendering and sending forth fruitful seed', anticipating Thomas Laqueur's famous dictum: 'Having a penis does not make the man.'[62] Possession of functioning testicles as well as a penis earned men their sexual identity. 'Take away a man's stones and he is no more the same man, but grows cold of constitution though he were never so hot before . . . also their voice grows shrill and feminine, and their manners and dispositions are commonly naught,' thought Sharp,

[59] J. Sharp, *The Midwives Book: Or The Whole Art of Midwifry Discovered* (London, 1671), ed. E. Hobby (Oxford, 1999), p. 25; and G. Archibald Douglas, *The Nature and Causes of Impotence in Men, and Barrenness in Women* (6th edn, London, 1772), pp. 18–19.

[60] Sharp, *The Midwives Book*, p. 25; Nicholas Venette, *Conjugal Love; Or, The Pleasures of the Marriage Bed* (London, 1750), p. 52; and A. Eccles, *Obstetrics and Gynaecology in Tudor and Stuart England* (London, 1982), p. 36.

[61] McLaren, *Reproductive Rituals*, p. 44; Venette, *Conjugal Love*, p. 67.

[62] J. Rueff, *The Expert Midwife* (London, 1637), pp. 11–12; T. Laqueur, *Making Sex: Body and Gender from the Greeks to Freud* (Cambridge, Mass., 1990), pp. 25, 115.

following the Hippocratic tradition that 'the stones are the strength and vigour of manhood'.[63]

Men needed to do all they could to preserve their supplies of seed. Too much pre-marital sex with 'mercenary harlots' was thought to deprive young men of the possibility of children when they married.[64] Similarly, on his wedding night, the bridegroom was advised to 'be careful that he does not spend his stock too lavishly', since men who engaged in too frequent love-making were thought to 'weaken and enervate themselves to that degree, [that] their seed becomes barren, and their privy parts refuse to obey them'.[65] It was also understood that old age affected men's fertility. Beyond the age of fifty-five 'the heat of procreating matter . . . begins to flag', leaving 'the seed by little and little being extinguished, and the humours dried up'. Thus, the way in which men could contribute to infertility was thought to vary over the life-cycle.[66] Ideas about semen were also shaped by changing anxieties about male sexuality. Hence in the eighteenth century, it was thought a man's supply of seed could be irreversibly depleted if he had engaged in 'the heinous sin of self-pollution', or masturbation. Such men had their 'blood and spirits impair'd, and the seed render'd infertile, so as to make them unfit for procreation', so that, in the unlikely event of their having children, they would be 'weakly little ones, that either die soon, or become tender, sickly people'.[67]

It was thought that seminal fluid needed to be 'substantial, entire, and glutinous', and 'sufficiently spirituous' to ensure conception.[68] However, as one eighteenth-century physician recognised, although 'absolute impotence' was easily discerned, detecting whether a man's 'liquor' was 'proper' for procreation was 'remote and difficult to be proved'.[69] Early modern people knew that it was the quality as well the quantity of semen that was important, but without modern technology they had no satisfactory means of testing it. 'This is one of those cases in which the cause being remote, the defect is usually laid upon the woman; while it is really in the man,' sympathised one male author.[70]

If the third way in which a man could contribute to infertility was difficult to prove, the fourth was even more so. For conception to occur,

---

[63] Sharp, *The Midwives Book*, pp. 70–1.   [64] Venette, *Conjugal Love*, pp. 84–5.

[65] *Aristotle's Compleat Masterpiece*, (23rd edn, London, 1749), p. 39; Venette, *Conjugal Love*, p. 101.

[66] *Aristotle's Master-Piece: Or, the Secrets of Generation* (London, 1694), p. 4.

[67] *Onania; Or, the Heinous Sin of Self-Pollution* (6th edn, London, 1722), pp. 15–16; John Hunter attracted controversy when he denied that there was a link between masturbation and impotence, in *A Treatise on the Venereal Disease* (London, 1786), p. 200.

[68] Venette, *Conjugal Love*, p. 52; *A Practical Discourse*, p. 63.

[69] Archibald Douglas, *The Nature and Causes of Impotence*, pp. 14–15.

[70] Ibid., pp. 14–15, 17, 18.

it was believed that the compatibility of the man and woman was all-important. Practitioners such as Sharp promoted the idea that emotional or sexual compatibility played a role in conception, so the cause of barrenness could be a 'want of love in man and wife'.[71] 'If their hearts be not united in love, how should their seed unite to cause conception?' asked Nicholas Culpeper.[72] It was essential if a couple wanted children that they banished all worries and cares, for the common saying was that 'love and laughter beget children'.[73] Most crucially, husbands had a duty to ensure that their wives were contented, for such was the power of women's imaginations that unhappiness 'oftentimes kills the fruit in the very bud'.[74] The popular belief that much depended on mind, as well as body, at the moment of conception continued well into the eighteenth century, as illustrated famously in the opening lines of *Tristram Shandy*.[75] 'Want of warm desire in the mind', wrote one physician, 'gives not, but as it were refuses, a suitable reception to the effluvia of the male semen, and so absolutely prevents conception'.[76] Although medical theorists came to reject the idea that for conception to occur a woman as well as a man had to produce seed during an orgasm, female sexual pleasure remained important. It was even argued that a woman would know if she had conceived 'as soon as the man ejects his seed, from the extraordinary pleasure she receives during the action'.[77] One physician postulated that 'If the wife shall receive a great contentment in the company of her husband', then it was a sure sign that she was pregnant.[78]

While there were recipes 'to increase lust, and to help conception', it was men's sexual techniques that were portrayed as central to their ability to give women pleasure, and so maximise their chances of having children. Men were warned against being over-hasty in their love-making, because this would mean that a woman would be insufficiently aroused and so

---

[71] Sharp, *The Midwives Book*, p. 79; see also *Aristotle's Master-Piece*, pp. 175–6.

[72] N. Culpeper, *A Directory for Midwives* (London, 1656), p. 70; Sharp, *The Midwives Book*, pp. 79–80; and *Aristotle's Compleat Masterpiece*, p. 50. Following the same logic, it was thought impossible for a conception to follow rape.

[73] *A Practical Discourse*, p. 57; see also Rueff, *The Expert Midwife*, pp. 38–42; *The Compleat Midwife's Practice Enlarged* (3rd edn, London, 1663), p. 220; and *Aristotle's Master-Piece*, pp. 176–7.

[74] Culpeper, *A Directory for Midwives*, pp. 93–4.

[75] The eponymous narrator laments: 'I wish either my father or my mother, or indeed both of them, as they were in duty both equally bound to it, had minded what they were about when they begot me', for their disposition shaped 'the happy formation and temperature of his body, perhaps his genius and the very cast of his mind'. Laurence Sterne, *The Life and Opinions of Tristram Shandy* (1759), p. 1.

[76] *A Practical Discourse*, p. 51.   [77] Venette, *Conjugal Love*, pp. 62–3.

[78] William Sermon, *The Ladies Companion, Or the English Midwife* (London, 1671), p. 19.

'not prepared to receive the seed with that delight which she ought'.[79] Similarly, men were advised that after they had ejaculated 'all is not done', for to withdraw from a woman too quickly would allow a rapid insertion of air, and more importantly give inadequate time for the woman's body to respond to impregnation.[80] Sexual positioning could also be a factor, since 'the laws of nature' determined that a man should be on top if their union was to be fertile.[81] Thus it was men's actions and behaviour that mattered most in baby-making. Men who only sought their own sexual pleasure, or who were clumsy and ejaculated prematurely, would never become fathers.

Medical theories about conception altered over this period, with discoveries of the fallopian tubes, ovaries and spermatozoa raising doubts over older humoral and 'two-seed' theories. One remarkable continuity, however, was the widespread acknowledgement that sexually functioning adult men could be infertile, as evidenced in the documentation of certain early modern fertility tests for men as well as women. 'The best experiment that ever I could find', wrote Sharp, was for man and wife to pass urine on some corn; whichever 'grows first is the most fruitful, and so is the person whose urine was the cause of it'.[82] Even those who advocated tests such as these were aware of their varying reliability, however, and so doubts could remain about a man's reproductive capabilities if a marriage continued without issue.

Much research on early modern masculinity has emphasised the importance of physical and sexual self-control to ideals of manhood, but childlessness raised the possibility of problems with the male body that men could believe they were unable to control.[83] The idea that men's imagination could be a cause of, and offer a cure for, their impotence was present in sixteenth-century texts, hence paternal as well as maternal imagination was thought to have a role in reproduction.[84] Within this mental world, the sedate academic could find his lifestyle disadvantageous if he wanted to have children. 'Those who constantly study and think too intensely',

[79] *Aristotle's Compleat Masterpiece*, p. 56.
[80] *Aristotle's Master-Piece*, p. 177; and Archibald Douglas, *The Nature and Causes of Impotence*, pp. 21–2.
[81] Venette, *Conjugal Love*, pp. 176–81.
[82] Sharp, *The Midwives Book*, pp. 127–8. For other tests, see *The Complete Midwife's Practice*, pp. 254–5; F. Mauriceau, *The Accomplisht Midwife, Treating of the Diseases of Women with Child, and in Child-Bed*, trans. H. Chamberlen (London, 1673), p. 5; *Aristotle's Master-Piece*, pp. 174–5.
[83] See for example Lyndal Roper, *Oedipus and the Devil: Witchcraft, Sexuality and Religion in Early Modern Europe* (London, 1994), ch. 5; and Fletcher, *Gender, Sex and Subordination*, Part II.
[84] M. de Montaigne, 'Of the power of the imagination' (1572–4), in *The Complete Works of Montaigne*, trans. D. M. Frame (Stanford, 1958), pp. 68–76.

it was argued, 'may reasonably suspect' that this was a cause of 'their not having children', since their constitutions would be overwhelmed with cold and moist humours.[85] These ideas were adapted to keep pace with changing modes of living at the end of the seventeenth century. John Graunt, in his commentary upon the *Bills of Mortality* (1662), speculated that it was because 'the minds of men in *London* are more thoughtfull and full of business then in the Country' that they had fewer children than their rural counterparts. Among country men, Graunt thought, hard physical labours 'promote Breedings', whereas for city men '*Anxieties* of the minde hinder it'.[86] Whereas urban myth held that it was a lack of physical exertion and the consumption of luxuries that rendered city women less fertile than more active and robust country women, it was the mental stress of city life that could harm men.[87] 'Fast living', especially in London, sapped men of all their strength so that their seed would never be 'sufficiently spirituous' to produce children. By the eighteenth century, increasing importance was laid upon what would now be called the psychological dimensions of male sexuality. The surgeon John Hunter wrote 'of impotence depending on the mind', which he argued could be cured by being 'perfectly confident of the powers of the body'.[88] Thus it was increasingly understood that men's mental and physical health were deeply connected, and that this had implications for their sexual and reproductive capabilities.

Medical texts documenting cures for infertility provide insights into prescriptive advice, but it is necessary to look elsewhere in order to find first-hand accounts by childless men of their experiences. Samuel Pepys's diary provides one of the few traceable links between the cures for barrenness found in midwifery manuals and the similar types of oral advice given to childless couples. Pepys recorded how he got drunk one afternoon with some gossips who had attended the birth of a friend's son, and took the opportunity to ask their opinions 'of my not getting of children', perhaps because he was the only man present.[89] The women obliged him 'freely

---

[85] *A Practical Discourse*, pp. 44, 63–4.

[86] John Graunt, *Natural and Political Observations . . . upon the Bills of Mortality* (1662), ch. VII, pp. 45–6. Particular thanks to Jeremy Boulton for this reference.

[87] Culpeper, *A Dictionary for Midwives*, pp. 91–2; *Aristotle's Compleat Masterpiece*, p. 42; Lisa Forman Cody, *Birthing the Nation: Sex, Science, and the Conception of Eighteenth-Century Britons* (Oxford, 2005), p. 8, footnote 13.

[88] Hunter, *Treatise on the Venereal Disease*, pp. 201–4; it was Hunter who in 1776 conducted the first ever successful attempt at human artificial insemination, but the procedure was so controversial that the results were not published until after his death, see W. Moore, *The Knife Man* (London, 2005), p. 204.

[89] Pepys, *Diary*, vol. V, p. 222 (26 July 1664).

and merrily' with their advice, which concerned three areas in particular; the timing and positioning of intercourse, diet, and clothing. Pepys noted he should not 'hug my wife too hard nor too much', and have sex 'when we have most mind to it', but especially on certain specified days of the month; that he should 'Eat no late suppers' and drink 'Mum and sugar' and 'Juyce of sage'. His wife was advised 'not to go too straight-laced' and he was told to 'Wear cool Holland-drawers'. The gossips also placed 'especial' importance on lying upside-down in bed, or at least raising the feet to above head-height. Pepys's lack of compunction about raising the issue of his childlessness with this tipsy crew of mature and experienced women is striking, although, having put himself at their mercy, he tried to regain some of his dignity with the rather superior observation, 'Very merry all, as much as I could be in such sorry company.'[90] The absence of recorded consultations about infertility in midwifery case books suggests that few sober men would have consulted a midwife or man-midwife for advice about this matter.[91] Even allowing for under-recording, there is evidence that men (if they could afford it) preferred to consult surgeons or physicians in reproductive matters, rather than midwives. This may have been because male medical practitioners enjoyed higher social prestige, but it could also have been easier for men to consult someone of their own sex about such a personal subject. Hence, Robert Allison, who faced an annulment suit for impotence in 1727, was said to have 'applied to several surgeons' for a cure, and Hugo Colley had visited a physician in Chester, accompanied, interestingly, by his wife, complaining of 'a weakness in his genital parts'. Hugo was prescribed 'some strengthening and provocative medicines' after he declared to the physician that 'in case he could get his wife with child, it would make everything easy'.[92]

The lack of effective medical solutions for infertility meant that many men, like Pepys, experimented with a variety of methods to boost their chances of having a child. Changes to diet were popular and easy to adopt. Since 'fulness of seed and plenty of wind' was thought necessary to achieve an erection, men were encouraged to eat plenty of food that would make them flatulent, including pulses, beans and peas.[93] Other

---

[90] Ibid.

[91] See, for example, S. Stone, *A Complete Practice of Midwifery. Consisting of Upwards of Forty Cases* (London, 1737); Wellcome Library, London MS 3820 'Richard Paxton's Case Book' (1753–87); W. Perfect, *Cases in Midwifery* (Rochester, 1781); J. Lane, 'A provincial surgeon and his obstetric practice: Thomas W. Jones of Henley-in-Arden, 1764–1846', *Medical History* 31 (1987), 333–48.

[92] London Metropolitan Archive (hereafter LMA), London Consistory Court (hereafter DL/C) 162 (1727), fols. 361v–362r; and LMA, DL/C/259 (1719/20), fol. 107.

[93] Sharp, *The Midwives Book*, p. 30; McLaren, *Reproductive Rituals*, pp. 35–8.

husbands concentrated their efforts upon eating foods that were known to be aphrodisiacs. Charles Schutz, for example, tried to comfort his new wife after he failed to consummate their marriage on their wedding night, by telling her that 'he hoped he should be better by eating of jellies and oysters'.[94] In addition, men and women could carry loadstones, the magnetic qualities of which were believed to promote marital harmony as well as fertility.[95] For the affluent, the spas at Bath and Tunbridge Wells were thought beneficial. It was not just the 'air and waters' of these locations that helped childless couples, but also the 'mirth and good humour that reigns at those celebrated places'. The result was just the right kind of positive mental as well as physical environment that was conducive to baby-making.[96]

The desire to have children also led couples to explore less conventional cures. Some popular medical lore was repeated in medical texts. Nicholas Culpeper, for example, wrote that he 'had heard' that a man could cure barrenness by 'making water through his wives wedding-ring'.[97] That infertility could have a magical cause was accepted in most early to mid seventeenth-century medical texts but firmly rejected by the century's end, when the writer of *Aristotle's Master Piece* disparaged such views as 'frivolous and vain'.[98] While witchcraft remained a popular and convenient explanation for childlessness, it was not one that was readily pursued or recorded by the English courts. Both men and women who were tried for witchcraft in England could be accused of causing harm to babies and children, and their cases could centre upon anxieties about bad parenting, but (unlike elsewhere in Europe) the crime of the English witch was not that she or he had prevented children being conceived in the first place.[99]

Popular healing magic offered a number of ways for couples to overcome childlessness. Trees were powerful symbols of fertility that were thought to produce strength and vitality, and couples were advised to make love in woodland, or dance around maypoles. Certain stones, found

---

[94] LMA, DL/C/278 (1771), fol. 134r.

[95] See, for example, Culpeper, *A Directory for Midwives*, pp. 90, 97; *Aristotle's Compleat Masterpiece*, p. 44.

[96] *A Practical Discourse*, p. 57.   [97] Culpeper, *A Directory for Midwives*, p. 90.

[98] For acceptance that magic could be a cause see, for example, Rueff, *The Expert Midwife*, p. 16; *The Compleat Midwife's Practice*, p. 220; Sharp, *The Midwives Book*, p. 81; for rejection, see *Aristotle's Master-piece*, p. 80.

[99] For the similarity of charges made against English male and female witches, see M. Gaskill, 'The devil in the shape of a man: Witchcraft, conflict and belief in Jacobean England', *Historical Research* 71, 175 (1998), 142–71. Trials of continental witches could, by contrast, focus upon anxieties about impotence and infertility. See Roper, *Oedipus and the Devil*, pp. 125, 136–8, 188, 208.

throughout Britain, were thought to have magical qualities, such as the 'Holed Stone' and 'Crick Stone' in Cornwall, on which a woman who wanted children was encouraged to sit or lie.[100] Visitors to the Tower of London at the end of the seventeenth century were encouraged to stick a pin in the display of Henry VIII's codpiece, which was believed to be an aid to conception.[101] The commercialisation of medicine only multiplied the number of reputed cures for infertility, many of which were advertised in eighteenth-century newspapers. The most sensational product in this market-place was offered in the 1770s by the infamous quack Dr James Graham, who for fifty pounds a night hired out 'The Celestial Bed', complete with an electrical mattress.[102]

Evidence from court records indicates that men may have been willing to go to these lengths to find a cure for infertility since some suffered humiliation if they were publicly exposed as unable to father children. A common theme of popular literature was the husband who failed to perform, but ballads could also be based on the real-life stories of marriages struggling with the problems of infertility. Stephen Seagar, a London joiner, had no children with his wife, Grace, after six years of marriage, when rumours began to circulate in 1669 that Grace had committed adultery with his apprentice, Tarrant Reeves. Several mocking ballads were composed about the pair, and a man was seen holding up a pair of ram's horns, the symbol of a cuckold, outside the Seagar household. Most humiliating of all was the discovery that Grace was pregnant, and the suspicion that it was Tarrant who was the father. When Tarrant was questioned about the affair, he did not deny having sex with Grace, but claimed to have slept with her only once. A fellow apprentice declared of Tarrant that 'he was a good workman to get her with child by lying but once with her . . . and the said Tarrant laughed thereat'.[103]

Like the fictional character of a seventeenth-century ballad, 'The West-country Wonder', who managed to get a sixty-seven-year-old widow pregnant in a single attempt, Tarrant proved himself a 'proper' man by the potency of his seed.[104] 'Proper' men were those who got their wives pregnant soon after marriage, and with little apparent effort. The assessment of who were 'proper' men could be made by other men, who did not

[100] D. Buchan (ed.), *Folk Tradition and Folk Medicine in Scotland: The Writings of David Rorie* (Edinburgh, 1994), pp. 65, 67–8; and Gélis, *History of Childbirth*, pp. 27–9.

[101] Capp, *When Gossips Meet*, p. 365.

[102] J. Peakman, *Lascivious Bodies: A Sexual History of the Eighteenth Century* (London, 2004), p. 265.

[103] Lambeth Palace Library (hereafter LPL), Court of Arches (hereafter CA), Case 8136 (1669), Ee3, fols. 605r, 606v, 613v; Eee4, fol. 6r.

[104] 'The West-country Wonder', in *The Euing Collection of Broadside Ballads*, introduction by J. Holloway (Glasgow, 1971), p. 644.

hesitate to discuss the sex lives of married couples, even when they did not know them personally. Hence when George Jackson, a York uphol-sterer, installed a new bed for a married couple, the Tiremans, 'he advised the said Mr Tireman to get his wife with an heir in the said bed'. The very next morning, George enraged Samuel Tireman by saying that he had heard that 'his wife was with child'. Samuel's angry response, that if his wife was pregnant 'it was with a bastard and not of his getting', betrayed his impotence.[105]

Without children, a married man's honour, reputation and credit were open to question. An impotent man was portrayed in medical texts as one who did not have the social skills to earn him the respect of others. Men with bodies that lacked potent heat were thought weak and ineffectual outside the bedroom as well as within it. Without the ability to control their sexual bodies, their management of undesirable emotions was also at risk. Impotent men were believed to be more likely to show anger and pick fights with others.[106] With no children to prove their potency, it could even be suggested that childless men would make inept politicians. Candidates who stood for political office laid their personal lives open to scrutiny and comment, a trend which accelerated during the course of the eighteenth century through the proliferation of popular election literature and newsprint. Lord Parker, for example, who stood as MP for Oxfordshire in 1754, was lampooned for being childless.[107] In the contested election for County Down in 1805, an address in verse to local freeholders undermined the credit of one of the candidates, the foreign secretary Lord Castlereagh, by drawing attention to his childless marriage and thus, it was implied, his impotence:

> There is only one virtue I see in this peer,
> A bounty from heaven, this country to cheer;
> His vices must cease, when his sun it has set,
> For 'tis not in his breeches, a son to beget.[108]

Generally, 'impotent' was a label attached to those who were economi-cally dependant. When applied to men, the term 'impotent' linked sexual

---

[105] Borthwick Institute of Historical Research, York (hereafter Borthwick), Consistory Court Cause Papers (hereafter CPI)/169 (1702–3).

[106] Foster, 'Deficient husbands', 731–2.

[107] Elaine Chalus, 'Kisses for votes: The kiss and corruption in eighteenth-century English elections', in Karen Harvey (ed.), *The Kiss in History* (Manchester, 2005), pp. 122–47 has highlighted the lack of research that has been done on the gendered rhetoric of election literature; see n. 50.

[108] Quoted in Judith S. Lewis, '1784 and all that: Aristocratic women and electoral politics', in Amanda Vickery (ed.), *Women, Privilege and Power: British Politics, 1750 to the Present* (Stanford, 2001), p. 91.

and economic incapacity, sometimes to devastating effect. In the viciously personal *New Athenian Comedy* (1693), for example, Elkanah Settle publicly attacked the childless marriage of the publisher and bookseller John Dunton. The play contains a thinly disguised character representing Dunton, who suffers 'Curtain Lectures for non-performance at home' from his wife. Using a metaphor that befitted the experiences of the middling sort in late-Stuart London, Settle suggested that Dunton was debarred from participating in the economy of family life as surely as a debtor was excluded from the stock exchange: 'a Childless Citizen looks so Bankrupt like, so forlorn a wretch, that poor trader in Love, as if he had neither City stock of his own, nor Court credit to supply him'.[109] The stereotypical idea, expressed in this as in so many other popular literary forms, was that unless a man could make his wife pregnant she would cuckold him with another man who had more 'corne' in his 'bushell'.[110]

Historians have shown how in practice men's creditworthiness could depend upon their status as householders or married men, but this has neglected the importance of fatherhood as another milestone of financial status.[111] When Samuel Tireman bought a watch in early eighteenth-century York, the agreement was that he was 'to pay for it at the day of the birth of his first child or the day of his death'. Here credit relations operated between men on the assumption that fatherhood would follow marriage, as surely as death would end life. Given Samuel's impotence, no wonder 'he seemed very well pleased' and 'as tho'' he had got a very good bargain'.[112] For the propertied, the honour of the family as well as the individual was at stake. It was the eldest son's duty to preserve his family's financial worth and security by producing an heir. If he failed in this duty, other siblings seem to have felt no compunction about openly discussing how sexual incapacity would affect the future distribution of family estate. The younger brother of Edward Weld, for example, was overheard boasting in London society that although Edward was due to marry, 'that would signify nothing', for knowing that his older brother was impotent gave him confidence that 'he should be heir to the estate'.[113]

Compensation for sexual incapacity could even be expressed in financial terms between husbands and wives. Informing his wife Jane that he was impotent, Robert Allison promised 'to make it up to her some other way for if he had or was worth £1,000 he would not give one shilling from

[109] Elkanah Settle, *The New Athenian Comedy* (1693), Act II, p. 16.   [110] Ibid.
[111] See Alexandra Shepard, 'Manhood, credit and patriarchy in early modern England c.1580–1640', *Past and Present* 167 (2000), 82–6.
[112] Borthwick, CP I/169 (1702–3).   [113] LPL, CA, Case 9764 (1730), Eee13, fol. 248r.

her'. Her response was significant: she claimed that it was because Robert had made them both bankrupt that she had brought the annulment case. She declared that she 'would never have published' his impotence 'if he had not robbed her of all that she was worth', for 'she had never heard of his base character till after she was married to him'. It was marriage that revealed Robert's 'base character' because it was only then that his sexual and financial skills were put to the test. Jane's discovery that her husband failed on both counts showed that in all ways he was fully 'spent'.[114]

Annulment cases can also give us insights into the personal costs of impotence for men. Charles Schutz, 'in a sighing sobbing tone of voice', told his wife of 'his sorrow' at his 'inability to perform' on their wedding night in March 1770.[115] When Jane Allison talked to her husband about his impotence, 'he sat down and cried and called [her] beast to upbraid him with what he could not help'.[116] The lack of heat in an impotent man's body was sometimes used metaphorically to describe cases where there was a want of emotional warmth in marriage: several impotent husbands were described as behaving in a 'cold and indifferent' manner towards their wives.[117] Husbands sometimes admitted that their sexual difficulties could be 'the cause of a great deal of uneasiness' in their marriages.[118]

Only a very small number of childless marriages ever reached the stage of legal proceedings, in part because annulment was only possible on the grounds of non-consummation through impotence or frigidity, not childlessness *per se*. Annulment cases suggest how marriages that experienced sexual difficulties and faced little prospect of bearing children were more broadly understood. There is little doubt, however, that there were many other childless marriages that were both sexually active and emotionally fulfilling. Clearly, happy marriages could be childless ones, and men who were not fathers were not necessarily disadvantaged in their career ambitions.[119] A childless thirty-nine-year marriage, for example, did not hinder the success of the man-midwife William Smellie (1697–1763). Indeed, members of the College of Physicians were more likely to marry later, or not at all, and were more often childless than the rest of the population. For these men, a lack of children seems to have been the intended

---

[114] LMA, DL/C/162 (1727), fol. 362r; DL/C/265 (1728), fols. 17v–18r.
[115] LMA, DL/C/176 (1771), fol. 229r.   [116] LMA, DL/C/547/144/1 (1727).
[117] See, for example, LMA, DL/C/158 (1719/20), fol. 332v; and LPL, CA, Case 9764 (1730), Eee13, fol. 252r.
[118] See, for example, LPL, CA, Case 5604 (1759), D1257, fols. 32, 122r.
[119] See, for example, evidence from the affectionate letters between Susanna Newdigate and her husband John Newdigate III written in the 1620s, in V. Larminie, 'Marriage and the family: The example of the seventeenth-century Newdigates', *Midland History* 9 (1984), 10–18.

result of a distancing from women and domesticity, which boosted manly professional status rather than weakening it.[120] Other men, like Jonas Hanway, took the opportunity of not having families of their own to engage in philanthropic activities that were concerned with improving children's lives. Hanway became governor of the Foundling Hospital in 1760, and founded the Marine Society, which was credited with placing more than 10,000 poor and orphaned boys in the Navy during the Seven Years War. Although he believed marriage to be a civic virtue, he defended his own single status and celibacy by devoting 'a large portion of his time and fortune to the service of the distrest, of both sexes, particularly in their infant state'.[121]

The process of accepting that childlessness was a permanent condition could be a lengthy one, but at some point the better off had to address the problem of their lack of an heir. Their property and assets were most usually inherited by close kin, most typically nephews or nieces. In a family with many children, it was not exceptional for a younger son or daughter to be adopted as an heir by childless relatives, as was the case with Jane Austen's brother Edward, whose entry into the custody of his wealthy uncle was marked by a silhouette picture depicting the boy being handed by his impoverished father to his newly adopted aristocratic parents, the Knights.[122] Ties of affect as well as blood were nurtured through the custom of godparenting, and the practice of naming children after childless aunts or uncles in order to cement close affiliation and the expectation of inheritance. Although the role of godparents was somewhat diminished after the Reformation, the tradition continued, and could be important within families where 'spiritual kinship' was deemed significant.[123] Samuel Pepys was godfather to his sister Paulina's son, named

---

[120] Margaret Pelling, 'The women of the family? Speculations around early modern British physicians', *Social History of Medicine* 8 (1995), 383–401; and 'Compromised by gender: The role of the male medical practitioner in early modern England', in H. Marland and M. Pelling (eds.), *The Task of Healing: Medicine, Religion and Gender in England and the Netherlands 1450–1800* (Rotterdam, 1996), pp. 101–33. For an alternative view, see Lisa Cody, who has argued that, rather than distancing themselves from women, man-midwives assumed female qualities to enhance their status, *Birthing the Nation*, esp. ch. 6.

[121] James Stephen Taylor, *Jonas Hanway, Founder of the Marine Society: Charity and Policy in Eighteenth-Century Britain* (London and Berkeley, 1985), pp. 63–6, 70–3, 82. Unlike the majority of men included in this chapter, neither Hanway nor William Stout (see below) was married, but their unusual levels of articulation of their own feelings about never being fathers merit inclusion.

[122] Austen's biographer comments, 'It is remarkable how little disturbance this dynastic transfer has caused to subsequent biographers and family historians'. David Nokes, *Jane Austen: A Life* (London, 1997), pp. 74–5.

[123] Will Coster, *Baptism and Spiritual Kinship in Early Modern England* (Aldershot, 2002), esp. ch. 8, pp. 222–45.

Samuel in his honour, with the expectation that he would be his heir.[124] William Stout lived with his spinster sister Elin, but always had two of their brother Leonard's children living with them, between the ages of two and six, when they were old enough to go to school.[125] Both Pepys and Stout attempted to exert influence as surrogate father-figures, and (perhaps significantly) both used the patriarchal threat of disinheritance with their wayward nephews and nieces when they refused to accept their authority over matters such as choice of spouse or career.[126] Godparents and guardians could thus redefine family life, with forms of adoption complementing or supplanting the influence of the biological mother and father within the nuclear family.

This chapter has examined the importance of paternity to early modern ideas of masculinity. Children were demonstrable proof of a man's sexual success *and* fertility. Medical theories made it clear that a sexually functioning husband could be responsible for a childless union, since his seed could contain faults that were not easily detected or cured. Certainly by the eighteenth century (well before the advent of modern psychology) the mind was increasingly understood to play a part in determining the chances of a fruitful union, and the consequences of childlessness could be mentally troubling and unsettling for men as well as women. Much as contemporary commentators may have liked, simply blaming women for childlessness was not the ready or automatic response of our early modern predecessors.

Alexandra Shepard has argued that the 'social practice of manhood was enormously diverse' in England at this time, and that not all men achieved manhood by following the hegemonic model of patriarchal masculinity, that is, by marrying and becoming fathers.[127] Certainly, the existence of significant numbers of never-married men and childless husbands suggests the impossibility of all men achieving manhood in the same way. But in contrast to Shepard's thesis, this chapter has shown that childless men did not find patriarchy an 'irrelevance', or pursue 'alternative codes' of masculinity. Instead, the misfortune and occasional ridicule suffered

---

[124] H. T. Heath (ed.), *The Letters of Samuel Pepys and His Family Circle* (Oxford, 1955), pp. xxix, 52–3.

[125] J. D. Marshall, *The Autobiography of William Stout of Lancaster, 1665–1752* (Manchester, 1967), pp. 142, 179, 196–201, 203–9. Stout occasionally seems to have regarded himself as another one of Elin's surrogate 'sones' (p. 142) but it is he who exerts quasi-patriarchal authority as a response to the children's perceived insubordination.

[126] Further research on the variety of alternative parenting arrangements in cases of childlessness is planned as part of 'The History of Infertility in Britain' – see the footnote at the start of this chapter.

[127] Shepard, *Meanings of Manhood*, p. 1.

by childless men in their families and in the wider community illustrates the continuing importance for men throughout this period of performing their social role as patriarchs. That men without children took measures to find different ways of exercising patriarchal manhood illustrates this point. In public life as philanthropists, or as godparents, guardians and adopted parents within their family circles, men could become father-figures without having their own biological children. In cases where they had responsibility for the training, discipline and well-being of young people who lived as domestic servants and apprentices in their households, childless men could also experience many of the trials and rewards of fatherhood. Thus childlessness could open a man's reputation to question, but he could still assume paternal roles and exercise patriarchal authority. The patriarchal model of masculinity remained intact, even though the fertility of men was variable. Being a patriarch was less easily achievable, but nevertheless was attainable for the childless man in early modern England.

8 Aristocratic women and ideas of family in the early eighteenth century

Ingrid Tague

One of Lawrence Stone's primary arguments in *The Family, Sex and Marriage* is that the late seventeenth and eighteenth centuries saw the decline of patriarchy and its replacement by affective individualism in the nuclear family. This thesis has been the subject of considerable debate over the years, as historians have questioned whether there was any such change, and if so, how great that change was and how it affected men and women. As Naomi Tadmor has recently pointed out, these debates appear to have reached something of a stalemate, with arguments in favour of the continuity of the English family apparently winning out; but it also seems that the discussion has simply been exhausted.[1] Stone's argument may now be so familiar that it hardly seems to merit attention. Yet it is worth re-examining his work to consider what exactly he meant by patriarchy and the implications of its decline.

The eighteenth-century aristocratic family is a particularly fruitful focus of discussion in this context because scholarship on the period encapsulates some of the central debates over Stone's tale of the demise of patriarchy. It is within the aristocracy, for instance, that some historians with views similar to Stone's have seen the rise of the affective nuclear family, with close emotional ties growing more important and broad kinship relations decreasing in significance.[2] Yet other scholarship on aristocratic women, particularly as political actors, has emphasised the survival of extended kin networks in the elite throughout the century and even beyond (indeed, some of this work comes close to reviving Lewis Namier's vision of politics in the period as factional conflicts between families).[3] The political work of aristocratic women on behalf of their

---

[1] Naomi Tadmor, *Family and Friends in Eighteenth-Century England: Household, Kinship, and Patronage* (Cambridge, 2001), pp. 5–6.

[2] See Judith Schneid Lewis, *In the Family Way: Childbearing in the British Aristocracy, 1760–1860* (New Brunswick, N.J., 1986); Randolph Trumbach, *The Rise of the Egalitarian Family: Aristocratic Kinship and Domestic Relations in Eighteenth-Century England* (New York, 1978).

[3] Lewis Namier, *The Structure of Politics at the Accession of George III* (2nd edn, New York, 1957). See for example Elaine Chalus, *Elite Women in English Political Life, c.1754–1790*

families at the end of the eighteenth century seems to resemble similar activities among Tudor aristocrats, as recently analysed by Barbara Harris.[4] To what extent, then, did the eighteenth century see significant changes in the aristocratic family? If women continued to work on behalf of their kin, did the patriarchal family survive intact?

In this chapter I will discuss change and continuity in the family by exploring how aristocratic women perceived the bounds of their families and their own roles within those families. Stone's argument about change over time presented three successive models: the medieval open lineage family, the seventeenth-century restricted patriarchal nuclear family, and finally the closed domesticated nuclear family. To him these models represented a transformation from a family that was extensive, public and political to one that was nuclear, private and domestic. The early eighteenth-century family did experience changes, but they were not as straightforward as Stone's work might suggest. Indeed, the aristocratic family was notable for the simultaneous – and frequently competing – presence of ideas embodied in each one of Stone's three paradigms. Kin networks, patriarchal power and domestic ideals co-existed, often uneasily, in the lives of aristocratic women. Many women were committed to patriarchal values and recognised the benefits of extensive family connections. At the same time, however, this period saw an increasing attempt on the part of didactic authors and other cultural critics to create a strong division between public and private life, with the ostensibly private, domestic household set off as a privileged but restricted realm for women.[5] These newer ideas also affected aristocratic women's understanding of their families, even though they often conflicted with older values. The many contemporary meanings of the word 'family', recently explored by Naomi Tadmor, in part reflect the various roles of women.[6] If the household-family of co-residents could be seen as the seat of patriarchal power in Stone's terms, by the eighteenth century it was increasingly being constructed as a woman's domain; she was offered control of her children and servants in return for ceding politics and public life to her husband.[7] On the other hand, both Tadmor's 'lineage-family' and 'kinship-family', in which

---

(Oxford, 2005); Judith S. Lewis, *Sacred to Female Patriotism: Gender, Class, and Politics in Late Georgian Britain* (New York, 2003); K. D. Reynolds, *Aristocratic Women and Political Society in Victorian Britain* (Oxford, 1998).

[4] Barbara J. Harris, *English Aristocratic Women, 1450–1550: Marriage and Family, Property and Careers* (Oxford, 2002).

[5] Ingrid H. Tague, *Women of Quality: Accepting and Contesting Ideals of Femininity in England, 1690–1760* (Woodbridge, Suffolk, 2002), chs. 1–2.

[6] Tadmor, *Family and Friends*.   [7] Tague, *Women of Quality*, pp. 44–7.

the family extended beyond the household and across generations, remained especially significant in aristocratic life throughout the eighteenth century, and these conceptions of family remained patriarchal.

Before we explore these various ideas about family, the term 'patriarchy' requires some discussion. Stone's definition of patriarchy is important because the expansion of feminist scholarship in the decades since he wrote his book has emphasised a somewhat different conception of the term, and this in turn has affected responses to his argument. Stone explicitly defined patriarchy as 'the despotic authority of husband and father', and he believed that it reached a peak during the period from 1550 to 1700.[8] He traced this dominance to a series of related factors: the state's deliberate reinforcement of an analogy between the state and the family (with the king as husband/father to his people, and the husband/father as monarch of his household); Protestantism's emphasis on the spiritual power of the household head; legal changes that gave the head of a family greater power to dispose of his property as he wished; and the male monopoly of education.[9] For Stone, then, 'In many pious upper-class households in the seventeenth century, the power of the head of the household was oppressive in its completeness.'[10] He also argued that this patriarchy was distinct from, although related to, medieval forms of authority: 'What seems to have happened is that a diffuse concept of patriarchy inherited from the middle ages that took the form of "good lordship" – meaning dominance over kin and clientage – was vigorously attacked by the state as a threat to its own authority' and was replaced by a stronger form of patriarchy that actually shored up the 'political order'.[11] Such patriarchy was, for Stone, intimately connected to the rise of the nuclear family; patriarchal dominance was over this nuclear family, not the extended kin network of the Middle Ages.

Stone's conception of patriarchy crucially informed his argument about changes to the family in the late seventeenth and eighteenth centuries, when, he suggested, affective individualism developed. Because patriarchy was reinforced by analogies between family and state, he claimed, the development of contract theory 'brought with it a severe modification of theories about patriarchal power within the family and the rights of the individual'.[12] Marriage became a contract of mutual obligations:

---

[8] Lawrence Stone, *The Family, Sex and Marriage in England 1500–1800* (New York, 1977); quotation p. 151.
[9] Ibid., pp. 152–9.   [10] Ibid., p. 155.   [11] Ibid., pp. 153–4.
[12] Ibid., p. 240. For similar arguments, see Margaret Sommerville, *Sex and Subjection: Attitudes to Women in Early-Modern Society* (New York, 1995), pp. 215–17; Susan Amussen, *An Ordered Society: Gender and Class in Early Modern England* (Oxford, 1988); Mary

wives must obey their husbands, but husbands must also care for and love their wives. Similarly, Stone perceived significance in the rise of thinking that stressed the importance of individual happiness, thus placing the contentment of individual bride and groom over the needs of their respective families. Stone also saw changes in property law as undermining patriarchy. The strict settlement, he argued, limited patriarchal power by guaranteeing property for all the children of a family – even though this property was distributed in a way that most benefited eldest sons. Marriage settlements creating pin money and trusts for wives, he believed, also protected the individual property rights of married women by legally limiting their husbands' control. Finally, the decline of family prayers was a manifestation of decreasing patriarchal power.[13] According to Stone, all these changes were made possible by new economic ideas that stressed individualism, by the rise of 'a wealthy entrepreneurial bourgeoisie', by the impact of Puritanism's emphasis on individual conscience, and by the political changes associated with the Glorious Revolution.[14] Stone's narrative of the rise of affective individualism was thus above all a story of progress, from despotism to egalitarianism, and in his view this transformation was particularly beneficial to women. Affective individualism implied the importance of the individual over that of the male-dominated family, and individual happiness in turn meant more loving, egalitarian relationships between husbands and wives.

Stone's argument has, of course, come under criticism from many different directions. Many historians have demonstrated the existence of loving families long before the eighteenth century, and have stressed the variety of factors that influenced familial relations.[15] Others have emphasised the importance of life-cycle changes in family relationships; early modern families might have different members at different times, and individual perceptions of these relationships might vary depending on one's age, marital status or occupation, as well as one's sex.[16] From

Lyndon Shanley, 'Marriage contract and social contract in seventeenth-century English political thought', *Western Political Quarterly* 32 (1979), 79–91.

[13] Stone, *Family, Sex and Marriage*, pp. 239–46. For very different readings of the impact of the strict settlement and separate property, see Susan Staves, *Married Women's Separate Property in England, 1660–1833* (Cambridge, Mass., 1990); Eileen Spring, *Law, Land, and Family: Aristocratic Inheritance in England, 1300 to 1800* (Chapel Hill, 1993).

[14] Stone, *Family, Sex and Marriage*, pp. 257–67; quotation, p. 260.

[15] The scholarship on the English family is vast; see the introduction to this volume for a summary. A typical survey that emphasises the diversity of individual experiences is Ralph A. Houlbrooke, *The English Family 1450–1700* (London, 1984).

[16] Tadmor, *Family and Friends*, esp. chs. 1–2; T. K. Haraven, 'The history of the family and the complexity of social change', *American Historical Review* 96, (1991), 95–124.

another point of view, some feminist scholars have accepted Stone's narrative of change while questioning whether or not this change was beneficial to women. Here the definition of patriarchy becomes particularly important. As we have seen, Stone's definition of patriarchy as despotism was central to his argument that the decline of patriarchy implied greater equality within the family. Later scholars frequently rely on more flexible conceptions of patriarchy, keeping the idea of the subordination of women to men, but allowing for a positive presentation of women's roles within that subordination. By this definition patriarchy is not incompatible with affective family relationships. Some historians thus distinguish between 'patriarchy' in this sense and 'patriarchalism', using the latter in the specifically political context of analogies between household and state, father and king.[17] Stone's notion of patriarchy conflated these two meanings: hence his use of the political term 'despotism' to refer to male control in the family, and his representation of the strict settlement, for instance, as a blow to patriarchy. In the view of feminist political theorists like Carole Pateman, by contrast, the decline of patriarchalism simply enabled the development of a different, more insidious, form of patriarchy.

For Stone, patriarchy and affective individualism were mutually exclusive: one replaced the other. Critics of Stone often emphasise continuity over change – either the continuity of familial affection or the continuity of female subordination. At the same time, as historians have explored early modern gender relations, they have increasingly emphasised the ways in which patriarchy could be contested and resisted. Anthony Fletcher, for instance, sees a powerful patriarchal system in place in early modern England, but he suggests that this system was strongest in public life, and often greatly modified or ignored in private relations between husbands and wives.[18] Bernard Capp goes further, arguing that 'there was no patriarchal *system*, rather an interlocking set of beliefs, assumptions, traditions, and practices' through which it is possible to see the basis and workings of patriarchy.[19] Yet if there was no such system, and if 'patriarchy' simply refers to women's subordination to men, then it may be that this sense of the word has outlived its

---

[17] On patriarchalism and patriarchy, see, e.g., Gordon J. Schochet, *Patriarchalism in Political Thought: The Authoritarian Family and Political Speculation and Attitudes, Especially in Seventeenth-Century England* (New York, 1975); Carol Pateman, *The Sexual Contract* (Cambridge, 1988); Rachel Weil, *Political Passions: Gender, the Family and Political Argument in England 1680–1714* (Manchester, 1999).

[18] Anthony Fletcher, *Gender, Sex and Subordination in England 1500–1800* (New Haven and London, 1995), esp. chs. 8–9.

[19] Bernard Capp, *When Gossips Meet: Women, Family, and Neighbourhood in Early Modern England* (Oxford, 2003), quotation p. 1.

usefulness as a tool of historical analysis: it is difficult to identify any
time, past or present, when women have not experienced some degree of
subordination.[20] In this chapter I will use a historically specific definition
of 'patriarchy', but one that does not replicate Stone's idea of paternal
despotism in the nuclear family. The patriarchal family, in the sense I
will be employing here, implied male dominance (but not necessarily
tyranny) along with a high regard for patrilineage and male inheritance.
In this context, extended kin networks remained extremely important.[21]
If ideas associated with the Glorious Revolution seriously undermined
analogies between state and family in the eighteenth century, these other
characteristics of patriarchy survived, especially among the elite.[22]

The patriarchal family could not be divorced from the public sphere
because of the connections between family and political power. In this
context, aristocratic marriage negotiations always involved political and
financial considerations, even in the eighteenth century when child-
betrothals were extremely rare and when most people accepted the power
of potential brides and grooms to veto marriage candidates. Even choices
that might seem purely symbolic or religious, such as who should serve
as godparents, demanded a careful consideration of political and status
implications.[23] Ensuring the safe inheritance of landed wealth through
generations was a further important consideration for aristocratic families. Ironically, the unbroken family line gained its significance in part
because aristocratic lineages were in reality so fragile; hence the use of
family portraiture, for instance, to celebrate successful lineages and even
to create the illusion of an unbroken family when no such line existed.[24]
The patriarchal family was thus simultaneously a private and a public
entity. Moreover, although by definition it subordinated the interests of

---

[20] Amanda Vickery makes a similar point about the concept of 'separate spheres' in her
'Golden age to separate spheres? A review of the categories and chronology of English
women's history', *Historical Journal* 36 (1993), 383–414.

[21] For similar ideas, see Tadmor, *Family and Friends*, ch. 3 (on the lineage-family); Harris, *English Aristocratic Women*; Vivienne Larminie, *Wealth, Kinship and Culture: The
Seventeenth-Century Newdigates of Arbury and Their World* (Woodbridge, Suffolk, 1995).

[22] On the impact of the Glorious Revolution on ideas about family, see Tague, *Women of
Quality*, pp. 7–9.

[23] See Will Coster, *Baptism and Spiritual Kinship in Early Modern England* (Aldershot,
2002), esp. pp. 144–51.

[24] Kate Retford, 'Sensibility and genealogy in the eighteenth-century family portrait: The
collection at Kedleston Hall', *Historical Journal* 46 (2003), 533–60; Shearer West, 'The
public nature of private life: The conversation piece and the fragmented family', *British
Journal for Eighteenth-Century Studies* 18 (1995), 153–72; Marcia Pointon, *Hanging the
Head: Portraiture and Social Formation in Eighteenth-Century England* (New Haven and
London, 1993), ch. 6.

women to those of the male-dominated lineage, women did play a significant role in this family. Many scholars have noted that the double standard is at least in part a result of relying on female chastity to ensure the
purity of the male line.[25] And because women's rank primarily reflected
that of their fathers or husbands, aristocratic women could feel a strong
investment in the success of their lineages.

We can see one particularly vivid example of a woman's commitment
to the patriarchal lineage in the letters of Lady Isabella Wentworth. During the period for which we have records, she was an elderly widow with
six grown children. After the death of Lady Wentworth's husband in
1692, her son Thomas took over the role of patriarchal head of the family, and Lady Wentworth's view of her family was deeply affected by her
son's domination.[26] She was crucially interested in the perpetuation of
the family line through Thomas's children, a concern that only increased
as he remained unmarried until he was nearly forty. Because he waited
so long to marry, there existed for many years the real possibility that
the children of his younger brother Peter would inherit the family estate.
This prospect depressed Lady Wentworth. 'Yesterday a Little before twoe
in the Morning your Sister Wentworth was brought to bed of a Lovly
great boy', she wrote in 1707; 'all his children Makse me Mallancolly to
thinck they are as your airs, for I see noe hopse of your having any of
your own.'[27] Not only was she disappointed by the thought, but she also
found it difficult, she claimed, to feel the proper affection for her other
grandchildren: 'when I thinck Peters children, ar Loockt upon as your
airs, I then hate them parfitly'.[28] She did not express this kind of resentment for her daughters' children, which suggests that it was above all the
patriarchal issues of inheritance of the family name and the perpetuation
of Thomas's line that concerned her.

Her relationship to her family becomes even clearer when we consider
her decision to settle her entire fortune on her son Thomas, leaving herself only an annual income of £200. Since she claimed that her jointure
had been worth £540 per year, she obviously believed that she had done
something special for him, and her decision was clearly connected to her

---

[25] The classic articulation is Keith Thomas, 'The double standard', *Journal of the History of Ideas* 20 (1959), 195–216.

[26] Thomas Wentworth held the Irish title Lord Raby before receiving the earldom of Strafford in 1711. For convenience, I refer to him throughout as Lord Strafford.

[27] Lady Isabella Wentworth to Lord Strafford, 12 December [1707], British Library (BL) Additional MS 22225, fol. 64r. In all quotations from manuscripts, I have silently expanded contractions such as 'yᵉ' for 'the', and I have sometimes added punctuation for clarity.

[28] Lady Wentworth to Lord Strafford, 15 February [1705/6], BL Add. MS 31143, fol. 140v. See also same to same, 22 December [1710], BL Add. MS 31143, fol. 623r.

view of Thomas as head of the family.[29] Yet the question of her money and her children's potential inheritance frequently bothered her. In response to a letter of his, she insisted with passion that she had no regrets, 'only for what I have for my own self, I would dispose, ether Leving or dead, as I Lyke, & not ether giv acount or doe it by derection . . . thear is noe sarvent but has the Leberty to dispose of thear waygis, & never giv any acount for it'. It seems that Thomas had been demanding of her, as he often did, an explanation of her spending habits. But she went on to stress that

for Peter & his Wife, Lett them take cair to provyde for thear Brood, thear is noe reson I should deny my self all manner of sattisfaction for them . . . but tell I see you have a child, God forgiv me for it, I can not have much Lov for that Brood, nether can I take it kindly to be trickt out of anything for any of them. This was always my openyon, althoe nothing can be kinder then both thay are to me. They have often invited me to thear hous & made me very welcom whe[n] thear . . . but when I fancy thear in exspectation of any of thears to be your airs it givs me an avertion to them.[30]

Her fears about Thomas's lack of offspring thus affected her relations with her other children, especially her son Peter, and made her worry that she might be 'trickt out' of part of her fortune to help them, who had to take care of their 'Brood' themselves. Her defensiveness about controlling her own money, which frequently flared up in the face of criticisms from Thomas, was always mitigated by her intense submissiveness toward him. Her remark in response to such criticism that 'one may be a very good parent & yett consult ons own eas as well as our childrens & not to be a slave for thear pleasures' was quickly followed by a postscript: 'I doe not reckon you in the number of the the [sic] rest of my children. I can thinck nothing to much to doe for you.'[31] Indeed, the extent of her devotion to one child over all others is most strikingly revealed in a letter she sent to him in 1706, asking permission to reveal her financial settlements to her other children. In justification she said that she feared that without their knowing the situation she could not 'be sure whoe Lovs me & whoe dus not'. 'I design to be very sencear with them in telling them, as I often have, that none showed me that Love, you did, & I shall ad that you aloan

29 See Lady Wentworth to Lord Strafford, 10 November [1706], BL Add. MS 31143, fol. 175r. For her claims about her jointure, see same to same, 11 December 1726, BL Add. MS 22225, fol. 502r. Her husband had died intestate: The National Archives (hereafter TNA): Public Record Office (hereafter PRO), PROB 6/71, Administration of Sir William Wentworth, 23 October 1695.

30 Lady Wentworth to Lord Strafford, 5 January [before 1711], BL Add. MS 31144, fol. 191r–v.

31 Lady Wentworth to Lord Strafford, 8 February [before 1708], BL Add. MS 31144, fols. 188r–189v.

stuck to me when al elc had forsaken me', she continued. 'Thearfore I put it out of my power beleeving when I had anything to dispose of they would Flatter me for the sake of what I had.'[32]

I have quoted from Lady Wentworth's letters at some length here because her language demonstrates both the strength of her devotion to her eldest son and his lineage, and the way in which this devotion obviously made her feel somewhat defensive and vulnerable to criticisms from her other children. To a modern eye, her language of love ('you aloan stuck to me when al elc had forsaken me') sits uneasily next to her clear concern with questions of lineage. It is worth noting that her financial decisions could not be seen to affect her other children adversely, since all but one of her children were married off and more or less financially independent. And in any event, in case of financial problems they inevitably turned to Thomas for assistance, not to her. Her comments in this context about the need for Peter and his wife to provide on their own for their 'Brood', and her 'avertion' to his children, suggest that her decision to turn her fortune over to Thomas was intimately bound up in her hopes for his procreation and the production of a male heir. Her energy was thus focused on providing for this hypothetical child, even to the exclusion of her other offspring and their children. Although she often pleaded on behalf of her other children, especially her daughters, for Thomas's help with both money and patronage, her notion of family was primarily defined in terms of patriarchy and lineal descent.

Similar views were expressed by many other aristocratic women, and primogeniture of course embodied these priorities in law. The patriarchal family was always complicated for women, however, by the competing demands of their families by birth and by marriage, and by the added complexities created by frequent deaths and remarriages. Remarriage by both men and women was an area of concern because of fears that the interests of children by a second marriage might trump those of the first union. Widows were seen as particularly vulnerable in this regard since remarriage was often seen as caving in to their sexual desires and abandoning their natural maternal instincts toward the children of their first marriage, but men were not immune from concern. Lord Chancellor Hardwicke counselled against a second wife, who, in 'contending for the interests of her own children, . . . will strive to gain more influence as old age and its concomitants may grow upon you; and everything which they acquire, your children will think themselves wronged and defrauded

---

[32] Lady Wentworth to Lord Strafford, 10 November [1706], BL Add. MS 31143, fol. 176r–v. Thomas's reply to her request has not survived.

of'.[33] Widowhood also added another layer of complexity: the shift to dowager status frequently transformed women's lives on the most basic level, requiring a widow to move out of her house while another woman took over her social position. Because aristocratic marriages inevitably combined questions of personal preference, wealth, status and political alliance, they were often fraught with tension. Yet even without such complications, aristocratic women's perception of familial ties could vary depending on circumstance, broadening or narrowing the scope of their family connections as needed. Indeed, this very fluidity in what constituted 'family' – from parents and siblings to in-laws, cousins and other kin – could be advantageous in an age when anything from political advancement to the outcome of lawsuits might depend on family influence.

The boundaries of the aristocratic family were thus extremely flexible. When Anne Johnson married into the Wentworth family and became countess of Strafford, she all but abandoned her connections to her family of birth. Since she did not come from the nobility, she did not bring the prestige of an important lineage to the marriage, but as Lady Strafford she was attached to the undisputed head of the family. Thus she expected submission and respect from Thomas's siblings, and frequently complained about their bad behaviour toward her. She promised 'to look upon your fameley as my own & I hope 'tis what I have allway's don, . . . but this I must say Again for my self that I ought to have som smalle returns of Civillity's Again as I am your Wife tho I ware the most despisable Creature living'. Indeed, she suggested, 'the only way to be well with som of your fameley is to be Civill to them at a distance as I dare say you'll see your self when you com to live at home'.[34] By referring to Lord Strafford's siblings repeatedly as 'your fameley', she pointedly distinguished between connections by blood and marriage even as she reaffirmed her sense of status as deriving from her marriage. Marriage into higher rank did not always give women an advantage, however. The countess of Hertford complained that her husband's family had always hated her because they considered her beneath their rank even though her marriage made her their superior. Her sisters-in-law, she said, 'could not bear to see a person whom they thought much their inferior (as in truth they did everybody) put before them, and took all opportunities to blame whatever I said or did, and endeavoured to bias everybody to look

---

[33] Cited in Trumbach, *Egalitarian Family*, p. 58.
[34] Lady Strafford to Lord Strafford, St James's Square, 17 February 1712/13, BL Add. MS 22226, fol. 297r–v.

upon me and treat me with the same contempt and aversion which they entertained for me themselves'.[35]

Yet if marriage could lead to tensions within families, it also brought opportunities by expanding the network of available kin from whom to seek assistance, and understandably most women seem to have looked wherever they thought such assistance might be forthcoming.[36] When Lady Mary Coke sought a way out of her marriage to her abusive husband, for instance, she turned for support to her father-in-law, the earl of Leicester, as well as other relations. Leicester initially professed his loyalty to her in terms that simultaneously acknowledged and denied the difference between affinal and consanguineal relations: 'I look upon you as my own Daughter married to another family & do feel for you as much as your own father cou'd.'[37] But when Leicester refused to agree to Lady Mary's demands for a separation, she next looked to her sisters and their husbands; and she eventually relied on the help of her brother-in-law, who was a lawyer.[38]

Such flexibility in the boundaries of family did not, however, outweigh the significance of patrilineage in the aristocratic family. The patriarchal family's emphasis on lineage can be seen most clearly in the frequent concern expressed by aristocratic women to ensure the continuation of the male line. Successful production of a male heir was widely accepted, by both men and women, as the primary duty of an aristocratic wife. When Lady Strafford was expecting her first child in 1712, Lady Wentworth eagerly anticipated a boy; she wrote to her son that her room in their new house was beautiful, but 'I shall with a great deal of Joy, giv it up to my Little Lord, but not with altogether soe much Joy to my Lady Anne, althoe she shall be welcom.'[39] Her comment summarised many families' attitudes toward babies: although girls were loved (and among Lady Wentworth's own children, she ranked her daughter Anne, not her younger son, as her second favourite child), boys were the priority. Lady Wentworth even understood these priorities to affect such matters as the traditional distribution of gifts to the lying-in assistants at the christening, and she was ashamed to find that she had given less than Lady Strafford's relations after the birth of Strafford's first child: 'it being but a Girle & I

---

[35] Frances, countess of Hertford to [recipient unknown], [n.d.], in Helen Sard Hughes (ed.), *The Gentle Hertford: Her Life and Letters* (New York, 1940), pp. 35–6.

[36] See Elizabeth Foyster, *Marital Violence: An English Family History 1660–1857* (Cambridge, 2005), pp. 173–84, for a discussion of the ways in which kin could intervene in marital conflicts as well as how differing ideas of family could themselves lead to conflict.

[37] Earl of Leicester to Lady Mary Coke, Holkham, 1 January 1747/8, BL Add. MS 22629, fol. 139v.

[38] See BL Add. MS 22629, fols. 143–80 *passim*.

[39] Lady Wentworth to Lord Strafford, 8 July [1712], BL Add. MS 22225, fol. 140r.

Noe Gossap I thought a ginney round was enough but Sir Harry & Lady Roysten [Lady Strafford's father and her grandmother Lady Rawstorn] gave duble'.[40] Although her remark that it was 'but a Girle' might seem to imply that she did not care about the baby, the remainder of her letter – and her behaviour throughout the rest of her life – demonstrated that she doted on the child. Her actions and this comment should be seen in the context of a convention that discriminated between boys and girls, but that did not dictate the ways in which parents and children actually interacted. When Lady Strafford appeared to be pregnant again in June 1713, Lady Wentworth remarked, 'I pray God grant it a boy, although it can not possable be a fyner child then Lady Ann.'[41] Nevertheless, the pressure to bear a son was intense. When Lady Catherine Wheler gave birth to a boy, her husband happily reported her as saying that 'though she had just gone through very severe pains . . . to have been sure of a boy she would willingly have gone through twice as much'.[42] It is also useful to remember that the concern with patrilineage could have material implications. Sophia, duchess of Kent, for instance, produced only one child in her marriage, a girl, much to the disappointment of her husband. The duke's determination to preserve his family line meant that he provided little for Sophia or their daughter, instead settling his estate on another relative. As the duke lay dying, Sophia's mother remarked that 'the little disposition he has shew'd to make [her] easyer, than she was by her joynture, makes her affliction much less, then if he had been kinder'.[43]

Not only did aristocratic women widely assume that their husbands preferred boys to girls, but they also frequently referred to their husbands' lack of interest or disappointment in female babies. Lord Strafford was chastised by both his mother and his wife for his attitude toward his newborn daughter. Lady Wentworth criticised him for not seeing his baby, who was born while he was on the Continent, for several months after her birth, complaining that if she had been a boy Strafford 'would not have been so patient'.[44] Lady Strafford felt obliged to preface the news of her daughter's birth with the comment that 'I wish at my heart I could wish you Joy of A Son but as it has pleas'd God it is A Daughter I hope

[40] Lady Wentworth to Lord Strafford, 27 March [1713], BL Add. MS 22225, fol. 252v. See also Peter Wentworth to Lord Strafford, London, 27 February 1712/13, BL Add. MS 31144, fol. 351, on Lady Wentworth's disappointment at the birth of a girl.
[41] Lady Wentworth to Lord Strafford, [June 1713], BL Add. MS 22225, fol. 302r–v.
[42] Granville Wheler to Lady Anne Hastings, in George Hastings Wheler (ed.), *Hastings Wheler Family Letters [Part 2], 1704–1739* (Wakefield, 1935), p. 107.
[43] Jane, countess of Portland, to William, Count Bentinck, BL Eg. MS 1715, fol. 143r.
[44] Lady Wentworth to Lord Strafford, 7 July [1713], BL Add. MS 22225, fol. 311r.

never the Less you will love it.'[45] Several months later, after her husband had returned to England, she remarked in an aside: 'I hope now you are better acquanted with our Daughter you are reconciled to her in som measure,' suggesting that Lord Strafford was having trouble overcoming his disappointment at not having a son.[46] One of Strafford's sisters wrote to him, after receiving the news of another daughter in 1717, that he had no right to complain: 'as for not having a Son whos fault is it for if you gott a son Ile engage my Lady can bring it forth as well as Daughters'.[47] She did not overtly criticise his prejudice, but, by gently mocking him, she drew attention to the pointlessness of his disappointment. Similarly, in 1734, when his first grandchild was a girl, his daughter wrote to him half-jokingly that she was certain that despite his disappointment, if he saw the baby he 'woud think her as worthy love as if she had been a son & I asure you I Woud not change her for one'.[48] She also expressed reservations shortly after the birth of a sickly son a year later; though she knew that her husband and 'his friends' were pleased at having a boy, his ill health made her afraid to become too affectionate, 'so my Pretty Girl is still my favourite'.[49]

The Bentinck family expressed similar mixed feelings about the birth of girls. When the countess of Portland wrote to her son William Bentinck with the news that he had a new niece, she noted that he was likely to be 'angry', though the husband had managed to overcome his disappointment 'and looks upon his little girle with so much affection, that whatever he may have wisht for, his outward behaviour shews his great kindness & esteem for his wife'.[50] Asking him to be godfather to her granddaughter, William's sister, the countess of Clanbrassill, remarked that 'we should all have been better pleased had it been a Son, and I tell you so that you may not tell it me, which you would undoubtedly have

---

[45] Lady Strafford to Lord Strafford, St James's Square, 10 March [1712/13], BL Add. MS 22226, fol. 93r.

[46] Lady Strafford to Lord Strafford, The Hague, 17 November 1713, BL Add. MS 22226, fol. 361v. Although this may have been intended humorously, Strafford's preference for boys is clear throughout the family papers.

[47] Lady Arabella Bellew to Lord Strafford, 28 August [1717], BL Add. MS 22228, fol. 43r–v.

[48] Lady Anne Conolly to Lord Strafford, Dublin, 16 February [1733/4], BL Add. MS 22228, fol. 145r. Lord Strafford had obviously expressed his disappointment, since Mr Conolly's aunt wrote to him that though she agreed with him that a boy would have been better, she was simply relieved at the safe delivery: Katherine Conolly to Lord Strafford, Dublin, 28 February 1733[/34], BL Add. MS 22228, fol. 170.

[49] Anne Conolly to Lord Strafford, Leixslip, 3 January [1734/5], BL Add. MS 22228, fol. 141r.

[50] Lady Portland to Count Bentinck, Whitehall, 20 January [n.y.], BL Eg. MS 1715, fol. 5r.

done if you recollected this is her fourth Daughter and that she has but one Son'.[51] Because for most aristocratic families the continuation of the family name and the inheritance of the estate depended on the presence of a male heir, the pressure on women to bear boys was enormous. But Lady Clanbrassill's sarcasm, like the gentle chiding by Strafford's female relations, suggests that women did not always agree with their husbands' priorities (though it was certainly easier to express favour for girls once a male heir was secured). By 1761, Lady Clanbrassill could enthusiastically welcome the news she had just heard of Bentinck's newborn grandchild, while humorously defending the sex in general:

> as it is only [news] of a Daughter you did not I suppose think it worth while to *annonce* her arrival. I desire to know whether you think I can patiently bear such an affront upon the Sex, and considering how fond you are of your Daughter in Law I wonder you are not rejoiced with the hopes of this childs growing up like her. For my part I have four Grandaughters, and delight in them. I am not sure I love my Grandson as well, to which I know you will answer that is a sign of my bad taste, but I wont agree to that, so this affair will remain to be disputed between us, for I dont suspect you will give up your side of the argument.[52]

It is possible that by the 1760s it had become easier to express favour for girls.[53] But for most early eighteenth-century women, producing male heirs remained a priority as well as an important source of pride. Daughters required explanation and apology, both because husbands wanted sons and because women identified with the dynastic priorities of their families, through which they were able to establish a significant role as the bearers of heirs.

Nevertheless, women could express their resistance to the patriarchal status quo, particularly when addressing other women, as we can see in the letters of Mary Delany and her circle. Thus Elizabeth Foley wrote to Mary's sister Ann about her imminent delivery, 'I think I must wish it may be a son, because that sex is generally most acceptable to the gentlemen, but for *yours* and *my own sake* I shall be *glad if it is a daughter*.'[54] On

---

[51] Harriet, Lady Clanbrassill to Count Bentinck, Dublin, 24 March 1761, BL Eg. MS 1722, fol. 171r.

[52] Lady Clanbrassill to Count Bentinck, Castletown, 26 September 1761, BL Eg. MS 1722, fol. 228r.

[53] Amanda Vickery notes that 'the darling daughter was patriarchy's Achilles heel'. Indeed, among the late eighteenth-century families she studied, 'the only positive preference which surfaces in genteel correspondence is for girls, although this may be because most of the matrons studied here had plenty of boys'. Vickery, *The Gentleman's Daughter: Women's Lives in Georgian England* (New Haven and London, 1998), pp. 49, 105.

[54] Elizabeth Foley to Ann Dewes, Stoke, 14 July 1741, in Lady Llanover (ed.), *The Autobiography and Correspondence of Mary Granville, Mrs. Delany: With Interesting Reminiscences*

another occasion, Mary commented, regarding a recent marriage, that

Mr. Forde, the father, has done very generously by his son, . . .; but there is one *error* which most fathers run into, and that is in providing *too little* for daughters; young men have a thousand ways of improving a little fortune, by professions and employments, if they have good friends, but young gentlewomen have no way, the fortune settled on them is all they are to expect – they are incapable of making an addition.[55]

Similarly, Mary's sole criticism of *Sir Charles Grandison* was that the eponymous hero insists that his sons be brought up as Protestants, while he allows his daughters to be raised as Catholics. 'Had a woman written the story', Mrs Delany complained to her sister, 'she would have thought the *daughters as of much consequence as the sons*.'[56] Their friend Elizabeth Robinson was especially bitter about her father's refusal to acknowledge her desire for financial independence. After spending a day riding out with him to view landscapes she found uninteresting,

I gently intimated to my papa that perhaps if time should make my eyes a little dim, a little land in possession was better than a great deal in prospect; but a quick apprehension in other matters is sometimes slow in taking a hint; and I find, if I sue for lands it must be under covert baron, as the widow Blackacre says. Is it not a sad thing to be brought up in the patriot din of liberty and property, and to be allowed neither?[57]

Comments like these and those of Lady Clanbrassill quoted above suggest that the eighteenth century was witnessing changes in attitudes toward female children, and indeed the period saw a growing emphasis on the family as a privileged, domestic arena in which women were dominant. As women's roles as mothers and household managers were increasingly emphasised and applauded, this vision of the family worked against the dominance of the traditional patriarchal family, even within the aristocracy. Motherhood was particularly powerful in this regard, since the eighteenth-century emphasis on women as mothers created a space to glorify women's contributions to family and nation. Women were, for instance, able to argue for special privileges when they were lying in, and they could use their devotion to their children as leverage with their male relatives.[58] As Count Bentinck remarked apologetically to his mother,

of King George the Third and Queen Charlotte, 6 vols. (London, 1861–2), vol. II, p. 162. Mary and Ann were the nieces of George Granville, Lord Lansdowne.
[55] Mary Delany to Ann Dewes, Mount Panther, 28 July 1750, ibid., vol. II, pp. 574–5.
[56] Mary Delany to Ann Dewes, Bulstrode, 21 December 1753, ibid., vol. III, p. 257.
[57] Elizabeth Robinson to duchess of Portland, [?] 1741, in Matthew Montagu (ed.), *The Letters of Mrs. Elizabeth Montagu, with Some of the Letters of Her Correspondents*, 3rd edn, 4 vols. (London, 1810–13), vol. I, pp. 240–1.
[58] Tague, *Women of Quality*, pp. 84–6.

when he said he was giving in to his wife's wishes to lie in with her own relatives, he found it easier to do what she asked than to create 'an *éclat*' and risk being blamed if there were a problem with the delivery.[59]

Women's involvement in the care of their children was so widely acknowledged as their duty that they were often careful to emphasise the extent of their attention and affection. Frances Boscawen, for instance, frequently wrote to her husband assuring him that her priorities lay with her family while he was away. In 1748 her relations invited her to the fashionable spa town of Tunbridge Wells for a fortnight but, she wrote, 'I shall not quit my peaceful groves, much less my pretty babes for that tumult. I shan't easily forget how ill my boy looked when I returned last year, nor shan't be easily persuaded to deprive him again of his mother's eye. Beside, Bess is toothing and requires care.'[60] Her refusal to indulge in fashionable leisure away from home demonstrated her concern, while her suggestion that her children became ill when she left them re-emphasised her importance to their well-being. When one of her children was being inoculated for smallpox in 1755, she again assured her husband that they were her chief interest, even when she had to go out. She regretted that she had promised friends to visit the pleasure gardens of Ranelagh at a time when 'You may believe my choice would have been a more solitary walk this evening.'[61] Presenting herself as taking no pleasure in entertainment provided a means of maintaining a virtuous appearance even when she was not directly caring for her children. Mary, Countess Cowper even used the love of her child as a weapon in her battle for her husband's affection. Sending him a letter in which she claimed to be resigning herself to the end of her marriage, she announced,

I desire to dedicate the rest of my days to the Education of my poor Child in a perfect retirement. For when I must quitt you I'm resolv'd to leave the world at the same time. I hope you wont deny me the priviledge of carrying her with me. Tho' I dont need the sight of the dear innocent to preserve the remembrance of my Dear lov'd husband. But I think it my duty to take care that she be instructed as she ought. & having said this let us part as people that have lov'd well.[62]

In fact the marriage lasted happily for seventeen years until Lord Cowper's death, but Mary sought to use her love for her daughter as

[59] Count Bentinck to countess of Portland, Sorgvliet, 30 August 1737, BL Eg. MS 1712, fol. 108.
[60] Frances Boscawen to Edward Boscawen, 23 June 1748, in Cecil Aspinall-Oglander (ed.), *Admiral's Wife: Being the Life and Letters of the Hon. Mrs. Edward Boscawen from 1719 to 1761* (London, 1940), p. 87.
[61] Frances Boscawen to Edward Boscawen, 17 April 1755, ibid., p. 167.
[62] Undated letter of Countess Cowper to William, Earl Cowper, Hertfordshire Record Office, D/EP F59.

a way of demonstrating her own moral righteousness and positioning herself as a victim.

Two cases of actual marital breakdown show in more detail how women could use maternal affection to counteract accusations of unfeminine conduct in their disobedience of their husbands. In seeking the optimum stance against their husbands, both Henrietta Howard and Henrietta Knight explicitly turned to maternal love for moral authority when they were accused of failing in wifely submission. Henrietta Knight was especially vulnerable because her husband Robert demanded a separation on the grounds of her adultery, and her claim to maternal care was one of her few rhetorical weapons. When the initial conflict broke out in 1736, she used her children as part of her plea to her husband for forgiveness and reconciliation, begging him, 'Think what a punishment it is for any crime to be deprived of your Esteem & of my Childrens company – The rest is not worth naming.'[63] Yet since she lost custody of her children, as was almost inevitable in the period, the strategy of emphasising her maternal affection was limited. Thus Robert announced, when requesting formal separation articles, 'You have nobody to maintain or provide for, but your self; I must maintain & give portions to *my* Son & Daughter.'[64] Nevertheless, Henrietta continued to exploit the rhetoric of maternal affection; in 1744, for example, she requested changes in their separation agreement with the comment that she had entered into it 'willingly as I thought it for the advantage of Our Children'. She justified her need for a larger allowance on the grounds that she was spending it on improvements to her estate: she 'might to be sure spare by living in a Town & by not laying out any thing on a Place which is to be my Sons, & therefore draws on the Expences of a gentlemans Seat but I regard my self less than Justice to all, & the advantage of my Children, which makes me propose this'.[65] By claiming that dynastic considerations came before her personal desires, she sought to present expenses on her own house as investments in her son's future and the need to maintain his status as a 'gentleman'. In later letters to her friends, she continued to emphasise her maternal role:

---

[63] Henrietta Knight to Robert Knight, 14 April [1736], BL Add. MS 45889, fols. 15v–16r. That she attempted unsuccessfully to keep custody of her children is evident from letters to her from her half-brother in which he told her to accept the necessity that they be somewhere where they could get a good education, not 'so far out of the world' as she was living: Henry, Lord Bolingbroke to Henrietta Knight, Argeville, 17 December 1736, BL Add. MS 45889, fol. 38r–v; same to same, 20 March [1736/7], BL Add. MS 45889, fol. 40r.

[64] Robert Knight to Henrietta Knight, Golden Square, 24 April 1742, BL Add. MS 45889, fol. 48r–v. Italics added.

[65] Henrietta Knight to Robert Knight, Henbury, 16 January 1743/4, BL Add. MS 45889, fol. 56r–v.

'I return thanks for your compliment about my Son, who is as *dear* to me as he is *dutiful*, and, I flatter myself, *deserving*.'[66] Without questioning her genuine love for her children, it is nonetheless clear that they became tools in her conflict with her husband, exploited by both parents as they fought for the moral high ground.

Henrietta Howard's separation from her husband Charles created a similar situation in which a child became a symbol of a woman's feminine duty, a symbol manipulated by both parents. In this case, Henrietta chose to remove herself from the marriage, and thus she accepted from the beginning that their separation would cause her to lose custody of her son. When she refused to return to Charles in 1727, he quickly reminded her of 'the small Posterity of A Child you seem'd to love', who would suffer because of her damaged reputation.[67] Henrietta responded with an equal emphasis on her love for her son, drawing on the conventionally close relationship between mother and child: 'I wish to God he was of a riper age to be a Judge between us, I cannot but flatter my self he wou'd have more duty and humanity than to desire to see his Mother exposed to Misery and want.'[68] And when faced with her son's apparent rejection of her, she created an image of herself as an ideal mother whose child had failed in his duty:

The case of my Son is a matter of that tenderness to me that I hardly dare trust my own weakness upon the Subject, . . . but I am not willing to sopose he will long neglect a parent who has not forfieted the duty he owes her, but if this of all other evils is yet reserved for me I must bear it with patience & submit to my fate, If I were now to dye he might say he had a mother to whom he had not paid the respect that was due, so on the other side if he deserts me however lemantable the stroke is to me, I must and will think as in cases of mortality that I once had a Son.[69]

Such rhetoric was possible through a cultural convention of strong mother–child bonds and filial duty. She sought to respond to accusations that she had failed in her duty as submissive wife by sketching a portrait of a son who had failed in his duty of submission to his mother. She turned again to this rhetoric in a conflict with Charles over his brother, who was planning to leave a considerable bequest to Henrietta: 'his not Complying to your demands, will not I hope ingage you to Endavour any Thing that may hereafter prove a disadvantage to [our] Child', she wrote

[66] Henrietta Knight to William Shenstone, Barrells, 27 June 1748, in *Letters Written by the Late Right Honourable Lady Luxborough, to William Shenstone, Esq.* (London, 1775), p. 31.
[67] Charles Howard to Henrietta Howard, 2 May [1727], BL Add. MS 22627, fol. 30r–v.
[68] Henrietta Howard to Charles Howard, [May 1727?], BL Add. MS 22627, fol. 31r–v.
[69] Henrietta Howard to Charles Howard, 15 May 1727, BL Add. MS 22627, fols. 37v–38r.

to Charles, adding, 'nor can you reflect upon my behavior and not beleive I cou'd have suffer'd any missery for you while it was your advantage and I and the Child not in the fears of starveing through the whole Course of our lives'.[70]

As Joanne Bailey's chapter in this collection shows, the rhetoric of maternal affection remained a powerful weapon in marital conflicts throughout the eighteenth century, one wielded by husbands and wives alike. Bailey's investigation of criminal conversation trials in this context also highlights the fact that it was not just within the family that maternal care could be employed as a source of moral authority. Such authority allowed motherhood to cross into the 'public' spheres of court and politics, as well as the law. In 1759, for instance, Elizabeth Egerton asked her brother Count Bentinck to help her get a sinecure for her daughter on the grounds that this would secure her daughter's future – even though Elizabeth herself planned to receive the income during her lifetime. This was one of many letters she wrote to him over the years, seeking his help in finding places for herself or her family, but in this instance she stressed her devotion to her daughter even while admitting that she would get the immediate benefit: 'what I much wish for, is something in my Daughters name (the income of which I should enjoy during my Life) that she might have a comfortable subsistance when I am Dead, for tho I can not do what I wish for her, yet she will find a great alteration when I am gone; she is so good and considerate towards me that she deserves every thing that I can do, or get done for her'.[71] Asking the countess of Suffolk to excuse her from her service in waiting on the queen, the countess of Bristol remarked that she hoped the queen was 'too indulgent a Mother, not to have her tendernes [*sic*] feel for me; I had an account last night that my poor Daughter Mansell was not like to last many days, this stroke (tho' long expected) coming so soon after my other has thrown me into such a disorder, that tho' I was in the coach, I was forc'd to be taken out of it again'.[72] In a 1744 letter to a male friend, Lady Mary Hervey explained that his discussion of politics would have fascinated her if her 'fears and concern' for her pregnant daughter 'did not exceed what I do or ever can feel for the public. She has engrossed my thoughts; but when *she* is *better*, I will tell you more at large how very sorry I am to find the

---

[70] Henrietta Howard to Charles Howard, [February 1727/8], BL Add. MS 22627, fol. 22r–v.

[71] Elizabeth Ariana Egerton to Count Bentinck, 20 December 1759, BL Eg. MS 1722, fol. 44r.

[72] Elizabeth, countess of Bristol, to countess of Suffolk, 12 August [n.y.], BL Add. MS 22629, fols. 128–9.

patriots are never likely to be so.'[73] Although men's privileged role in the public world of politics was often presented as superior to women's private role, Lady Hervey exploited the moral authority of women's role in the family in order to reverse those priorities – and it is worth noting that she did not provide the usual caveat expressing her ignorance in public affairs.

Finally, even in those aristocratic families where the ideals of feminine domesticity seem least significant, other realities could complicate the apparent dominance of the patriarchal model. I have already noted that blood and birth families could compete for the allegiance of aristocratic women. Even more important was the role that could be played by the relative wealth of individual women, enabling some to continue to exercise great power over their children's lives even after the period of early childhood usually designated as mothers' particular domain. The degree to which this was possible depended primarily on the mother's financial status, particularly whether her children remained financially dependent on her. Women were perhaps marginally more likely to maintain such authority over their daughters than over their sons, but this seems to have been of much less importance than the strength derived from economic advantage. Thus, just as social status and wealth were essential factors enabling them, for example, to exercise power over servants in the household, so even within the family money was a significant factor in determining the nature of familial ties. It was when women possessed financial power that the limits of patriarchy were most clearly visible. As the dowager duchess of Portland replied to her son when he wanted to exploit some of the land she held in her own right, 'as by mother's will I am independent, I am determined to keep myself so, and must beg you will never mention it to me again'.[74] The impact of wealth on women's authority may suggest that the virulence of male attacks on pin money and marriage settlements designed to maintain women's financial independence was not unfounded: such independence could indeed alter traditional gender hierarchies.[75]

Sarah, duchess of Marlborough is one extraordinary example of a woman who sought, often successfully, to dominate her family through her control of its wealth, thus creating a family that might almost be termed matriarchal. Her strong will combined with political clout and

---

[73] Lady Mary Hervey to Mr Morris, Ickworth, 22 February 1744, in *Letters of Mary Lepel, Lady Hervey. With A Memoir, and Illustrative Notes* (London, 1821), pp. 35–6.

[74] Quoted in Trumbach, *Egalitarian Family*, p. 83.

[75] For complaints about pin money and women's financial independence, see Tague, *Women of Quality*, pp. 35–42.

spectacularly generous financial settlements meant that she wielded (rightly, in her view) tremendous authority over generations of her extended family. Not only did the duke allow her great financial freedom while he was alive, he also left her a £20,000 annual jointure and made her the major trustee of his estate.[76] Ironically, the strongest historical evidence of Sarah's authority exists in her many letters regarding perceived slights and a flouting of her power in the family, the result of her demand for unquestioning obedience. One daughter, Lady Monthermer, felt obliged to defend herself against Sarah's accusations of disrespect, insisting that 'I think I always make a chursy, or a bow, when I see you, & that one aught not to be out of Bedlam if one cou'd think it not reasonable to doe so, or if one did, not to doe it when one was bid.'[77] Even allowing for the emotional overstatement, the passage shows that she understood the significance of such conventional gestures of deference and obedience. On a more material level, Lady Monthermer protested shortly after her marriage that she had not complained about the pin money her mother had allowed her – 'tho' I confess I was just at that minute that I rec'd your letter, surprised to find it was to be five hundred, because I had all along understood from you it was to be eight hundred pound a year'.[78] The passage shows not only that Sarah determined her daughter's pin money allowance, but also Lady Monthermer's total powerlessness to complain except for the faint plea of 'surprise'. Other occasions prompted further assurances of such obedience to maternal authority. Sarah's daughters frequently wrote that they had obeyed her commands to cease visiting women who had offended her, or to visit others.[79] Even in such apparently trivial social situations they were constantly reminded of their duty to obey.

On occasions when the duchess explicitly discussed her expectations regarding her authority, its extent becomes more visible. In 1732 she insisted that her grandson John Spencer should stand in the Woodstock election rather than at Hampshire, since it was right for him to be elected 'as my Son and Heir'.[80] Here she referred to him not simply as the primary

[76] Frances Harris, *A Passion for Government: The Life of Sarah, duchess of Marlborough* (Oxford, 1991), p. 246.

[77] Lady Monthermer to duchess of Marlborough, [1705–9], BL Add. MS 61450, fol. 33v.

[78] Lady Monthermer to duchess of Marlborough, [early 1705?], BL Add. MS 61450, fol. 17r–v.

[79] See, e.g., Mary, duchess of Montagu to duchess of Marlborough, [after 1709], BL Add. MS 61450, fols. 64r–65r; Henrietta, countess of Godolphin to duchess of Marlborough [June–July 1703?], BL Add. MS 61432, fol. 66r–67r.

[80] Duchess of Marlborough to duchess of Bedford, Marlborough House, 5 December 1732, BL Add. MS 61448, fol. 77r.

male heir of the family, the successor to her husband, but as a successor to herself. Her rage at an engagement between two of her grandchildren in 1733 led to its being broken off after she threatened to disinherit her grandson. Asking for forgiveness, her granddaughter wrote revealingly, 'my only fault has been Loveing a Man, I was fool enough to believe would be Miserable if I did not Marry him; But I find I was a Fool indeed to Venture Your being in the least Angry with me, for the Sake of Mr Spencer.'[81] While the comment is clearly meant to express her regret at doing anything to offend her grandmother, it also suggests the enormous risks involved in making the duchess 'the least Angry'. Sarah's own accounts of her involvement in the marriage negotiations of her female relations equally emphasised her financial power and her leniency in using it wisely. She claimed that the duke gave her the major responsibility for marrying off their children: 'when a Match was considerable in the whole, he never minded the Settlements, & left it to me: And it was entirely by my means that they were so great,' thus preventing her daughters from marrying 'some Country Gentleman of fifteen hundred or two thousand Pounds a year'.[82] On the other hand, when she was offered a great match for her granddaughter, Lady Godolphin, she accepted Lady Godolphin's refusal, and 'Took her in my armes & Assured her That she need not be in any trouble, for I would not ask her, to Marry the Emperour of the World if she did not like him'.[83] There was apparently no question of the girl's parents intervening in this affair. In her account of such marriage negotiations, responsibility for finding a match was left entirely to her, and she sought to portray her actions as the benevolent exercise of absolute power. The expected return for such benevolence was absolute obedience. Sarah's strong will and financial clout enabled her to claim a level of authority ordinarily expected to be exercised only by a man.

On a smaller scale, Jane, countess of Portland also wielded significant authority over her family even after her two sons were grown. By Lord Portland's will, Jane received possession of a house at Whitehall for life, plus an income of 11,000 guilders a year. Because of the lawsuits filed by Lord Portland's children by his first marriage, it is unclear how much of this money Jane actually received, though her daughters ultimately

---

[81] Anne, dowager duchess of Bedford to duchess of Marlborough, Cheam, 7 January 1733, BL Add. MS 61449, fol. 139r.

[82] Duchess of Marlborough to Jane Hammond, 17 November 1739, BL Add. MS 61450, fol. 162r–v.

[83] Duchess of Marlborough, personal narrative, BL Add. MS 61451, fol. 25v.

did receive the portions bequeathed to them.[84] What is most significant, however, is the fact that she was financially independent herself, and that her eldest son, William Bentinck, depended heavily on her throughout his life not only for advice but for financial assistance. Lady Portland was not willing, as Lady Wentworth had been, to favour her eldest son exclusively over her other children or to sacrifice herself on his behalf. In response to an idea he had for her to provide him more financial assistance, she reminded him that she had already given him much more than she had her other children, and said she could offer him no more: 'I am sure you wont think it unreasonable, in me, to consider that I must look, upon my self, as mother to you all, & not because, expences have been imprudently run on in, by one; to make the others suffer from it.'[85] In contrast to Lady Wentworth's defensive tone, Lady Portland's continued firm control of the family finances enabled her to criticise her son for his extravagance and to refuse the help he had requested. Bentinck's letters to his mother contain frequent assertions of his continued respect and obedience. Thus, shortly before his marriage in 1732, he wrote to her asking her to remain in The Hague long enough for him and his new wife to return there from Germany and live under her good influence for some time: 'As little as you have seen me orderly [i.e., financially responsible] hitherto, as much would I try to make my self so at the very first, and I should be very *embarrassé* without you, having firmly resolved to putt my self entirely under your direction.' He also took her advice in his negotiations over marriage settlements.[86]

Lady Portland, in turn, continued throughout their correspondence to give her son detailed advice in the management of his affairs, struggling constantly against his improvidence. When his marriage failed and he was left heavily in debt thanks to his own and his wife's poor economy, she wrote in 1740 reminding him once more that he must be careful about money. She was the one who provided him with what money he had, but 'I have nothing more, then what I am engag'd for, & have given up so much, of my fortune already, as that I should be obligd to retrench, in my way of living, if I did any thing more.'[87] In response to another letter, she listed her many expenses and financial difficulties,

---

[84] See BL Eg. MS 1709, fols. 4–74 (copy of the earl's will and papers relating to the lawsuits); BL Eg. MS 1708, fols. 399–401 (receipts for the payment of Lady Portland's daughters' portions).

[85] Lady Portland to Count Bentinck, Whitehall, 25 April [1740], BL Eg. MS 1715, fol. 123r.

[86] Count Bentinck to Lady Portland, Varel, 7 September 1732, BL Eg. MS 1712, fols. 14r–15r; same to same, Varel, 19 December 1732, BL Eg. MS 1712, fol. 29r–v.

[87] Lady Portland to Count Bentinck, Whitehall, 12 February 1740, BL Eg. MS 1715, fol. 95r.

concluding, 'you may imagine how cruel I find it, after all I have done for you, to see I must be squeesing my self on to assist you still'.[88] Her natural right to give advice as concerned mother continued into adulthood because of his financial dependence on her. Indeed, she thought it should continue even after death, as she left a note asking him to be sure to follow the details of her will even if it did not conform to legal niceties.[89]

The Wentworth family provides two contrasting maternal figures in the persons of Lady Wentworth, the earl of Strafford's mother, and Lady Rawstorn, his wife's grandmother. As we have seen, Lady Wentworth had made herself entirely financially dependent upon her son, and clearly saw herself as subordinate to him in every respect. Rather than demanding and receiving signs of deference from her children, she deferred to Thomas and Lady Strafford frequently remarked on the lack of respect shown Lady Wentworth by her other children.[90] Lady Rawstorn, on the other hand, maintained control of a large sum of money to which Lady Strafford was the presumptive heir – but because Lady Rawstorn refused to commit herself in a will, the need to keep in her good graces remained. Thus Lady Strafford was unable to go to The Hague to visit her husband until she found a way to do so without offending Lady Rawstorn.[91] Her concern was obvious in a remark to Lord Strafford that 'indeed I don't think you need be under the Least fear of her doing us any harm in her will for she seemes very well pleased with me & extremly so with you'.[92] Although Strafford was the titular head of his family and dominated his mother and siblings, he was unable to ignore the financial power vested in Lady Rawstorn, needing her permission even to have his wife visit. Once Lady Strafford arrived at The Hague in 1713, she continued to try to placate her grandmother through letters reiterating both her and her husband's continued respect and obedience. Promising to return home soon, she wrote:

'I can Asure [you] if my Lord ware your own son he cou'd not have more concern than he has, & I doe realy believe we shall be over very soon for as an instance that my Lord desires to be over with all the speed that is posible at the same time

[88] Lady Portland to Count Bentinck, Kensington, 26 August 1741, BL Eg. MS 1715, fol. 287r.
[89] Lady Portland, note accompanying her will, Whitehall, 5 June 1729, BL Eg. MS 1708, fols. 405–6.
[90] E.g., Lady Strafford to Lord Strafford, St James's Square, 3 February 1712/13, BL Add. MS 22226, fols. 285v–286r.
[91] See Lady Strafford to Lord Strafford, St James's Square, 27 November 1711, BL Add. MS 22226, fol. 32r.
[92] Lady Strafford to Lord Strafford, St James's Square, 14 March 1712, BL Add. MS 22226, fol. 99r.

he write to desire the Queen to recall him he desired the secatary of state as soon as he had the Queen's Answere to order A yatch for us.[93]

It was only when Lady Rawstorn died intestate in 1713 and the inheritance was secured that Lord Strafford could be freed from her control.[94] Lady Rawstorn did not seek to dominate her entire extended family in the way that the duchess of Marlborough did, nor did she wield such tremendous political and financial power. But the financial control that she did maintain meant that she continued to influence her granddaughter's life even after Anne married.

Paradoxically, then, the early eighteenth-century aristocratic family combined elements of the three paradigms that Lawrence Stone presented as succeeding one another. In its emphasis on male lineage and extended kin networks, and in its use of those networks to preserve and increase political power, it was similar to Stone's open lineage family. In the primacy it placed on masculine authority, it resembled his restricted patriarchal nuclear family. And in its growing insistence on a special role for women, it held some of the characteristics of his closed domesticated nuclear family, with its affective individualism. Aristocratic families thus bore the hallmarks of both change and continuity. Any grand narrative of change in the family, moreover, must take into account the many ways in which family dynamics were complicated by events such as marriages and deaths; by individual personalities; and even by such mundane factors as personal wealth. The complexity was only increased in the aristocratic family, which in many ways depended on the permeable boundaries between public and private life. Nonetheless, while it may be tempting to dismiss Stone for his whiggish narrative and for his sometimes astonishing ideas about women, he did draw attention to significant transformations in family structure, and his work remains especially useful for helping us conceptualise the interactions of social, cultural, and emotional change over time. Perhaps the apparent triumph of narratives of continuity has less to do with convincing historical argument than with the extraordinary difficulty of constructing an alternative narrative of change that accounts for the many complexities of the early modern family.

---

[93] Lady Strafford to Lady Rawstorn, The Hague, 4 October 1713, BL Add. MS 22226, fol. 345r–v.
[94] TNA: PRO, PROB 6/89: Administration of Dame Alice Rawstorn, November 1713.

9 Reassessing parenting in eighteenth-century England

Joanne Bailey

The last thirty years of scholarship on parent–child relationships in England have been shaped by Lawrence Stone's narrative of evolution in family life. He identified three successive family types between 1500 and 1800, in which parents' emotional attitudes towards their children played a central role in distinguishing the different stages from one another, changing over time from indifference to devotion.[1] Stone's broader thesis has been dismantled, with patriarchy, courtship, married life, kinship, and relationships between parents and offspring coming under close scrutiny. 'Revisionists' attacked Stone's problematic and limited use of sources and demolished his chronological thesis by showing that the early modern family was as affectionate as its eighteenth-century successor.[2] The debate has entered a 'post-revisionist' phase in the last decade, shaped by gender, the inter-active relationship between cultural forces and everyday life, and the influence of both material and emotional factors on people's actions, and also by the attempt to uncover historical subjects' agency and dismantle simplistic concepts such as public and private.[3]

Many thanks to Alysa Levene and John Stewart for reading and making valued comments on this chapter, and to the editors of this volume for their measured, informed criticism and friendly support.

[1] L. Stone, *The Family, Sex and Marriage in England 1500–1800* (abridged edition, London, 1979). His formative position is equivalent to Philippe Ariès's in the European historiography of childhood.

[2] R. Houlbrooke, *The English Family 1450–1700* (London, 1984); A. Macfarlane, *The Family Life of Ralph Josselin, a Seventeenth-Century Clergyman: An Essay in Historical Anthropology* (Cambridge, 1970); L. Pollock, *Forgotten Children: Parent–child Relations from 1500–1900* (Cambridge, 1983); K. Wrightson, *English Society 1580–1680* (London, 1982).

[3] J. Bailey, *Unquiet Lives: Marriage and Marriage Breakdown in England, 1660–1800* (Cambridge, 2003); A. Fletcher, *Gender, Sex and Subordination in England 1500–1800* (New Haven and London, 1995); L. Gowing, *Domestic Dangers: Women, Words and Sex in Early Modern London* (Oxford, 1996); D. O'Hara, *Courtship and Constraint: Rethinking the Making of Marriage in Tudor England* (Manchester, 2000); A. Shepard, *Meanings of Manhood in Early Modern England* (Oxford, 2003); N. Tadmor, *Family and Friends in Eighteenth-Century England: Household, Kinship, and Patronage* (Cambridge, 2001); D. Turner, *Fashioning Adultery: Gender, Sex and Civility in England, 1660–1740* (Cambridge, 2002); A.

Parent–child relationships, however, have still not moved beyond the revisionist phase.[4] Though many aspects of childhood studies have developed in sophisticated and stimulating ways,[5] research into parenting has continued to 'measure' the degree of parental affection and emotional intimacy through the same key milestones: pregnancy and childbirth (including infanticide and abandonment); infant-care practices; discipline; child-independence (training and education); marriage-making; and finally death.[6] From these criteria, to characterise the debate somewhat crudely, traditionalists like Stone concluded that parents were indifferent or neglectful until a 'turning point' (generally either post-Locke or post-Rousseau) after which the child-centred family gained predominance. Revisionists, like Linda Pollock, on the other hand, analyse parents' responses to these stages of childhood within their social, cultural and economic context to demonstrate continuity in parental love. This is a valuable approach since it acknowledges that parents can implement practices that might be disapproved of in other times and places as a result of love for their children and in an attempt to act in their best interests.[7] Yet it has left research into English parenting in something of an historical 'cul-de-sac'.[8] This chapter suggests some ways forward by asking new questions about fatherhood and motherhood informed by gender history and by using matrimonial litigation, a new source material for the experience and portrayal of parenting.

Gender is a category of analysis that is ripe for sustained application to parenting. While it has been used to good effect in examining childrearing practices, decoding the meaning of gendered clothing, toys, education, training, and parental expectations, it has yet to be fully considered in

---

Vickery, *The Gentleman's Daughter: Women's Lives in Georgian England* (New Haven and London, 1998).

[4] The two phases have been described variously as ideas versus experience, H. Cunningham, *Children and Childhood in Western Society since 1500* (2nd edn, Harlow, 2005), p. 7; as domination versus affection, I. K. Ben-Amos, 'Reciprocal bonding: Parents and their offspring in early modern England', *Journal of Family History* 25, 3 (July 2000), 291; and as 'black legend' versus 'white legend', R. Dekker, *Childhood, Memory and Autobiography in Holland from the Golden Age to Romanticism* (Basingstoke, 2000), p. 4.

[5] For example, S. Hussey and A. Fletcher (eds.), *Childhood in Question: Children, Parents and the State* (Manchester, 1999).

[6] An innovative approach to interpreting the impact of the death of children, which sensitively explores the role of children in the family and the self-identity of parents and other adult members of their communities, is found in K. Mizoguchi, 'The child as a node of past, present and future', in J. Sofaer Dervenski (ed.), *Children and Material Culture* (London, 2000), pp. 148–9.

[7] For an overview of these stances see Cunningham, *Children and Childhood*, pp. 5–15; Pollock, *Forgotten Children*.

[8] Dekker's phrase, *Childhood, Memory*, p. 4.

terms of parenting.[9] Literary scholars and historians of art have led the way by investigating the cultural construction and representation of motherhood, linking it to emerging discourses about nation, empire building and class.[10] Historians of lower-ranking lone mothers and the role of gender in the formation of the middle class also touch upon its influence.[11] Even so, the role of gender in shaping the experience and representation of parenting is in its infancy, especially where fatherhood is concerned.[12] This chapter will thus examine gendered representations of paternity and maternity in matrimonial litigation to propose that while there is no firm evidence to argue that affection between parents and children was growing during the eighteenth century, as Stone asserted, there is evidence that the depth of parental emotional intensity was increasingly the focus of attention in conveying the tensions and ideals of elite parenting. The chapter will then conclude by recommending new directions for future work.

Sources

This chapter draws upon seventy-two cases of cruelty and adultery separation cases that came before Durham and York ecclesiastical courts and fifty-eight adultery and 'criminal conversation' (crim. con.) trials[13] heard at Doctors' Commons and King's Bench respectively that were

---

[9] For example see E. A. Foyster, 'Boys will be boys? Manhood and aggression, 1660–1800', in T. Hitchcock and M. Cohen (eds.), *English Masculinities 1660–1800* (London, 1999); L. A. Pollock, '"Teach her to live under obedience": The making of women in the upper ranks of early modern England', *Continuity and Change* 4, 2 (1989), 231–58; K. Calvert, *Children in the House: The Material Culture of Early Childhood, 1600–1900* (Boston, Mass., 1992).

[10] T. Bowers, *The Politics of Motherhood: British Writing and Culture 1680–1760* (Cambridge, 1996); E. J. Yeo, 'The creation of "motherhood" and women's responses in Britain and France, 1750–1914', *Women's History Review* 8, 2 (1999), 201–17; K. Retford, *The Art of Domestic Life: Family Portraiture in England* (New Haven and London, 2006).

[11] L. Davidoff and C. Hall, *Family Fortunes: Men and Women of the English Middle Class, 1780–1850* (London, 1987); T. Evans, *'Unfortunate Objects': Lone Mothers in Eighteenth-Century London* (Basingstoke, 2005), ch. 4.

[12] For the lack of studies of fatherhood see K. Harvey, 'The history of masculinity, circa 1650–1800', *Journal of British Studies* 44 (2005), 310. A similar criticism about the history of French parenting is made by R. G. Fuchs, 'Introduction to the forum on the changing faces of parenthood', *Journal of Family History* 29, 4 (Oct. 2004), 331. For an excellent example of a work that does consider fatherhood from the mid-nineteenth century, see J. Tosh, *A Man's Place: Masculinity and the Middle-Class Home in Victorian England* (London, 1999).

[13] Criminal conversation was a civil action brought by a husband against his wife's lover for financial damages. For details about separation cases before the ecclesiastical courts see Bailey, *Unquiet Lives*, pp. 46–52.

published in two series of adultery trials: *Trials for Adultery* (1779–81) and
A New Collection of Trials for Adultery (1799).[14] Using matrimonial litigation for a study of parenting is novel since most studies of parent–child
relationships focus on ego-documents. Legal records are usually used to
address aspects of childhood such as the employment and apprenticeship of youths, crime committed against or by children and youths, or
what Alysa Levene calls 'liminal' childhood (children outside the normal
family environment), rather than parenting.[15] The most detailed matrimonial cases are useful in several ways to explore parenting because
they frequently include information about spouses' roles as fathers and
mothers. First, they contain empirical evidence that permits a more fluid
and dynamic study of parenting. This is because cases could occur at
several stages in a marriage, giving insights into parenting of younger
and older children, as well as the interaction between step-parents and
step-children.[16] While the most useful cases usually concern wealthy families, since the information appears in defended cases, which were most
expensive, there are glimpses into lower-ranking parental relationships
too. Second, though these were dysfunctional households, they still provide valuable insights into the relationship between ideas and practice
in parenting because, in demonstrating the shortcomings of fathers and
mothers, they indicate prevailing norms. Third, published trials demonstrate how parenting was represented discursively since litigants and their
counsels tactically deployed images of ideal fatherhood and motherhood.
This chapter will focus on two features of parenting that are exposed
by matrimonial litigation: the tensions that parenting caused between

[14] *Trials for Adultery: or, the History of Divorces*, 7 vols. (London, 1779; new edn New York
and London, 1985); *A New Collection of Trials for Adultery: Or, General History of Modern
Gallantry and Divorces* (London, 1799), vol. I. For an analysis of the Trial series and
the significance of adultery in public culture I have consulted S. Lloyd and G. Russell,
'"From Books learn precepts of adult'rate art": An overview of adultery trial literature,
1760–1799' (unpublished paper). My sincere thanks to Sarah Lloyd and Gillian Russell
for allowing me to read this.

[15] I. K. Ben-Amos, *Adolescence and Youth in Early Modern England* (London and New
Haven, 1994); A. Levene, 'Family breakdown and the "welfare child" in nineteenth-
and twentieth-century Britain', in *History of the Family* 11, 2 (2006); H. Shore, *Artful
Dodgers: Youth and Crime in Early Nineteenth-Century London* (London, 1999); J. Warner
and R. Griller, '"My Pappa is out, and my mamma is asleep". Minors, their routine
activities, and inter-personal violence in an early modern town, 1653–1781', *Journal of
Social History* 36 (Spring 2003). Many thanks to Alysa Levene for letting me consult her
review article before publication.

[16] E. A. Foyster, 'Marrying the experienced widow in early modern England: The male
perspective', in S. Cavallo and L. Warner (eds.), *Widowhood in Medieval and Early Modern
England* (Harlow, 1999), 108–24; A. Laurence, 'Intergenerational relations in a complex
family: The case of the Hastings family in the seventeenth and eighteenth centuries'
(unpublished conference paper). Many thanks to Anne Laurence for letting me see this
paper.

spouses and the ways in which ideas about gender influenced parenting as the eighteenth century progressed.

Tensions caused by parenting

A detailed separation case spanning the 1760s and involving one of the leading gentry families in Sunderland has been selected to examine the tensions that differing expectations about appropriate parenting caused between spouses. William Ettrick (1726–1808), a justice of the peace, inherited his estate at High Barnes, Bishop Wearmouth, in 1752, the same year that he got married to Catherine Wharton (?–1794), the daughter of a mayor of Durham. They had two children, also Catherine (1752–1823) and William (1757–1847).[17] Catherine initiated a separation against William on the grounds of cruelty in 1765 at Durham consistory court; William appealed to the provincial court at York resulting eventually in cause papers amounting to approximately 2,000 pages.[18] Six of the nineteen articles making up Catherine's Libel dealt specifically with William's failings as a father and drew comments from numerous deponents.[19] The court case reveals the main sources of tension relating to the Ettricks' parenting: Catherine's pregnancies, the children's christenings, William's interest in his children as infants, and their upbringing and correction. Given the limitations of space, the last two of these issues will be addressed here.

Catherine Ettrick was pregnant almost immediately after her wedding and this seems to have created considerable strains between her and her husband.[20] According to Catherine, William would not see his daughter after her birth on 24 October 1752 and 'if he chanced to pass or go where the Child was then the Nurse always covered the Child up to prevent his seeing it'.[21] Moreover he would not 'suffer it to be brought to his house till it was three quarters of a year old, but sent it to nurse' with Isabel Young, at Newbottle, a few miles away, and did not go to

---

[17] They were a family notable for their longevity and their eccentricity. See E. Watts Moses, 'The Ettricks of High Barnes', *Antiquities of Sunderland*, vol. xx, 1932–43 (1951), and J. W. Summers, *The History and Antiquities of Sunderland* (Sunderland, 1858), vol. I, pp. 186–95.

[18] Catherine's proctors then appealed to the court of Delegates. The case consulted here is that held in the Borthwick Institute of Historical Research (BIHR), Trans.CP.1765/4, *Ettrick c. Ettrick* and related cause papers.

[19] All depositions referred to hereafter as Trans.CP.1765/4 are found pp. 193–572 of the transmitted cause book and are identified by the name of the deponent.

[20] For the tensions that pregnancy could cause in their most extreme form, see E. Foyster, *Marital Violence: An English Family History 1660–1857* (Cambridge, 2005), pp. 135–8.

[21] BIHR, CP.I/1503, *Ettrick c. Ettrick*, Catherine Ettrick's Answers to William Ettrick's Allegation, 10 April 1767.

see his daughter at the nurse's house.[22] Deponents who responded to the Libel supported her accusations against her husband. Ingrid Tague shows that aristocratic families were eager to secure a male heir and that fathers were sometimes criticised by their wives for their lack of interest in female babies.[23] Although William was interested in the Ettrick family's lineage, celebrating his links with his male forbears in his memorial stone, there is no conclusive evidence that he distinguished between his children by sex.[24] He even attempted to break the entail on the family estate and disinherit his son, who later in life described in his diary that he had decamped from 'the cave of despair' when he left his home at the age of twenty-one.[25]

Indeed, Catherine attacked William's lack of interest and affection for both his children as infants. Admittedly she did not make specific complaints about his treatment of his baby son, but this was probably because William 'Determined to leave her and go to the East Indies' as a Purser in the Royal Navy when he discovered she was pregnant again and was absent for four years from 1757 to 1761.[26] Catherine drew attention to William's failings in behaviour toward his children when they were older too. Clearly expressing normative expectations that a father should demonstrate his love for his children, she alleged that he would 'frequently Threaten to Spitt in their Mouths forcing them open, and he frequently Spitt upon their faces and Necks but more frequently upon his Daughter'. George Applegarth recalled seeing William order his children to do something when they had guests. When they did what they were bid, 'some of the Company did say Mr Ettrick shou'd kiss them upon which he said if the Children wou'd come to him he wou'd Spitt in their Mouths and that was the way to kiss them'.[27]

The children's discipline was another area of contention. Here, Catherine offered two kinds of evidence attacking William's actions as a father. First was his capricious and unpredictable exercise of physical punishment. Thus she depicted his correction of his children as an arbitrary act rather than objecting to his paternal authority *per se*. When William was in a 'good humour' he would often lay his daughter across his knee

---

[22] BIHR, Trans.CP.1765/4, *Ettrick c. Ettrick*, Thomasine Walker's and Ann Fawcett's depositions.

[23] See pp. 195–6 of this volume.

[24] An illustration and transcription of the marble cenotaph is included in R. Surtees, *The History and Antiquities of the County Palatine of Durham*. 4 vols. (1816–40), vol. II, p. 239.

[25] Cited by J. Corder in his account of the family. Sunderland Local Studies Library (SLSL), The Corder Manuscripts, No. 28, Bishopwearmouth, Vol. 1 A–L, p. 253.

[26] BIHR, Trans.CP.1765/4, *Ettrick c. Ettrick*, Catherine Ettrick, Libel, pp. 95–182, article 7.

[27] Ibid., Catherine Ettrick, Libel, article 17; ibid., George Applegarth's deposition.

and tickle her about the waist. However, when he was in an 'ill humour', whether she was guilty of any fault or not, he would 'suddenly Curse her, Beat her, throw her upon the Ground and Kick her about the Floor, Telling her he knew she would be a Whore and that she wou'd be Hang'd and once he Kick'd her with so much Violence upon the Belly that some Blood came from her and she complained of being in Great Pain'. Catherine also accused him of frequently beating their son when he was five years old.[28] It was not necessarily that Catherine disagreed that the children needed reprimanding at times. This was demonstrated by Sarah Beadnel's report that William 'took a Hazel Rod and Beat his Daughter in such a Manner that the flesh did rise in Several Parts of her Sides, Back and Arms to thickness of one's Little finger' as punishment for insulting Mary Beadnel by telling her she was an 'ugly Bitch and that her Father had said so'. Sarah explained that it was his wife Catherine who 'told Mr Ettrick of it Least the Child should be Spoiled for abusing the Servants'.[29] This would indicate that Catherine was concerned that her daughter's character as an adult would be damaged if such conduct went uncorrected. However, the physical correction William then applied was considered by his wife and by their servants as far too severe. At other times they felt it was applied to an act that did not require punishment. The proportionate correction of children paralleled attitudes towards the correction of wives where physical chastisement was legitimate but constrained by powerful cultural 'rules' about the degree of force permitted.[30]

The servants' depositions reveal that they discussed William's severity in correcting his children, and, apparently, judged his actions according to the age of the child, the marks left upon its skin, and the presence of blood. Indeed, the servants often introduced new examples of William's ill-treatment of his children in their depositions or elaborated at length on the events about which they were questioned. Mary Reevely explained that she once saw Mr Ettrick give his fifteen-month-old daughter 'a Blow upon the Buttocks with the flat of his Hand with such force that it left the Marck of his hand upon the Buttocks of the Child and saith that the Mark was not gone of[f] in a Day or two afterwards when she show'd the same to Jacob Trotter . . . [her] Brother and Robert Calvert, an acquaintance . . .'[31] Emphasising the disproportionate nature of the father's correction, Mary Beadnel, a former maid, recalled how, when Catherine's

---

[28] BIHR, Trans.CP.1765/4, *Ettrick* c. *Ettrick*, Catherine Ettrick, Libel, article 17.
[29] BIHR, Trans.CP.1765/4, *Ettrick* c. *Ettrick*, Sarah Beadnel's deposition.
[30] Foyster, *Marital Violence*, pp. 39–46.
[31] BIHR, Trans.CP.1765/4, *Ettrick* c. *Ettrick*, Mary Reevely's deposition.

reading did not please her father, 'He with his hand Struck the Child and knock't her down to the Ground.'[32] The servants were prepared to intervene to mediate the treatment if they considered it inappropriate. George Applegarth set the young William to school on Mondays. He recalled taking the boy's breakfast for him when his father had ordered him out in such haste that he missed it at home.[33] Similarly, Isabel King took boiled milk to him when he walked to school 'down the park on the back side of the house where Mr Ettrick could not see him'. She and Ann Wilde brought in Catherine when William locked her outside in the dark and put the frightened child to bed 'in the nursery unknown to the said William Ettrick'.[34] In other words, all members of the extended 'household-family' monitored parenting, even while outwardly conforming to patriarchal forms of discipline.[35]

The other aspect of William's behaviour as a father that was at odds with his household and his wife's expectations was his failure to protect his children. His lack of care in preparing his young son before sending him to school has already been mentioned. On several occasions, William responded to some perceived insubordination by leaving his daughter alone outside. On one occasion, in August 1764, when Catherine junior was eleven, the Ettricks were travelling to Durham assizes in their chaise. In the midst of a sudden thunderstorm, he began to swear at his daughter and beat her 'and then taking the Stool which she satt upon from under her, Struck her with it, so that her Nose bled, and ordering the Chaise to Stopp Putt his Daughter out, tho' it then Rained Hard and she was four Miles from Home and must be up to the Anckles in Dirt upon the High Road before she could Reach any House or shelter'. Deponents stressed that he ordered the chaise on and ignored what became of her.[36] John Arrowsmith remembered a similar occasion when Catherine was riding behind her father on a horse on a family visit to Westoe. Without warning, William suddenly ordered her off the horse and rode away, leaving the child alone. Catherine emphasised her daughter's vulnerability, stating that she was left upon the road 'in a Place where she was an intire Stranger and must Cross the River Wear in a Ferry-Boat before she could get to Sunderland which is above two Miles from Barnes'. William ignored his wife's pleas not to leave their daughter, who was eventually taken care

---

[32] Ibid., Mary Beadnel's deposition.   [33] Ibid., George Applegarth's deposition.
[34] Ibid., Isabel King's and Ann Wilde's depositions.
[35] N. Tadmor, 'The concept of the household-family in eighteenth century England', *Past and Present* 151 (1996), 111–40.
[36] BIHR, Trans.CP.1765/4, *Ettrick* c. *Ettrick*, Jane Nicholson's deposition. Nicholson, the landlady of a nearby public house, got her servant to follow Catherine and looked after her for a few hours before sending her back with someone who boarded with her brother.

of by John Chapman, a passer-by, who found her wandering alone and carried her to his house.[37]

What was William's motivation? Though described as capricious, he does not seem to have been without a formal structure of behaviour guiding him. Where disciplining was concerned he accepted Catherine's allegations, but cast them in a somewhat different light. He denied 'Chastizing his Daughter otherwise then is Incumbent upon a Parent to Chastize and Correct his Children'. He said he did not do this as often as his wife requested him to, and that 'such Chastizement of his . . . Daughter was Generally by giving her a Slap on the face with his open Hand'. He claimed that he hurt her accidentally because she had got into a habit of throwing herself on the floor to avoid the slap. On these occasions he'd give her 'a kick on the Backside and once unluckily hit her in such a manner that he believes two or three Drops of Blood did come from her, since which time he hath never once kicked her'.[38] Where Catherine saw neglect and abandonment, William seems to have believed in the influence of 'Nature', giving freedom to his daughter to walk. For example, in his interrogatories (questions addressed to the deponents answering the articles in Catherine's Libel) he asked whether or not young Catherine regularly walked two miles anyway, with her mother's approval, when she went to collect her brother from school. He implied that the pub was close to where Catherine was ordered out of the chaise and that the weather was not particularly bad.[39] In answer to disapproval of his letting his son walk to school on an empty stomach, he said that his son only missed breakfast once and 'is at Present Healthy and Strong'.[40]

Untangling William's approach to fatherhood is difficult. Why did his view of parenting differ from Catherine's and his servants'? Part of the answer to this question is that, as the Ettricks' statements indicate, a range of views of childrearing could be held by the same family, even perhaps by the same individual. This is important since there was an evolution in attitudes towards childhood over the course of the eighteenth century. Three key 'stages' in thinking have been identified: the 'Puritan' conviction that the child was born in original sin, which permitted corporal punishment as a means to train the child; the Lockean concept that the child entered the world as a clean slate in terms of ideas, which required that the child be moulded by reason and negotiation and only in extremity by physical correction; and the Rousseauian celebration of a distinct phase of

---

[37] Ibid., John Arrowsmith's deposition; Catherine's Positions Additional, p. 612.

[38] Ibid., Personal Answers of William to 17th article of Catherine's Libel, p. 642.

[39] Ibid., William Ettrick's Interrogatories, p. 572.

[40] Ibid., Personal Answers of William to 17th article of Catherine's Libel, p. 642.

childhood in which nature knew best, which promoted a less interventionist form of parenting.[41] None entirely replaced its predecessor, however, and traditional ideas remained in circulation alongside more novel ones.[42]

Thus it seems that some of William's ideas were traditional. In stressing that he had a right as a parent to chastise his children he adhered to the authoritarian image of the father who could deploy physical correction.[43] This was not the dominant discourse of the eighteenth century, however, following John Locke's influential work that rejected physical punishment except in cases of obstinacy.[44] So William's attitudes were possibly 'old-fashioned' by the mid-eighteenth century and certainly departed from his wife's and servants' views. Yet, in his promotion of the physical freedom of his children, he had much in common with Locke's and Rousseau's recommendations that boys be exposed to the cold and wet, and introduced to physical exercise in order to harden them for adult life. By including his daughter in a regime intended for boys, however, he was still out of step with current advice. We need not be surprised by the apparent contradictions in his practice. Modern childhood studies show that where there are several discourses available, parents will often hold internally competing and conflictual views.[45] It would seem that in the eighteenth century the co-existence of several contrasting views about childrearing provided more opportunity for conflict between parents.

The existence of different attitudes towards childrearing within a single household may have also been the result of differing experiences of being parented. William's conduct seems to have reflected inherited beliefs. Somewhat ambivalently, Isabella Ettrick, William's mother, answered Catherine's complaints that William did not see his baby daughter Catherine by asserting that he saw her while she was in the house before nursing 'and took as much Notice of it as parents generally do of children that age'.[46] This rare insight suggests that William was

---

[41] These were followed with the Romantic view of childhood in the early nineteenth century. C. Heywood, *A History of Childhood: Children and Childhood in the West from Medieval to Modern Times* (Cambridge, 2001), pp. 22–7; Dekker, *Childhood, Memory*, pp. 89–90; Cunningham, *Children and Childhood*, pp. 52–72.

[42] Heywood, *History of Childhood*, p. 27; Cunningham, *Children and Childhood*, pp. 59, 66.

[43] Interestingly, he held similar beliefs about chastising his wife. See Bailey, *Unquiet Lives*, p. 121.

[44] J. Locke, *Some Thoughts Concerning Education* (1693), E-text from J. W. Adamson, *The Educational Writings of John Locke* (Cambridge, 1922), letter 78, accessed on www.socsci.kun.nl/ped/whp/histeduc/locke/.

[45] Extract from J. Ribbens, 'Mothers' images of children and their implications for maternal responses', in M. Woodhead and H. Montgomery (eds.), *Understanding Childhood: An Interdisciplinary Approach* (Milton Keynes, 2003), pp. 75–9.

[46] BIHR, CP. I/1475, *Ettrick c. Ettrick*, Isabella Ettrick's deposition, August 1767.

following his own family's model of childrearing, which perhaps diverged from Catherine's understandings. The hypothesis that one's exposure to parenting shaped one's behaviour as a parent is hardly addressed at all in existing historical studies and needs to be more fully explored through research in family archives and more 'self-reflexive' sources such as auto-biographies.

Representing fatherhood

As the Ettrick case study shows, the evaluation of spouses' roles as parents offers empirical evidence of the experience of parenting. It also reveals that such cases can be analysed for what they reveal about changing representations of elite fatherhood and motherhood as well. Introducing a father's ill-treatment of his children was not an unusual tactic in cruelty separation cases, since it aided a woman's case if her husband was a cruel father. Elizabeth Foyster observes that 'providing evidence of how an adult had behaved as a parent was regarded as indicative of their attitudes and conduct in other personal relationships'.[47] This is no doubt part of the reason for the amount of space given over to William Ettrick's paternal role in his wife's cruelty separation against him. Yet in singling out his behaviour as a father in such detail it illustrates that a new emphasis was being placed upon men's behaviour as fathers in the second half of the eighteenth century.

If expectations about appropriate parenting were shaped by prevailing views about the nature of childhood, they were also influenced by gender. The portrayals in matrimonial cases of men and women as spouses and parents correlated closely with dominant ideas about masculinity and femininity. In order to be fully rounded examples of manhood, early-modern men needed to be married and, importantly, to be 'good' husbands and fathers. While respect and affection for wives was advocated in advice literature, much emphasis was placed on discipline and material provision.[48] The primary role of the father in a patriarchal society was as the centre of authority, organising the education, training and discipline of children over the age of seven.[49] Society and the law also demanded

---

[47] Foyster, *Marital Violence*, p. 153.
[48] Bailey, *Unquiet Lives*, p. 63; A. Shepard, 'Manhood, credit and patriarchy in early modern England c.1580–1640', *Past and Present* 167 (2000), 83.
[49] Heywood, *History of Childhood*, p. 104; Loftur Guttormsson, 'Parent–child relations', in D. I. Kertzer and M. Barbagli (eds.), *Family Life in the Long Nineteenth Century 1789–1913* (New Haven, 2002), pp. 266–7. The 1839 Custody of Infants Act allowed women to petition for custody of their children up to the age of seven, Foyster, *Marital Violence*, p. 156.

that men adequately maintain their wives and children.[50] Thus in the cases that came before Durham and York ecclesiastical courts before the mid-eighteenth century, descriptions of inadequate fathering highlighted their failure to provide subsistence.[51] A letter from 'Mrs Heartfelt', published in the *Gentleman's Magazine*, 1732, reflects this view of the duties of fathers. Complaining about young gentlemen who fail in their responsibilities, the author's account of good fatherhood recommended 'the Care of his Family, and feeding his children [which] is more reputable and prudent than the Care of his Hunters, and the feeding his Cocks and other Animals'.[52]

This aspect of fathering continued to be a significant feature of the responsibilities of paternity.[53] The Libel from a 1775 case brought by Anne Parkyns against her husband George Parkyns, esquire, an army captain, for example, stated that he left her in February 1765 'and never paid any regard or attention to their children'.[54] This was clearly intended to demonstrate that he had failed to support them financially. Such images of fatherhood were deployed in crim. con. trials by the husband's counsel against the defendant, the wife's alleged lover. For example, Thomas Erskine, representing Lord Cadogan against the Reverend Mr Cooper in 1794, explained that Cooper's violation of Christian virtues was worse 'as a husband, and as a father of innocent children, who have a right to look up to him for protection'. As he advised the jury, Cooper had already ruined his family himself so that the damages they awarded would not make them suffer worse.[55] Those lower-ranking fathers who deserted their families were also condemned for failure to provide materially for their children and were prosecuted by the quarter sessions.[56] By the 1760s, as Catherine Ettrick's separation case indicates, however, the role of genteel fathers was being expanded to include other attributes.[57] In addition to financial protection and the application of calm and consistent correction, formal written depictions also included emotional closeness as an indicator of a good father.

[50] Bailey, *Unquiet Lives*, pp. 36–7, 63–7, 170–8.
[51] For an example focusing on failure to support their children's education, see BIHR, CP.H/3264, *Allenson c. Allenson*, 1676.
[52] *Gentleman's Magazine* 2 (Feb. 1732), pp. 618–19.
[53] For such continuities in portraits of fathers, see Retford, *Art of Domestic Life*, pp. 126–38.
[54] *Trials for Adultery*, vol. v, *Parkyns c. Parkyns*, 1775, Libel.
[55] Trial of Rev. Mr Cooper for Adultery with the Lady of the Right Honourable Lord Cadogan of Hanover Square, *New Collection of Trials*, pp. 7, 12.
[56] For economic causes of desertion see Bailey, *Unquiet Lives*, pp. 170–8. For evidence from popular literature see Evans, *'Unfortunate Objects'*, p. 58.
[57] It is not suggested that a sentimental version replaced a traditional one. For the point that an emphasis on paternal intimacy could co-exist with patriarchy, see Retford, *Art of Domestic Life*, pp. 13, 16, 126–9.

This more elaborate version of fatherhood was shaped by the cultural phenomena of 'sensibility' and 'domesticity' in two broad ways. First these cultural phenomena elevated fatherhood as a more important element of masculine identity.[58] As Kate Retford illustrates through family portraiture, public portrayals of men's 'properly tender devotion to their offspring' signified their civility and virtue.[59] This seems to have applied to William Ettrick too. In 1782, twenty-six years *before* he died, the *Newcastle Courant* published an announcement of his death:

Died last week at High Barnes near Sunderland, William Ettrick Esq deeply regretted by all who had the singular happiness of his friendship. In the paternal and conjugal character he was eminently remarkable; his pretensions to hospitality and all the social virtues are too well known to require any eulogium.[60]

A subtle lampoon underlay the conventional language of this 'obituary'. In the Bishop Wearmouth area William was admired for his uprightness in carrying out his professional duties as a justice of the peace, but was nonetheless considered personally eccentric due to a tendency to reject norms of sociability.[61] Furthermore, as his wife's cruelty case against him demonstrates, his behaviour towards her and his children was fairly widely known, discussed and often condemned by locals. He also spent much of his time making enemies, carrying out feuds and litigation against neighbours.[62] Thus it is clear that the 'obituary's' author intended it to be read ironically without risking libel. What is important here is that in the 1780s William's inadequacies as a father were considered as significant in judging his character and standing as his relationships with his wife and neighbours.

Secondly, 'sensibility' and 'domesticity' emphasised the freer display of emotions and prized familial intimacy. This contributed to a shift in ideals from an authoritarian father to one who incorporated more 'feminine' characteristics of nurturing and caring. Art historians have delineated the pictorial version of this shift. In British, French and American family portraits the distant, patriarchal authority figure of the father was replaced by a more relaxed, physically and emotionally engaged

---

[58] P. Carter, *Men and the Emergence of Polite Society: Britain 1660–1800* (Harlow, 2001), pp. 96–100; for Europe: Guttormsson, 'Parent–child relations', p. 260.

[59] Retford, *Art of Domestic Life*, pp. 116–21.

[60] Cited in SLSL, Corder Manuscripts, p. 254.

[61] William refused to serve second courses to friends dining with him and reacted furiously when Catherine made a custard for a visiting family. He threw a dish at her, kicked her bottom and had the custard tipped down the necessary. BIHR, Trans.CP.1765/4, *Ettrick c. Ettrick*, William Ettrick's Personal Answers to Libel, p. 642. The story was well known, see SLSL, Corder Manuscripts, pp. 252–3.

[62] Dorset Record Office (DRO), Mrs Sherwood, 'Account of William Ettrick's Life', D1854/3; Watts Moses, 'Ettricks of High Barnes', p. 12.

father–child relationship from the mid-eighteenth century.[63] There are other hints that fatherhood was moving in these directions. The medical profession condemned paternal indifference. William Buchan's *Domestic Medicine* (1785) asserted that fathers had an equal interest in their offspring's welfare and should assist in whatever related to the improvement of their bodies or minds. He disparaged the elite father's 'distance from even the smallest acquaintance with the affairs of the nursery'. Echoing the complaint made thirty years earlier that men paid more attention to their animals than their children, he condemned the man who was prepared to direct the management of his dogs and horses but 'would blush were he surprised in performing the same office for that being who derived its existence from himself, who is heir of his fortunes, and the future hope of his country'.[64] This was a demand that fathers recognise the importance (both personally and nationally) of their offspring and get more closely involved both physically and emotionally.[65]

The new expressions of fatherhood shaped other public images of paternity by the later eighteenth century. In 1793, the *Gentleman's Magazine* published a letter, which was written by J. G. Stedman to his son in 1787 when he thought he was dying. Its sender recommended the letter as 'useful' because the father advised the son how to live a virtuous, temperate life. It also repeatedly stressed the father's love for his son; envisioning meeting with him and his mother 'in the presence of our Heavenly Father . . . [when] our joy and happiness shall be eternal and complete', and signing off 'with an affectionate heart to eternity'.[66] When the *Lady's Magazine* serialised an 'interesting history' of the Monmouth family in 1780 it condemned George Monmouth, originally a shipwright who won a half-share in the lottery, for his unkindness to his eldest children. It contrasted this with his idolisation of his 'little ones'; he 'would still them in the night, nurse them in sickness, and study their accommodation and amusement'.[67] Though rarely analysed systematically, private expressions of loving paternal involvement also abound in the later

---

[63] Retford, *Art of Domestic Life*, ch. 5; 'The Georgian family and the parental role' in 'The new child: British art and the origins of modern childhood', www.bampfa.berkeley.edu/exhibits/newchild/index.html; C. Duncan, 'Happy mothers and other new ideas in eighteenth-century French art', in N. Broude and M. Garrard (eds.), *Feminism and Art History: Questioning the Litany* (New York, 1982), p. 208; Calvert, *Children in the House*, p. 90.

[64] This was an extremely popular medical book in the home, with numerous editions. W. Buchan, *Domestic Medicine* (London, 1785), digitised text, accessed at www.americanrevolution.org/medicine.html, p. 5.

[65] The role of the father in the welfare of the nation was highlighted in art and literature in the same period, Retford, *Art of Domestic Life*, pp. 127–8.

[66] *Gentleman's Magazine* 62 part 2 (1793), p. 802.

[67] *Lady's Magazine* 11 (Aug. 1780), p. 418.

eighteenth century.[68] The relationship between the increasing emphasis on a tender paternal role and lived experience is yet to be unrav-
elled. Nonetheless one exists, for the fact that men were supposed to pay
more attention to their offspring before they reached the age of seven
explains the weight placed upon Catherine Ettrick's complaints about
her husband's lack of interest in his children when they were babies and
infants.

Representing motherhood

The language of motherhood also underwent transformation in the second half of the eighteenth century. For early modern women, 'motherhood conferred reputation of a different sort [from men], underlying their
devotion and tenderness rather than power over their children'.[69] This
continued, but the rhetoric of maternity became more intensely emotional during the eighteenth century.[70] The 'ideal of the tender, noble,
self-sacrificial, and ever-nurturant mother' was codified in the first half
of the eighteenth century and consolidated in the second, when it was
glamorised, morally elevated and put to a wider range of politicised uses.[71]
The developing middle-class ideology of domesticity also shaped images
of motherhood by placing an intensified mother–child relationship at the
core of the new 'self-conscious familialism'.[72] Conveyed in art, fiction
and conduct literature, similarly emotive images of motherhood were also
deployed in adultery separation cases and crim. con. actions where the
behaviour of the accused woman was held up to close scrutiny. This was
particularly so in the latter which were performative in style, examined the
quality of the marital relationship, and deployed often contrasting images
of wives according to whether it was the accused lover's or husband's version of events.[73] As such, these legal cases forcefully demonstrate the

---

[68] Several are mentioned in Vickery, *Gentleman's Daughter*, pp. 122–3.

[69] Ben-Amos, 'Reciprocal bonding', 298.

[70] For the interplay between change and continuity in portrayals of maternity see Retford, *Art of Domestic Life*, chapter three.

[71] Bowers, *Politics of Motherhood*, p. 15; R. Perry, *Novel Relations: The Transformation of Kinship in English Literature and Culture, 1748–1818* (Cambridge, 2004), p. 337; Vickery, *Gentleman's Daughter*, p. 93; Yeo, 'The creation of "motherhood"', *passim*.

[72] For the influence of domesticity on motherhood see M. J. Maynes, 'Class cultures and images of proper family life', in Kertzer and Barbagli, *Family Life*, pp. 195, 198. For the self-sacrificing qualities of motherhood see J. Popiel, 'Making mothers: The advice genre and the domestic ideal, 1760–1830', *Journal of Family History* 29, 4 (Oct. 2004), 340; J. S. Lewis, *In the Family Way: Childbearing in the British Aristocracy, 1760–1860* (New Brunswick, N.J., 1986), pp. 57–9.

[73] S. Staves, 'Money for honor: Damages for criminal conversation', *Studies in Eighteenth Century Culture* 11 (1982), 282–3.

growing importance of idealised motherhood in symbolising domestic and marital harmony.

The 'good mother' was nurturing and self-sacrificing. Adulterous wives were neither since they chose a life of 'depravity' and sin over their children and domestic life.[74] Indeed they shared many of the features of the 'bad mother' utilised in French didactic literature: 'selfish, unnatural, undisciplined, and externalized', whose children 'paid the price for her selfishness'.[75] Adulterous women's elevation of their lovers over their children was a case in point. In the separation case against Sarah Payne, brought in 1776, the deponents called by Edward Payne deposed that when the alleged lover, a JP and officer in the militia, visited Mrs Payne in the parlour she sent out her children. The eldest child would go into the kitchen and say that her mamma had given her a halfpenny to leave the room.[76] The attempt to conflate sexual immorality with bad motherhood was explicit in the very public breakdown of Andrew Robinson Stoney Bowes's marriage to the countess of Strathmore. In response to her case against him on the grounds of cruelty and adultery in 1785, he condemned her on three counts: her sexual behaviour, her financial profligacy, and her inadequate mothering. He produced as evidence her *Confessions* (published in 1793), which he had forced her to write in 1778. In this she admitted guilt for her 'unnatural dislike' of her eldest son and her endeavours to miscarry four pregnancies using medicines. Of the witnesses appearing for Andrew Bowes, one damagingly reported that she had said she loved her cats better than her children. These claims were circulated in pamphlet form and in the press during the couple's extended legal dispute. For example, The *Ton Gazette* reported Mary Bowes's alleged preference for her cats and stated that she had abandoned her eldest son.[77] The accusations were still being circulated in 1799 in a new adultery trial publication.[78]

[74] By being adulterous and/or eloping they lost legal rights to have any access to their children.

[75] Popiel, 'Making mothers', 343. For a visual rebuttal to satirical images which accused Georgiana, duchess of Devonshire of being a bad mother by portraying her as an attentive, devoted mother, see Retford, *Art of Domestic Life*, pp. 196–202.

[76] *Trials for Adultery*, vol. VI, *Payne c. Payne*, Sarah Allen's deposition. Also, *New Collection of Trials*, The Trial of Robert Gordon, Esq., for adultery with Mrs Biscoe, wife of Joseph Seymour Biscoe, Esq., cross examination of housekeeper.

[77] Contained in the voluminous collection of material pertaining to the scandal collected by Judith Baker, University of Durham, University Library, Palace Green Section, Baker–Baker papers, 71/428, fol. 248v.

[78] *New Collection of Trials*, The Trial between countess of Strathmore and her husband Andrew Robinson Stoney Bowes including his allegations against the countess for criminal intercourse with George Gray, Esq.

Motherhood was emblematic enough by the later eighteenth century to be skilfully manipulated by the plaintiff's counsel, who acted for the husband in crim. con. trials. In blackening the character of the alleged seducer, he emphasised the defendant's culpability: seducers were not just denying husbands their wives; they were now tearing mothers from their children.[79] Thomas Erskine, plaintiff's counsel in the trial of Francis Sykes for adultery with the wife of Captain Parslow in 1789, denounced Sykes for denying the couple the joys of parenthood (they had a daughter of four) and sought to increase sympathy for his client by observing that the Parslows' beautiful daughter was a poignant reminder to the husband of his wife and his sorrow due to her loss.[80] Counsels for the plaintiff also increasingly deployed wives' roles as mothers in similarly dramatic ways to establish that women were coercively seduced. In the Duberly v. Gunning trial of 1792, Erskine depicted James Duberly's wife as penitent victim by reading to the court the letter she wrote to her husband after her infidelity, in September 1791. She begged: 'Take care, my dear James, of our offspring. Teach them not to despise their mother . . .' Erskine was apparently so moved by this letter that he was unable to continue his cross examination. It certainly aided his case for large damages for his client against General Gunning whom he cast as old, gouty and lecherous. As he emotively concluded:

you will see how much the scale preponderates in favour of my client. He has been deprived of every thing that could render life dear to him. An affectionate couple in the bloom of youth, and happy in the embraces of each other, have been separated for ever; and this by a MUMMY, who could never have been suspected of such conduct.[81]

While these strategies were intended to facilitate full damages, their publication for a popular audience produced more sympathetic narratives of adulterous wives' maternal plight. For example Joseph Biscoe's counsel (Bearcroft) portrayed Mrs Biscoe's unwilling elopement by suggesting that her lover got her drunk and browbeat her, crowning it all with the report that she was overhead crying 'My God! My God! Can

---

[79] For other strategies employed by plaintiff's counsel to achieve full damages see Staves, 'Money for honor', *passim*.

[80] *New Collection of Trials*, The Trial of Francis William Sykes, Esq., for adultery with the wife of Captain Parslow of the Third Regiment of Dragoons. This, along with the Gunning–Duberly and Bingham–Howard trials, was one of the most highly publicised cases of the period 1789–94. Lloyd and Russell, 'An overview of adultery trial literature', p. 35.

[81] *New Collection of Trials*, The Remarkable Trial of General Gunning for adultery with Mrs Duberly, the wife of James Duberly, Esq.

I leave my child?'[82] Lord Kenyon summed up the Parslow–Sykes case
in 1789 by describing the adulteress as a seduced victim whose voice of
conscience revealed the enormity of her offence via the domestic roles she
had rejected: 'The misery she has entailed upon her family – the thorns
she has planted in the bosom of her husband – an alien from her children – deprived of the sight of them, and their society – taught from their
infancy to look on her with loathing and disgust!'[83] These women were
the ultimate sinners, but also the ultimate losers. The anguish of losing
access to children was conveyed acutely to the reading public through
the Heatley case, published in *Trials for Adultery* between 1779 and 1781.
Richard Heatley sued his wife Arabella for separation in 1770 after her
affair with John Jolly. The letters' original purpose was to offer the ecclesiastical court proof of adultery since in them Arabella regretted and
apologised for her infidelity. Yet the main subject of the twelve letters
written to Richard was her forced separation from her baby Tom, whom
she left when he was around six months old. Offering advice on Tom's
weaning, worrying about his care and health, the letters are eloquent,
agonising accounts of her feelings at being parted from her son. In one
she explained that her heart was bleeding for 'the loss I feel in my child:
nothing but a mother that loves as I do, can tell'. In another she pleaded:

Oh, my dear Heatley, think what I suffer in thus being separated from you both.
Oh my child, my child – My tears make me blot the paper so, that I hardly know
what I have written. Perhaps you will say, I deserve it, and that I brought it on
myself – I own the justness of your argument, but that still makes it the more
terable to bear.[84]

Overall, these images functioned to neutralise the dangerous figure of the
adulteress by returning her to conformity with the self-sacrificing ideal of
the good mother.

New directions in research into parenting

By applying recent conceptual and methodological insights and practices
it is possible to indicate a new agenda for research into parenting. This
chapter has shown that, in addition to intense emotional closeness, the

---

[82] *New Collection of Trials*, The Trial of Robert Gordon, Esq., for adultery with Mrs Biscoe,
wife of Joseph Seymour Biscoe, Esq.

[83] *New Collection of Trials*, The Trial of Francis William Sykes, Esq., for adultery with the
wife of Captain Parslow of the Third Regiment of Dragoons in the court of King's Bench,
1789.

[84] The case was published in volume III and sixteen letters that were submitted to the
ecclesiastical court were published in the final volume, VII. *Trials for Adultery*, vol. III and
vol. VII, pp. 74, 85.

prevailing characteristic of elite motherhood by the late eighteenth century was self-sacrifice.[85] What is more unusual, however, is that it also suggests that fathers seem to have been expected to move closer to this model.[86] Continental historiography offers a hypothesis against which these findings can be tested, which is that ideals of parenting shifted over the 'Romantic' period. Rebekka Habermas proposes that 'disinterested parenting' came into existence in the first few decades of nineteenth-century Germany. This was 'characterized by an absence of parental needs' and entailed a move from traditional reciprocal relationships of mutual dependence to an ideal of parents as devoid of any needs, devoting themselves to their children's wants.[87] Habermas notes that the shift was signified by critiques of cruelty inflicted upon children, greater attention to children's education, condemnation of selfish parents who focused on their own needs, and by changes in the significance children came to have in relationships between spouses.[88]

Such indicators are certainly apparent in English culture in the last quarter of the eighteenth century.[89] For example, although forced marriage was extremely rare, there was a vein of criticism that alleged that aristocratic parents coerced grown children into loveless marriages as a means to further family interests. Instead they were supposed to promote their children's personal happiness.[90] This change of expression is not just evident in parents' relationships with older children. For example, the *York Chronicle* published a poem titled 'The Power of Innocence, A True Story' in 1785. It described the gradual erosion of love between a married couple, 'Sir John' and his 'Lady'. Through familiarity, then complaisance, and finally neglect, they fell to trifling quarrels, which led to anger. Ultimately, 'Love's throne by baseless rage possess'd; / [they] Resolv'd to part, they'd meet no more'. A private separation was drawn up and the day came for the final parting. A delay ensued, however, in

---

[85] In some ways this also characterised public images of lower-ranking plebeian mothers. See discussion of the images that were used to depict the activities of the Foundling Hospital, Evans, *'Unfortunate Objects'*, pp. 77–85.

[86] For a similar finding in English portraiture see Retford, *Art of Domestic Life*, p. 4.

[87] R. Habermas, 'Parent–child relationships in the nineteenth century', *German History* 16, 1 (1998), 44, 46. For the model of reciprocal parenting see Ben-Amos, 'Reciprocal bonding', *passim*; and S. Marshall, '"Dutiful love and natural affection": Parent–child relationships in the early modern Netherlands', in J. B. Collins and K. L. Taylor, *Early Modern Europe: Issues and Interpretations* (Oxford, 2006), pp. 138–52.

[88] Habermas, 'Parent–child relationships', 47–9, 50.

[89] For reactions to cruelty against children in the late eighteenth and early nineteenth centuries see Cunningham, *Children and Childhood*, pp. 152–3.

[90] For this line of criticism see D. T. Andrew, '"Adultery à-la-mode": Privilege, the law and attitudes to adultery 1770–1809', *The Historical Association* (1997), 14; Evans, *'Unfortunate Objects'*, p. 63.

the form of their 'one lovely girl', 'The father's, mother's darling'. Ready to depart for his new home in town, Sir John turned 'to the darling of his heart' and asked her to bid her Mama goodbye. His wife cried out 'No', that Betsey would live with her. Sir John asked Betsey to choose. In the face of her little girl's tears and indecision, and forced to spell out the plan to live apart, the mother's 'grief o'erflow'd her breast,/ And Tears burst out, too long suppress'd'. Betsey thus supposed her father was unhappy and tried to get him to relent, lisping, '"Papa! Do Love dear Mama – Mama loves you!"' This did the trick and Sir John's 'manly pride' was cast aside; he and his wife realised they still loved each other and 'Breast rush'd to breast, and heart to heart, / Each clasp'd their Betsey o'er and o'er, / And Tom drove empty from the door'.[91] It is clear that the notion of a small child's ability to rescue adults from disaster and to awaken them to love was not just a product of nineteenth-century Romanticism.[92] Also, the poem celebrates parents who eventually prioritised their daughter's desires over their own. Such indications of parental 'affect' have been interpreted as a 'sign of merit' in family portraiture in the same period.[93] This sentimental poem also tells its readers that parents who put their children's needs first would be rewarded with stronger love for each other. Jean-Jacques Rousseau's *Emile*, published in instalments in 1780 in the *Lady's Magazine*, made the same point. Rousseau asserted that the presence of infant children in the house (nursed by their mothers) 'makes the father and mother more useful, dearer to one another, and strengthens the conjugal union'.[94]

This chapter has focused on deploying gender as a category of analysis. Another theoretical model is offered by European historians' exploration of the way that the memory of childhood was exploited to construct adult self-identity from the turn of the eighteenth century.[95] While this is part of the wider field of interest in 'the relationship between identity and biography' it would be fruitful to apply linguistic analysis of autobiography and memory to uncover more about the impact of the process of individualism upon parenting in England at such a formative period.[96]

---

[91] *York Chronicle* (14 Oct. 1785), p. 3.   [92] Cunningham, *Children and Childhood*, p. 69.

[93] Retford, *Art of Domestic Life*, p. 8.

[94] *Lady's Magazine* 11 (March 1780), p. 148. A similar didactic message that parental devotion brought benefits was conveyed in art too. James Steward, 'The family and sentiment' in 'The new child: British art and the origins of modern childhood', www.bampfa.berkeley.edu/exhibits/newchild/index.html.

[95] For specific relationship with childhood see J. Schlumbohm, 'Constructing individuality: Childhood memories in late eighteenth-century "empirical psychology" and autobiography', *German History* 16, 1 (1998); R. Dekker, *Childhood, Memory*, ch. 13.

[96] For this and its influence upon the use of 'life stories as historical source' see M. Chamberlain, 'Small worlds: Childhood and empire', *Journal of Family History* 27, 2 (2002), 187–8.

As Mary Chamberlain observes in her work on the relationship between attitudes to childrearing and wider social values, 'how people recount childhood reflects not only their experiences but also the assumptions and attitudes to childhood that they have inherited or acquired in their adult lives'.[97]

The concept that parenting is shaped by experience and inherited or acquired assumptions and attitudes is another inspiration for formulating new questions about parenting in the early modern period. The key, as suggested above, is to move beyond the static approach to parenting that arises out of the focus on fixed points of childhood. Studies of parenting need to incorporate current research in the social and behavioural sciences that demonstrates that parent–child relationships are interactive.[98] An analysis of the interplay of relationships would be rewarding; for example the 'triangle' between father–mother–child 'where the relation within each pair had a strong impact on the third person', or alternative groupings where more children are included. This approach could be applied to most forms of ego-documents from correspondence through journals to autobiographies to offer new insights into the way that the relationships between all protagonists shaped parenting and to give clues about how far parents' relationships with their offspring differed according to the child's sex and birth order.[99]

Studies of parent–child relationships in the early modern era are usually chronologically fixed in particular periods, such as infancy from around 0–2 years, childhood from 2–7 years, and then from around 7 to mid-teens.[100] Most end their research when children gained some form of independence, leaving home to carry out training, paid labour or 'higher' education. With the exceptions of Illana Ben-Amos and Elizabeth Foyster, who examine early modern parents' ongoing relationships with their children during adulthood, interaction between parents and offspring usually emerges in 'snapshots' such as at the time of a child's courtship or at the moment of inheritance upon a parent's death; both events

---

[97] Ibid., 188.

[98] M. Woodhead, 'The child in development', in Woodhead and Montgomery, *Understanding Childhood*, pp. 113–20; Heywood, *History of Childhood*, p. 4; J. Sofaer Dervenski, 'Material culture shock: Confronting expectations in the material culture of children', in *Children and Material Culture*, pp. 11–12.

[99] For the potential of this approach see Ingrid Tague's chapter in this volume. Also see Schlumbohm, 'Constructing individuality', 37, 38. Patricia Crawford posed the question that mothers may have had different types of relationships with their children in 'The construction and experience of maternity in seventeenth-century England', in V. Fildes (ed.), *Women as Mothers in Pre-Industrial England: Essays in Honour of Dorothy McLaren* (London, 1990), p. 27.

[100] See the structure of Heywood, *History of Childhood*, part II.

that emphasise the instrumental features of parent–child relationships.[101] These approaches are directed in part by the availability of sources; yet there is ample evidence in correspondence, journals and litigation that parenting continued into a child's adulthood and this still needs to be fully analysed to understand how far parents' emotional and power relationships with their children changed over the life-course.[102]

The generational aspects of parenting also need to be studied, as the Ettrick case hints. Although current childhood studies tackle the question of how far the experience of being parented directs modes of parenting, it is largely absent from many existing historical studies of parenting.[103] Given that parents had a significant role in rearing and educating offspring, there is scope to examine how far children's identification with parents' values or rejection of them shaped their own behaviour as parents. This is easier to achieve from the later eighteenth century when, as Rudolf Dekker observes from Dutch evidence, people were more likely to reflect on their memories of their childhood and to discuss their own children in more detail.[104] Furthermore, this era was one in which successive generations were influenced by novel ideologies of childhood.

Finally, questions about interaction across generations raise the almost entirely neglected subject of grandparenting.[105] The proportion of people aged sixty and over declined from around 10 per cent to 7 per cent across the eighteenth century, but since the population was rising fast by the late eighteenth century the absolute number of people over sixty was growing. Moreover, as the age of marriage was falling so was the age of grandparenthood for some sections of society and, in any case, this stage of the life-course could start in the fifties.[106] Whatever their number, there is evidence from historians of old age and kinship that the elderly were

---

[101] E. Foyster, 'Parenting was for life, not just for childhood: The role of parents in the married lives of their children in early modern England', *History* 86 (2003), 313–27; Ben-Amos, 'Reciprocal bonding'.

[102] Schlumbohm describes 'Schack Fluur's changing feelings from conflict to identification with his father', in 'Constructing individuality', 37–9.

[103] H. Montgomery, 'Childhood in time and place', in Woodhead and Montgomery, *Understanding Childhood*, pp. 48–9.

[104] Dekker, *Childhood, Memory*, ch. 13.

[105] An exception is the brief but interesting section in S. Ottaway, *The Decline of Life: Old Age in Eighteenth-Century England* (Cambridge, 2003), pp. 155–65. For an analysis of the vital role of grandparents in other cultures see Chamberlain, 'Childhood and empire', 192–5.

[106] E. A Wrigley and R. S. Schofield, *The Population History of England, 1541–1871: A Reconstruction* (London, 1981), pp. 216–17. Ottaway, *Decline of Life*, pp. 21–3. I am grateful to Steve King for explaining and clarifying the demographic status of the elderly in the long eighteenth century.

an increasingly important section of society.[107] Thus, scattered about the historiography there are numerous glimpses of grandparents assisting their children by caring for their grandchildren, or taking over when their children died.[108] A sustained analysis of parents' roles in their children's and grandchildren's lives would answer important questions, such as: was the experience of parenting dissimilar from grand-parenting; did grandparents treat their children differently from their grandchildren; and, did grandparents play an important part in cultural transference?[109]

The opening out of the category of parenting also draws in other carers, who can be loosely defined as 'surrogate parents'. This incorporates a range of relationships involving the temporary or permanent acts of caring, nurturing and maintenance. This is only really addressed critically with regard to wet nursing. As recent studies of the structure of the household and concept of family and kin demonstrate, the family was a far more complex, fluid unit than the concept of 'nuclear' would allow.[110] Although there is evidence in many of the usual sources for parenting and childhood, the presence of servants and other family members in caring for children is rarely investigated. For the early modern period, at least, and continuing into the eighteenth century, there were also foster parents who cared temporarily for children due to economic or physical need, and frequently during a child's education. For example, William Ettrick junior was boarded out with his aunt when he attended school in York at the age of nine.[111] Moreover, remarriage forged new relationships with the introduction of step-parents and siblings, and marriage itself created in-law relationships. While the material and demographic aspects of these have been touched upon, their emotional ones have not.

Conclusion

In his sweeping historical narrative of the family, Lawrence Stone documented several of the shifts in representations of parenting in the historical record that are discussed in this chapter. He identified a greater

---

[107] S. Ottaway, 'The old woman's home in eighteenth-century England', in L. Botelho and P. Thane (eds.), *Women and Ageing in British Society Since 1500* (Harlow, 2001), pp. 125–6; Ottaway, *Decline of Life, passim.*

[108] Ben-Amos, 'Reciprocal bonding', 295; K. Charlton, 'Mothers as educative agents in pre-industrial England', *History of Education* 23, 2 (1994), 149–5, 152; Crawford, 'Construction and experience of maternity', pp. 25–6; Lewis, *In the Family Way*, p. 52; Ottaway, *Decline of Life*, pp. 158–65.

[109] For the point that the overlap between generations facilitates cultural transference and innovation see G. Lilehammer, 'The world of children', in J. Sofaer Dervenski, *Children and Material Culture*, pp. 22–3.

[110] Tadmor, *Family and Friends, passim.*

[111] Watts Moses, 'Ettricks of High Barnes', p. 12.

emphasis on parental affection towards children in both art and social commentary in the second half of the eighteenth century.[112] Matrimonial litigation reveals something similar. In addition to heightened emphasis on self-sacrificing motherhood, these court records suggest that more was demanded of fathers too. Fatherhood was becoming multi-faceted with expectations of emotionally close, nurturing behaviour. Stone's interpretation of such cultural shifts as transformations in attitudes that conformed to chronological stages has been justly condemned. Yet this line of research still needs to be pursued, not only to open up to enquiry the still-neglected subject of fatherhood, but also to delineate more clearly the changing ideological formulations of parenting in England. It is proposed here that fathers were being brought into line with mothers to put their children's individual interests ahead of their own. While this could be said to have been an enduring feature of the parental–offspring relationship, measurable in the way that middling-sort parents were determined to take on considerable financial burdens to further their children's future livelihoods, its emotional aspects were increasingly prioritised.[113] As Retford's work shows, it is crucial to analyse why people sought to present their emotional lives in new ways.[114] It is also essential to consider more fully the complex relationship between discourse in newspapers, periodicals and didactic literature and the experience of parenting.

Finally, it is time to set aside Stone's agenda for research into English parent–child relationships and seek new directions. This chapter has suggested that the study of parenting needs to explore the role of gender in moulding mothers and fathers and their interaction with their children, and must recognise that children influenced parents as well as vice versa. It is also crucial to move beyond parent–child relationships as a set of 'benchmarks' to a more fluid and dynamic picture of parenting that expands our chronological and definitional boundaries to include a variety of parenting relationships across life-courses, across generations, and (where servants were concerned) across class.[115] With a new research agenda, more sophisticated models of change should emerge that sensitively locate both the enduring and the changing faces of parenting within a century shaped by four formative stages in thinking about childhood and by the key concepts of 'sensibility' and 'domesticity'.

[112] Stone, *Family, Sex and Marriage*, pp. 259, 275–8, 286–8.
[113] M. Mascuch, 'Social mobility and middling self-identity: The ethos of British autobiographers, 1600–1750', *Social History* 20, 1 (1995), 45–61.
[114] Retford, *Art of Domestic Life, passim*.
[115] I plan to address these issues in a book-length research project entitled 'Parenting in England, *c*. 1740–1840'.

Select bibliography

This select bibliography is intended as a guide to further reading. Publications are arranged thematically, and listed by date of publication.

LAWRENCE STONE AND FAMILY HISTORY

Stone, L., *The Crisis of the Aristocracy 1558–1641*, Oxford, 1965.
Stone, L., *The Family, Sex and Marriage in England 1500–1800*, London, 1977; abridged edition, London, 1979.
Stone, L. and Stone, J. C. F., *An Open Elite? England 1540–1880*, Oxford, 1984.
Stone, L., *The Road to Divorce: England 1530–1987*, Oxford, 1990.
Stone, L., *Uncertain Unions: Marriage in England 1660–1753*, Oxford, 1992.
Stone, L., *Broken Lives: Separation and Divorce in England 1660–1857*, Oxford, 1993.

WRITING FAMILY HISTORY

Anderson, M., *Approaches to the History of the Western Family, 1500–1914*, London, 1980.
Haraven, T. K., 'The history of the family and the complexity of social change', *American Historical Review* 96, 1(1991), 95–124.
Wrightson, K., 'The family in early modern England: Continuity and change', in S. Taylor, R. Connors and C. Jones (eds.), *Hanoverian Britain and Empire: Essays in Memory of Philip Lawson*, Woodbridge, Suffolk, 1998, pp. 1–22.

GENERAL SURVEYS

Wrightson, K., *English Society 1580–1680*, London, 1982.
Houlbrooke, R. A., *The English Family 1450–1700*, London, 1984.
Abbott, M., *Family Ties: English Families 1540–1920*, London, 1993.
Coster, W., *Family and Kinship in England 1450–1800*, Harlow, 2001.

DEMOGRAPHIC APPROACHES TO THE FAMILY

Laslett, P. and Wall, R. (eds.), *Household and Family in Past Time*, Cambridge, 1972.
Laslett, P., *Bastardy and its Comparative History*, London, 1980.

Wrigley, E. A. and Schofield, R. S., *The Population History of England, 1541–1871: A Reconstruction*, London, 1981.

Schofield, R. S., 'English marriage patterns revisited', *Journal of Family History* 10 (1985), 2–20.

Wrigley, E. A., Davies, R. S., Oeppen, J. E. and Schofield, R. S., *English Population History from Family Reconstitution, 1580–1837*, Cambridge, 1997.

Sharpe, P., *Population and Society in an East Devon Parish*, Exeter, 2002.

GENDER, PATRIARCHY AND THE FAMILY

Schochet, G. J., *Patriarchalism in Political Thought: The Authoritarian Family and Political Speculation and Attitudes, Especially in Seventeenth-Century England*, New York, 1975.

Amussen, S., *An Ordered Society: Gender and Class in Early Modern England*, Oxford, 1988.

Pateman, C., *The Sexual Contract*, Cambridge, 1988.

Hindle, S., 'The shaming of Margaret Knowsley: Gossip, gender and the experience of authority in early modern England', *Continuity and Change* 9, 3 (1994), 391–419.

Fletcher, A., *Gender, Sex and Subordination in England 1500–1800*, New Haven and London, 1995.

Gowing, L., *Domestic Dangers: Women, Words and Sex in Early Modern London*, Oxford, 1996.

Mendelson, S. H. and Crawford, P., *Women in Early Modern England*, Oxford, 1998.

Pollock, L. A., 'Rethinking patriarchy and the family in 17th-century England', *Journal of Family History* 23, 1 (1998), 3–27.

Foyster, E. A., *Manhood in Early Modern England: Honour, Sex and Marriage*, Harlow, 1999.

Weil, R., *Political Passions: Gender, the Family and Political Argument in England 1680–1714*, Manchester, 1999.

Shepard, A., 'Manhood, credit and patriarchy in early modern England, c.1580–1640', *Past and Present*, 167 (2000), 75–106.

Berry, H., *Gender, Society and Print Culture in Late-Stuart England: The Cultural World of the Athenian Mercury*, Aldershot, 2003.

Capp, B., *When Gossips Meet: Women, Family, and Neighbourhood in Early Modern England*, Oxford, 2003.

Gowing, L., *Common Bodies: Women, Touch and Power in Seventeenth-Century England*, New Haven and London, 2003.

Crawford, Patricia, *Blood, Bodies and Families in Early Modern England*, Harlow, 2004.

POOR FAMILIES

Wrightson, K. and Levine, D., *Poverty and Piety in an English Village: Terling 1525–1700*, London, 1979; second edition 1995.

Sharpe, J. A., 'Plebeian marriage in Stuart England: Some evidence from popular literature', *Transactions of the Royal Historical Society*, 5th series, 5 (1986), 69–90.

Hitchcock, T., King, P. and Sharpe, P. (eds.), *Chronicling Poverty: The Voices and Strategies of the English Poor 1640–1840*, Basingstoke, 1997.

Sokoll, Thomas (ed.), *Essex Pauper Letters, 1731–1837* (Records of Social and Economic History, new ser., 30), Oxford, 2001.

Hindle, S., *On the Parish? The Micro-Politics of Poor Relief in Rural England c.1550–1750*, Oxford, 2004.

MIDDLING-SORT FAMILIES

Davidoff, L. and Hall, C., *Family Fortunes: Men and Women of the English Middle Class, 1780–1850*, London, 1987.

Earle, P., *The Making of the English Middle Class: Business, Society and Family Life in London, 1660–1730*, London, 1991.

Barry, J. and Brooks, C. (eds.), *The Middling Sort of People: Culture, Society and Politics in England, 1550–1800*, Basingstoke and London, 1994.

Hunt, M. R., *The Middling Sort: Commerce, Gender, and the Family in England, 1680–1780*, London, 1996.

ELITE FAMILIES

Trumbach, R., *The Rise of the Egalitarian Family: Aristocratic Kinship and Domestic Relations in Eighteenth-Century England*, New York, 1978.

Pollock, L. A., '"Teach her to live under obedience": The making of women in the upper ranks of early modern England', *Continuity and Change* 4, 2 (1989), 231–58.

Heal, F. and Holmes, C., *The Gentry in England and Wales 1500–1700*, Basingstoke, 1994.

Vickery, A., *The Gentleman's Daughter: Women's Lives in Georgian England*, New Haven and London, 1998.

Harris, B. J., *English Aristocratic Women, 1450–1550: Marriage and Family, Property and Careers*, Oxford, 2002.

Tague, I. H., *Women of Quality: Accepting and Contesting Ideals of Femininity in England, 1690–1760*, Woodbridge, Suffolk, 2002.

Chalus, E., *Elite Women in English Political Life, c.1754–1790*, Oxford, 2005.

COURTSHIP AND MARRIAGE

Outhwaite, R. B. (ed.), *Marriage and Society: Studies in the Social History of Marriage*, London, 1981.

Gillis, J. R., *For Better, For Worse: British Marriages, 1600 to the Present*, Oxford, 1985.

Macfarlane, A., *Marriage and Love in England: Modes of Reproduction 1300–1840*, Oxford, 1986.

Ingram, M., *Church Courts, Sex and Marriage in England, 1570–1640*, Cambridge, 1987.

Fletcher, A., 'The Protestant idea of marriage in early modern England', in A. Fletcher and P. Roberts (eds.), *Religion, Culture and Society in Early Modern Britain: Essays in Honour of Patrick Collinson*, Cambridge, 1994, pp. 161–81.

Outhwaite, R. B., *Clandestine Marriage in England 1500–1850*, London, 1995.

Hindle, S., 'The problem of pauper marriage in seventeenth-century England', *Transactions of the Royal Historical Society*, 6th series, 8 (1998), 71–89.

O'Hara, D., *Courtship and Constraint: Rethinking the Making of Marriage in Tudor England*, Manchester, 2000.

CHILDREN, CHILDHOOD AND ADOLESCENCE

Ariès, P., *Centuries of Childhood*, London, 1962.

Smith, S. R., 'The London apprentices as seventeenth-century adolescents', *Past and Present* 61 (1973), 149–61.

Plumb, J. H., 'The new world of children in eighteenth-century England', *Past and Present* 67 (1975), 64–95.

de Mause, L. (ed.), *The History of Childhood: The Untold Story of Child Abuse*, London, 1976.

Thomas, K., 'Age and authority in early modern England', *Proceedings of the British Academy* 62 (1976), 205–48.

Pollock, L., *Forgotten Children: Parent–Child Relations from 1500–1900*, Cambridge, 1983.

Capp, B., 'English youth groups and "The Pinder of Wakefield"', in P. Slack (ed.), *Rebellion, Popular Protest and Social Order in Early Modern England*, Cambridge, 1984, pp. 212–18.

Thomas, K., 'Children in early modern England', in G. Avery and J. Briggs (eds.), *Children and Their Books: A Celebration of the Work of Iona and Peter Opie*, Oxford, 1989, pp. 45–77.

Rushton, P., 'The matter in variance: Adolescents and domestic conflict in the pre-industrial economy of northeast England, 1600–1800', *Journal of Social History* 25, 1 (1991), 89–107.

Calvert, K., *Children in the House: The Material Culture of Early Childhood, 1600–1900*, Boston, Mass., 1992.

Mitterauer, M., *A History of Youth*, Oxford, 1992.

Ben-Amos, I. K., *Adolescence and Youth in Early Modern England*, London and New Haven, 1994.

Fletcher, A., 'Prescription and practice: Protestantism and the upbringing of children 1560–1700', in D. Wood (ed.), *The Church and Childhood*, Studies in Church History 31, Oxford, 1994, pp. 325–46.

Cunningham, H., *Children and Childhood in Western Society since 1500*, Harlow, 1995; second edition 2005.

Griffiths, P., *Youth and Authority: Formative Experiences in England 1560–1640*, Oxford, 1996.

Hussey, S. and Fletcher, A. (eds.), *Childhood in Question: Children, Parents and the State*, Manchester, 1999.

Heywood, C., *A History of Childhood: Children and Childhood in the West from Medieval to Modern Times*, Cambridge, 2001.

PARENTING

Lewis, J. S., *In the Family Way: Childbearing in the British Aristocracy, 1760–1860*, New Brunswick, N.J., 1986.
Fildes, V. (ed.), *Women as Mothers in Pre-Industrial England: Essays in Honour of Dorothy McLaren*, London, 1990.
Bowers, T., *The Politics of Motherhood: British Writing and Culture, 1680–1760*, Cambridge, 1996.
Ben-Amos, I. K., 'Reciprocal bonding: Parents and their offspring in early modern England', *Journal of Family History* 25, 3 (July 2000), 291–312.
Foyster, E., 'Parenting was for life, not just for childhood: The role of parents in the married lives of their children in early modern England', *History* 86 (2003), 313–27.
Cody, L. F., *Birthing the Nation: Sex, Science, and the Conception of Eighteenth-Century Britons*, Oxford, 2005.
Evans, T., *'Unfortunate Objects': Lone Mothers in Eighteenth-Century London*, Basingstoke, 2005.

KINSHIP

Wrightson, K., 'Household and kinship in sixteenth-century England', *History Workshop Journal* 12 (1981), 151–8.
Cressy, D., 'Kinship and kin interaction in early modern England', *Past and Present* 113 (1986), 38–69.
Wolfram, S., *In-Laws and Outlaws: Kinship and Marriage in England*, London, 1987.
Larminie, V., *Wealth, Kinship and Culture: The Seventeenth-Century Newdigates of Arbury and Their World*, Woodbridge, Suffolk, 1995.
Tadmor, N., *Family and Friends in Eighteenth-Century England: Household, Kinship, and Patronage*, Cambridge, 2001.
Coster, W., *Baptism and Spiritual Kinship in Early Modern England*, Aldershot, 2002.
Perry, R., *Novel Relations: The Transformation of Kinship in English Literature and Culture, 1748–1818*, Cambridge, 2004.

SINGLE WOMEN

Peters, C., 'Single women in early modern England: Attitudes and expectations', *Continuity and Change* 12, 3 (1997), 325–45.
Bennett, J. M. and Froide, A. M. (eds.), *Singlewomen in the European Past 1250–1800*, Philadelphia, 1999.
Sharpe, P., 'Dealing with love: The ambiguous independence of the single woman in early modern England', *Gender and History* 11, 2 (1999), 209–32.
Hill, B., *Women Alone: Spinsters in Britain 1660–1850*, London, 2001.

Froide, A. M., *Never Married: Singlewomen in Early Modern England*, Oxford, 2005.

THE FAMILY ECONOMY

Clark, A., *Working Life of Women in the Seventeenth Century*, London, 1919.

Thompson, E. P., 'The moral economy of the English crowd in the eighteenth century', *Past and Present* 50 (1971), 76–136.

Levine, D., *Family Formation in an Age of Nascent Capitalism*, New York, 1977.

Smith, R. M. (ed.), *Land, Kinship and Life-Cycle*, Cambridge, 1984.

Roberts, M., '"Words they are women, and deeds they are men": Images of work and gender in early modern England', in L. Charles and L. Duffin (eds.), *Women and Work in Pre-Industrial England*, London, 1985, pp. 122–80.

Houlbrooke, R. A., 'Women's social life and common action in England from the fifteenth century to the eve of the civil war', *Continuity and Change* 1 (1986), 171–89.

Wall, R., 'Work, welfare and family: An illustration of the adaptive family economy', in L. Bonfield, R. M. Smith and K. Wrightson (eds.), *The World We Have Gained: Histories of Population and Social Structure*, Oxford, 1986, pp. 261–94.

Levine, D., *Reproducing Families: The Political Economy of English Population History*, Cambridge, 1987.

Hill, B., *Women, Work, and Sexual Politics in Eighteenth-Century England*, Oxford, 1989.

Sharpe, P. (ed.), *Women's Work: The English Experience 1650–1914*, London, 1998.

Wrightson, K., *Earthly Necessities: Economic Lives in Early Modern Britain*, London, 2000.

Grassby, R., *Kinship and Capitalism: Marriage, Family, and Business in the English-Speaking World, 1580–1740*, Cambridge, 2001.

Agren, M. and Erickson, A. L. (eds.), *The Marital Economy in Scandinavia and Britain 1400–1900*, Aldershot, 2005.

FAMILIES AND PROPERTY

Macfarlane, A., *The Origins of English Individualism: The Family, Property and Social Transition*, Cambridge, 1979.

Weatherill, L., 'A possession of one's own: Women and consumer behavior in England, 1660–1740', *Journal of British Studies* 25 (1986), 131–56.

Staves, S., *Married Women's Separate Property in England, 1660–1833*, Cambridge, Mass., 1990.

Spring, E., *Law, Land, and Family: Aristocratic Inheritance in England, 1300 to 1800*, Chapel Hill, 1993.

Erickson, A. L., *Women and Property in Early Modern England*, London, 1995.

Stretton, T., *Women Waging Law in Elizabethan England*, Cambridge, 1998.

Finn, M., 'Men's things: Masculine possession in the consumer revolution', *Social History* 25, 3 (2000), 133–55.

Wright, N. E., Ferguson, M. W. and Buck, A. R. (eds.), *Women, Property, and the Letters of the Law in Early Modern England*, Toronto, 2004.

MARRIAGE BREAKDOWN, SEPARATION AND DIVORCE

Thomas, K., 'The Puritans and adultery: The Act of 1650 reconsidered', in D. H. Pennington and K. Thomas (eds.), *Puritans and Revolutionaries: Essays in Seventeenth-Century History Presented to Christopher Hill*, Oxford, 1978, pp. 257–82.

Ingram, M., *Church Courts, Sex and Marriage in England, 1570–1640*, Cambridge, 1987.

Phillips, R., *Putting Asunder: A History of Divorce in Western Society*, Cambridge, 1988.

Hunt, M., 'Wife beating, domesticity and women's independence in eighteenth-century London', *Gender and History* 4, 1 (1992), 10–33.

Amussen, S. D., '"Being stirred to much unquietness": Violence and domestic violence in early modern England', *Journal of Women's History* 6, 2 (1994), 70–89.

Turner, D., *Fashioning Adultery: Gender, Sex and Civility in England, 1660–1740*, Cambridge, 2002.

Bailey, J., *Unquiet Lives: Marriage and Marriage Breakdown in England, 1660–1800*, Cambridge, 2003.

Foyster, E., *Marital Violence: An English Family History 1660–1857*, Cambridge, 2005.

WIDOWHOOD

Carlton, C., 'The widow's tale: Male myths and female reality in 16th and 17th century England', *Albion* 10 (1978), 118–29.

Todd, B. J., 'The remarrying widow: A stereotype reconsidered', in M. Prior (ed.), *Women in English Society, 1500–1800*, London, 1985, pp. 54–92.

Brodsky, V., 'Widows in late Elizabethan London: Remarriage, economic opportunity and family orientations', in L. Bonfield. R. M. Smith and K. Wrightson (eds.), *The World We Have Gained*, Oxford, 1986, pp. 122–54.

Cavallo, S. and Warner, L. (eds.), *Widowhood in Medieval and Early Modern England*, Harlow, 1999.

OLD AGE

Pelling, M. and Smith, R. M. (eds.), *Life, Death and the Elderly: Historical Perspectives*, London, 1991.

Botelho, L. and Thane, P. (eds.), *Women and Ageing in British Society Since 1500*, Harlow, 2001.

Ottaway, S., *The Decline of Life: Old Age in Eighteenth-Century England*, Cambridge, 2003.

DEATH

Wiener, C. Z., 'Sex roles and crime in late Elizabethan Hertfordshire', *Journal of Social History* 8, 4 (1975), 38–60.

Ariès, P., *Western Attitudes Towards Death*, London, 1976.

Ariès, P., *The Hour of Our Death*, London, 1981.

Hoffer, P. C. and Hull, N. E. H., *Murdering Mothers: Infanticide in England and New England, 1558–1803*, New York, 1981.

Sharpe, J. A., 'Domestic homicide in early modern England', *Historical Journal* 24, 1 (1981), 29–48.

Gittings, C., *Death, Burial and the Individual in Early Modern England*, London, 1984.

Llewellyn, N., *The Art of Death: Visual Culture in the English Death Ritual c.1500–c.1800*, London, 1991.

Amussen, S. D., '"Being stirred to much unquietness": Violence and domestic violence in early modern England', *Journal of Women's History* 6, 2 (1994), 70–89.

Dolan, F. E., *Dangerous Familiars: Representations of Domestic Crime in England, 1550–1700*, Ithaca, N.Y., 1994.

Kermode, J. and Walker, G. (eds.), *Women, Crime and the Courts in Early Modern England*, London, 1994.

Cressy, D., *Birth, Marriage and Death: Ritual, Religion, and the Life Cycle in Tudor and Stuart England*, Oxford, 1997.

Gowing, L., 'Secret births and infanticide in seventeeth-century England', *Past and Present* 156 (1997), 87–115.

Houlbrooke, R., *Death, Religion and the Family in England 1480–1750*, Oxford, 1998.

Lawson, P., 'Patriarchy, crime and the courts: The criminality of women in late Tudor and early Stuart England', in G. T. Smith, A. N. May and S. Devereux (eds.), *Criminal Justice in the Old World and New World: Essays in Honour of John Beattie*, Toronto, 1998, pp. 16–57.

Walker, G., 'Rereading rape and sexual violence in early modern England', *Gender and History* 10, 1 (1998), 1–25.

Gammon, J., '"A denial of innocence": Female juvenile victims of rape and the English legal system in the eighteenth century', in A. Fletcher and S. Hussey (eds.), *Childhood in Question: Children, Parents and the State*, Manchester, 1999, pp. 74–95.

Walker, G., *Crime, Gender and Social Order in Early Modern England*, Cambridge, 2003.

FAMILY PORTRAITURE

Hopkins, J. T., '"Such a likeness there was in the pair": An investigation into the painting of the Cholmondley sisters', *Transactions of the Historic Society of Lancashire and Cheshire* 141 (1992), 1–38.

Pointon, M., *Hanging the Head: Portraiture and Social Formation in Eighteenth-Century England*, New Haven and London, 1993.

West, S., 'The public nature of private life: The conversation piece and the fragmented family', *British Journal for Eighteenth-Century Studies* 18 (1995), 153–72.

Retford, K., *The Art of Domestic Life: Family Portraiture in England*, New Haven and London, 2006.

Index